Efficient Radiology

Daniel Rosenthal • Oleg Pianykh

Efficient Radiology

How to Optimize Radiology Operations

Springer

Daniel Rosenthal
Department of Radiology
Massachusetts General Hospital
Boston, MA
USA

Oleg Pianykh
Department of Radiology
Massachusetts General Hospital
Boston, MA
USA

ISBN 978-3-030-53612-1   ISBN 978-3-030-53610-7   (eBook)
https://doi.org/10.1007/978-3-030-53610-7

This Springer imprint is published by the registered company Springer Nature Switzerland AG
The registered company address is: Gewerbestrasse 11, 6330 Cham, Switzerland

"To my wife, Jacqueline M. Rosenthal, who encouraged this project by believing in it more than I did."

Daniel Rosenthal

"To my dear family for their unlimited patience and unconditional support"

Oleg Pianykh

Preface

This is an amoral book.

We are not going to tell the reader what he or she (or his or her department) should be hoping to achieve with respect to the delivery of healthcare services. Instead, our approach is to describe how to determine what it is you are *actually doing* and, from there, how to optimize your efforts so you are accomplishing everything you want to accomplish.

Who should read this book?

You may not realize that you need this information. Managing a radiology department is not likely to be part of the training received by the doctors, nurses, or technologists who work in the department. While the radiologist's role today can encompass economic gatekeeping, patient safety, quality-of-care improvement, and information technology [1], radiology training programs are only just beginning to consider these issues. There are structural issues, as well, in determining who should be interested in how to make a radiology department function more efficiently. In healthcare, lines of responsibility can be difficult to pin down. The much-vaunted "matrix" structure, while conceptually appealing, can be ambiguous. The Chairman of the Department, while certainly its major voice as well as its moral and aspirational leader, may or may not have direct responsibilities for its operation.

Complicating matters, the search process for a chairman at a major medical center, which is often led by an academic, typically undervalues leadership and management skills, despite their importance to the hospital or medical center [2]. As a result, the chosen leader may end up "offloading" these responsibilities to an "administrator" to avoid spending too much time on them. The administrator might have the managerial skills needed but will lack the necessary "domain expertise" and may require years of on-the-job training to acquire it. As a result, insufficient attention to management can have deleterious effects on every aspect of a department, from patient and physician satisfaction to new equipment requests.

Not so very long ago, the concept of healthcare quality did not extend to mundane matters of service. For example, a senior member of the faculty in one of the authors' training programs would speak caustically of patients complaining about the food in the hospital. His attitude toward these patients was, essentially, "You come to the hospital to get well, not to have a good meal." Similarly, care providers believed that "mere logistical matters such as capacity planning, staffing to demand

and waiting times were not quality issues, despite the fact that they clearly influence patient satisfaction and hospital efficiency" [3].

All of this has been changing rapidly. In the United States, the Joint Commission launched the first national program for measurement of hospital quality in 1998. By 2002, hospitals were required to collect and report data on two of four core measurement sets. Despite the modest nature of this requirement, hospitals strongly resisted the proposals at the time. In the years since, a number of further reporting requirements have been added, including requirements related to patient satisfaction and outcomes for certain conditions. A small army of performance measurement system vendors has emerged to help satisfy these requirements. Unfortunately, there is still disagreement as to which of them capture the key performance elements that draw the line between good and less good care [4].

Facing a need to learn quickly, the healthcare industry has looked to the large body of management literature (and consultants) developed for the business world. The language used to describe the methods for ensuring quality changes frequently. The Joint Commission recommended the "Plan, Do, Study, and Act" cycle that grew out of the work done at Bell Labs and by Deming. Six Sigma, introduced by Motorola in the 1970s, focuses on reducing variation. General Electric popularized the approach in healthcare using a technique called DMAIC (Define, Measure, Analyze, Improve, and Control). The System of Profound Knowledge was created by Deming and includes four components: appreciation of the system, a theory of knowledge, psychology of change, and knowledge about variation. Lean production, from Toyota, centers on eliminating waste and improving value to customers (waste due to variation, overburdening or placing stress on people and systems, and processes that do not add value). The theory of constraints identifies the bottlenecks that prevent a process from reaching its ultimate goal [5]. The groundbreaking work of the Institute for Healthcare Improvement has pioneered a uniquely pragmatic approach that they call the "science of improvement" [6].

Can any of these methods work in healthcare? And if so, does any one of them work better than the others? It would be impossible to answer these questions with the available evidence. Dozens of papers have been published reporting the success of one method or another with respect to cost savings, reducing appointment wait time, reducing in-department wait time, increasing patient volume, reducing cycle time, reducing defects, and increasing staff and patient safety and satisfaction. All of them have demonstrated improvements. However, because of high rates of systematic bias and imprecision, one could never really say whether the improvements were due to the method or simply due to the scrutiny that the process received [7]. Given the relatively low bar, any or all of these approaches can be successful in improving efficiency. Healthcare tends to be inefficient because processes evolve over time with little or no thought given to how to make them efficient. The more we understand this, and the more we get involved, the more opportunities there are for improvements. The key to success is the willingness to recognize a problem and take steps to address it [8].

So who should read this book?

We intend this book for readers interested in how a radiology department works and how it can be made to function more efficiently. A well-run, high-functioning radiology department is in the interests of everyone in healthcare. We hope that all radiology chairmen, vice chairmen, and division heads, as well as other medical leaders, will find it useful. At the same time, lay administrators and managers who work in radiology departments, or whose role within a hospital includes oversight of a radiology department, might also learn a thing or two from it.

We are motivated by certain basic concepts:

- *Complexity*: People take both pleasure and pride in being able to execute complex tasks. It should be obvious, though, that the more complex the task—and the greater the skill needed to accomplish it—the more likely it will result in error. Simplicity is always preferable to complexity.
- *The law of unintended consequences*: Many of the actions taken in the name of improved patient care cannot be shown to actually improve it—and may even make it worse. The more complex the system, the greater the probability of unintended consequences.
- *Murphy's law*: If anything can go wrong, it will. This doubly applies to healthcare because of the potential risks associated with mistakes.

In this book, we will walk the reader through the process of an imaging encounter, from the moment that the examination is requested until the findings are reported. At each step along the way, we will comment on some of the many things that can go wrong, as well as some of the metrics that can be used to determine whether or not the process is "under control."

We are not concerned with "utilization management," or whether the imaging study is appropriately ordered. These concepts are certainly related to efficiency, but they are matters of medical practice, not operations. Nor will we trouble ourselves with how the information created by the study is used. Therefore, though we will think carefully about costs, we will not consider cost/benefit ratios.

The organization of the book follows the process of ordering a study, scheduling it, "protocoling" (customizing) it, performing it, and reporting it. Each chapter will describe the main steps in the process and metrics that can be used to evaluate it. The metrics are generally divided into two categories: those that can be applied retrospectively and are used for determining normative data and establishing trends, and those that need to be applied in real time as a management tool. In order to avoid data overload, real-time metrics (reported actively, for example, by pagers) should be used sparingly.

References

1. Knechtges P, Carlos R. The evolving role of radiologists within the healthcare system. J Am Coll Radiol. 2007;4(9):626–35.
2. Arenson R, Garzio C. A practical guide to leadership and management in academic radiology. Springfield: Charles C Thomas; 2012.

3. Nickel S, Schmidt U. Process improvement in hospitals: a case study in a radiology department. Qual Manag Health Care. 2009;18(4):326–38.
4. Chassin M, Loeb J, Schmaltz S, Wachter R. Accountability measures-using measurement to promote quality improvement. N Engl J Med. 2010;363(7):683–8.
5. Rawson J, Kannan A, Furman M. Use of process improvement tools in radiology. Curr Probl Diagn Radiol. 2016;45(2):94–100.
6. Martin L, Mate K. IHI innovation system. IHI White Paper; 2018.
7. Amaratunga T, Dobranoski J. Systematic review of the application of Lean and Six Sigma quality improvement methodologies in Radiology. J Am Coll Radiol. 2016;13(9):1088–95.
8. Dowell J, Makary M, Brocone M, Sarbinoff J, Vargas I, Gadkari M. Lean six sigma approach to improving interventional radiology scheduling. J Am Coll Radiol. 2017;14(10):1316–21.

Boston, MA, USA   Daniel Rosenthal
Boston, MA, USA   Oleg Pianykh

Abstract This book offers a critical analysis of radiology operations. It walks the reader through the process of an imaging encounter, from the moment that the examination is requested until the findings are reported. At each step along the way, we comment on many things that can go wrong, as well as the metrics that can be used to evaluate these problems.

Keywords Radiology, Quality control, Quality improvement, Efficiency, Six sigma

Contents

Part I

Data and Sense

A Word About Numbers

1

"Everything is number"

Pythagoras

"If you torture the data long enough, it will confess to anything"

Darrell Huff, "How to Lie with Statistics" [1]

Content

It is often said that if you cannot measure something, you cannot manage it. Whatever the merit of this idea, the contrapositive (if you can measure, you can manage) is certainly wrong.

Healthcare is moving away from qualitative, seat-of-the-pants management toward more objective, data-derived metrics: dashboards, key predictor indicators, and the like. To be sure, these have their uses. But beware: Data is complex! To derive knowledge from it, the data first needs to be organized and simplified. When that is done, though, subtleties can be obscured, and meaningful patterns lost.

Consider the humble "average." We use averages all the time in operational management—to demonstrate the need for change and to provide evidence of success, among other things. Averages offer a comforting simplicity: A single number seems to tell a whole story. And who can argue with numbers, right?

© Springer Nature Switzerland AG 2021
D. Rosenthal, O. Pianykh, *Efficient Radiology*,
https://doi.org/10.1007/978-3-030-53610-7_1

Keep It Real!

For some purposes medians are preferred to arithmetic averages, because medians are not sensitive to outliers. Medians are particularly popular when one is trying to minimize some metric—such as turnaround time—since medians tend to be smaller than averages, thus making everything look better. However, not caring about the outliers is a dangerous habit! In fact, in many cases the only way to improve the average performance is to work on reducing the outliers.

Well, numbers—certainly the ways we wield them—can be deceiving. We, as a species, often prefer to view the world through rose-tinted glasses, and nothing helps us see what we *want* to see more than superficial number tricks—hiding the unwanted, obscuring details that do not conform to our preconceptions.

But what is generally a harmless practice in our everyday lives can have grave consequences in healthcare. The "average" mammogram is normal, but the rare cancer is the reason for doing the examination. One slip of the scalpel outweighs hundreds of flawless surgeries. If only 1 of every 1000 imaging examinations is misinterpreted, it will be obscured by averaging—a "negligible" 0.1% error. But you would not want this negligible examination to be yours, would you? The cost of "averaging" in healthcare can be high—really, unacceptably high. Ultimately, achieving quality in healthcare, perhaps more so than in most other fields, is dependent on outliers and individual patterns, not on averages.

Simplifying data for analysis, as with averaging, can lead to any number of pitfalls. In a 1973 paper, F. J. Anscombe offered an example of four entirely different datasets, sharing nearly identical simple descriptive statistics (averages, means, deviations) yet representing completely dissimilar trends [2] (Fig. 1.1). He used this

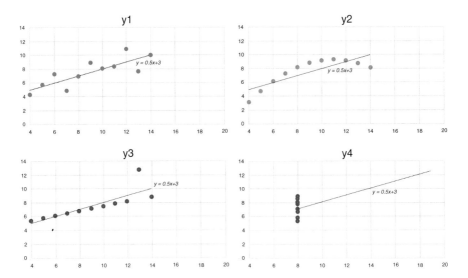

Fig. 1.1 "Anscombe's quartet"—four very different datasets (11 points each) with nearly identical means, variances, covariances, and regression fits

example to emphasize the importance of graphical data representation, to better understand data features and trends.

This 50-year-old number paradox has become important in our age of Big Data and artificial intelligence, alerting us to the need for thoughtful data pattern analysis. Data—healthcare data, in particular—*has to be understood.* It cannot just be reduced to a small number of conveniently aggregated statistics, dropped into a colorful executive summary. It cannot just be analyzed without the analyst being intimately familiar with the operations it describes (one of the reasons the use of consultants, so common in other businesses, is rarely successful in medicine). Even imperfect data can become valuable if its origins are understood: erroneous records, noise, and strange outliers can be exceptionally informative. It is worth the effort to try to decipher their hieroglyphs. Only in-depth understanding can save us from drawing naïve conclusions.

Let us consider a practical and seemingly trivial task: measuring the duration of a magnetic resonance imaging (MRI) study. Knowing how long an examination should take is essential for scheduling, assessing facility productivity and utilization, and assigning resources.

In our institution (and probably in most) the examination "begin" time Tb and "end" or "complete" time Tc are determined by policy: The examination is considered to have begun when the patient enters the scanner room and to have ended when the patient leaves. MRI technologists manually enter the Tb and Tc time points into the radiology information system (RIS). With these two timestamps in the RIS database, one can easily compute the examination duration as $D = Tc - Tb$. Using our data, we calculated that the MRI average duration was about 45 min. This time included the imaging acquisition and all other patient/technologist activities needed to make it happen.

We knew that some examinations would be longer and some shorter. However, we naively believed that equal numbers of examinations would fall into each category (i.e., a "normal" distribution). If delays occurred, they would represent random events and would tend to "even out" over time. Therefore, based on the average we had calculated, patients were scheduled at regular 45-min intervals.

However, when we looked at the data more carefully, our perception changed completely. The actual distribution of our MRI examinations turned out to be as shown in Fig. 1.2—far from being "normal," and definitely not nicely centered on the 45-min mean.

Take a moment to examine this chart. The more you look at it, the more questions arise:

- Why do some exams seem to take zero minutes to perform? The number is small, but 0.2% exams have a zero-minute duration.
- Why do some examinations appear to be performed in less than 10 min?
- Similarly, why do some examinations take up to 2 h and even longer?
- What accounts for the asymmetrical shape of the curve, with a long right-hand tail appearing to indicate very long examinations?
- Why does the curve have a strange "jagged" contour, with peaks in the numbers of exams occurring in multiples of 5 min (20, 25, 30, 35, 40, etc.)? Note that had we plotted this distribution with larger time bins (such as 5 min, as shown in the inset), we would not even notice this oddity. Why do we see it now?

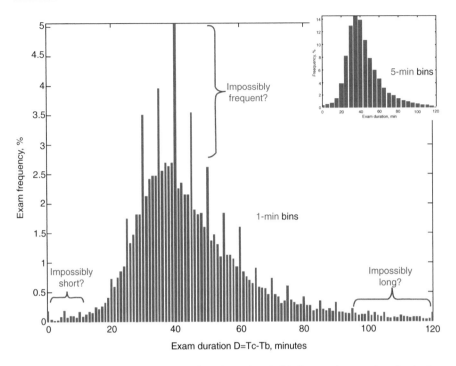

Fig. 1.2 Distribution of MRI exam durations in our hospital before any intervention, 1-min time bins. Inset: same distribution but with 5-min time bins (thicker 5-min bars)

Let us try to *understand* what we are seeing. In order to do so, it is necessary to actually observe the way in which the data was created. This is a somewhat laborious process because an individual must be present at the time of data collection and entry, making notes and entries regarding the relationship between workflow and the data that is meant to describe it.

First, consider the extremely short examinations. A brief observation period revealed that, for each examination, the technologist-patient interaction required a minimum of 10 min to prepare for and then to wrap up the scans—the inevitable housekeeping activities. Therefore, an examination that requires less than 10 min is essentially impossible.

Why do we see such "impossible" events in our chart? From observations of the workflow, three possibilities suggested themselves. Perhaps the short entries represent examinations that were never completed—for instance, examinations aborted because of claustrophobia or a contrast reaction. Another possibility is that data entry errors led to the apparently short durations: The technologist forgot to enter the begin time Tb until after the patient scan was completed and then entered Tb equal to Tc, resulting in $D = 0$. Third, it is possible that some of the examinations might have been "linked" to the main study without requiring additional scanner time (as with scanner-side reformats, for example) or multiple body part examinations derived from a single scan session (such as multiple spine segments)—which could have made them "zero-time" examinations. Based upon your own experience you might be able to suggest any number of other explanations.

As the possibilities begin to multiply, our simple task does not look so simple anymore. What do we do? People often talk about "curating" data to make it more straightforward, but this is a slippery slope. Too often, we talk about curation when we really just want to remove something that does not meet our expectations. "Oh, it must be some kind of error," we declare, as we delete everything we do not like.

> **Keep It Real!**
> Look back at the history of applied science: Those who refused to curate "errors" made some of the most interesting discoveries. This is how tiny oddities in Uranus's orbit led to the discovery of Neptune; failed photographic images, to radioactivity; barely detectable particle traces, to gravitational waves; and accidentally contaminated Petri dishes, to penicillin. With sufficient data curation, the theory of a flat Earth sitting on three elephants might not look too bad at all!

In this age of deep pattern analysis, one should avoid deleting (that is, *ignoring*) data at all possible costs. You can think of deleting a small number of records if and only if:

1. You can prove that they represent data entry errors.
2. These errors can be removed without distorting the other important patterns.

This is a serious challenge. How one addresses these questions can significantly impact the results of any analysis. For example, if we failed to eliminate the impossibly short records in Fig. 1.2, they would drive the overall average down, but would that be better or worse? As is frequently the case, the answer is: "It depends."

If inclusion of the impossibly short times results in a false, better-than-reality picture, we will want to remove them. For example, it seems inappropriate to include "linked" examinations in the computation of mean duration if we intend to use that number to determine the best scheduling interval. The linked time is already included in the main examination workload and does not need to be counted twice. However, should we also remove the examinations that were aborted due to patient claustrophobia and other unplanned events? There seems to be an irreducible minimum of such occurrences that will periodically (but erratically and unpredictably) result in very brief scanning appointments. But this is exactly what happens in reality, and including the aborted cases in our analysis could make practical sense. For instance, if we were studying examination durations to improve our scheduling, we would be able to consider better strategies—such as overbooking—on the expectation that a certain number of examinations would take much less time than expected.

Considering all of the above, we see that we cannot ignore data simply because it looks abnormal—we can do so only when we know what caused the abnormality. Yet, even this is not enough. What if, instead of improving our scheduling, we are trying to determine the examination durations associated with various scanning protocols (the amount of time needed for scans of the brain, knee, prostate, etc.)? Then we would have to *exclude* any aborted cases because they do not correspond to particular protocols. However, if we wanted to study something like waiting time, we would once again need to *include* the aborted examinations: After all, the claustrophobic patients who would eventually have to stop their scans still spend time sitting in the waiting room. In other words, we cannot just remove our impossibly short records—we will have to *exclude* or *include* them based upon the problem that we are trying to solve. Consequently, we cannot compute the average MRI exam duration unless we know in what context, and for what problem, this average will be used. This fundamental lesson was learned by simply looking at one tail of the examination duration histogram.

And we are not done yet.

The longer exams in the right-hand tail of Fig. 1.2 tell their own story. Some of these could also be due to data entry errors. However, unlike impossibly short examinations, excessively long exams are many, and can be real. Although some of the longest examinations *might* represent data entry errors, MRI cases can sometimes require 2 h to complete.

Not surprisingly, even a single 2-h case can wreak havoc on a schedule based on 45-min intervals. Even worse than this, though, the asymmetrical shape of the curve shows us that 60% of our exams took longer than the average 45 min to complete. In plain terms, this meant that our 45-min MRI slots would be insufficient 60% of the time. Thus, if a scan runs late, it is not really due to the clustering of "unfortunate outliers," as we postulated earlier. Scheduling a high percentage of cases that exceed the allotted time is an almost certain recipe for failure, even if the amount of time by which the mean is exceeded is counterbalanced by the time saved in short cases.

Unfortunately, in a tightly packed schedule, a case that overruns its scheduled time casts a long shadow over the rest of the day—a huge source of dissatisfaction for both patients and staff. Studies have shown that wait times have a strong positive correlation with the utilization rate for the device, and a strong negative impact on patient satisfaction [3]. But, you may ask, what about our naturally short and aborted cases? Don't they allow for at least some "catchup"? Alternatively, might we leave one or two appointments unfilled, hoping this will accomplish the same goal?

Not really. This is the approach that seems to be selected by most healthcare facilities, where the day is a never-ending cycle of falling behind and then catching up. An unfortunate sequence of long cases can lead to progressively accumulating delays, but it is never possible to get very far ahead, since the ability to begin is limited by when the next patient is available.

Finally, let us look at the most bizarre Fig. 1.2 oddity: the excessive frequency of examination durations that are multiples of 5 min. For example, notice the very large number of examinations that appear to last for 45 min, but the durations near it (44 or 46 min) are barely half as frequent. High peaks are also seen at 40 and

50 min. This does not make any sense, and one of us, after computing this chart, spent a good hour looking for an error in his code. Gradually, the explanation became clear: The technologists, having forgotten to enter the time stamps as required, were guessing them after the fact. Just like any human would, they were rounding up their math, making it easier to subtract from the complete time—"Did I start this exam 30 minutes ago?" Those "guesstimated" timestamps are clearly approximations of unknown veracity. The scope of this problem was so huge that we started a separate project to educate our technologists about accurate time entry, and on cleaning the "5-min garbage" from our data analyses. As a result, 2 years later the number of round-offs in our data was significantly lower, although still present (Fig. 1.3, compare to Fig. 1.2).

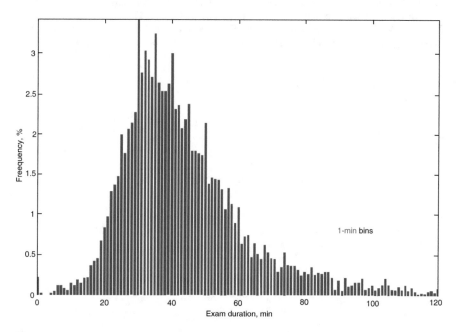

Fig. 1.3 Distribution of MRI exam durations, 1-min time bins after a 1-year educational program emphasizing the importance of correct data entry (compare to Fig. 1.2)

Keep It Real!
If you think that manual time round-offs are the exception rather than the rule, consider yourself an optimist. When we started this study, we discovered that, in one of our facilities, exams apparently always began at exactly 8:30 AM. When we asked the technologists why they were entering 8:30 instead of the actual time, the reply was, *"Because they told us to."* Needless to say, no one could say who *"they"* were. Without a doubt, "errare humanum est"—to err is human—as we will see so many times throughout this book.

Let us summarize.

We began this chapter by cautioning readers against an oversimplified math. We would like to conclude by affirming that we do in fact believe in math as long as it stays *real*. Indeed, we think that anyone who runs an operation should be expected to have access to and use certain metrics. Every manager needs to understand both the power and the limitations of the metrics that are used.

Understand your data! Question it, prod it, shake it, see if it makes real-life sense.

References

1. Huff D. How to lie with statistics. New York: W. W. Norton & Company; 1993.
2. Anscombe F. Graphs in statistical analysis. Am Stat. 1973;27(1):17–21.
3. Loving VA, Ellis RL, Steele JR, Schomer DF, Schoemaker S. Time is not on our side: how radiology practices should manage customer queues. J Am Coll Radiol. 2017;14(11):1481–8.

Mining Your Own Business

2

"All models are wrong, but some are useful"

George Box, British statistician

Contents

2.1 Collecting the Data

"Some are useful"—this can be said of data as well. Indeed, finding the most useful dataset is one of the principal challenges in data-driven management. Complete, valid, honest information is the fuel that propels operational success; you will not get far on low-quality substitutes.

But where does this data come from?

Imagine you have been tasked with determining the size requirement for a hospital waiting room [1]. In order to do so, you will have to know patient arrival patterns and how many companions (family members, friends, medical staff) will accompany each patient. Also, you will need to be aware of the frequency and magnitude of any delays that could keep the patient in the waiting room longer than anticipated. And to really get it right, you will have to know the patterns of unscheduled arrivals (walk-ins, urgent cases, etc.), so they can be added to the expected patient flow.

© Springer Nature Switzerland AG 2021
D. Rosenthal, O. Pianykh, *Efficient Radiology*,
https://doi.org/10.1007/978-3-030-53610-7_2

Needless to say, coming up with all of this information is not trivial (as you will soon see in the pages that follow). Depending on how much time and energy you have, you will need to do one of the following: try to extract the information from records of patient encounters (if available), guesstimate (in other words, make a huge number of assumptions that may or may not reflect reality), or do the hard work of directly observing the number of waiting patients and family members.

In the "good old days," observation was the only way to collect information. One had to intrude upon an operation in order to observe it, with stopwatch and notepad in hand, jotting down numbers. It would be hard to know how long you had to continue in your observations before you had seen the full range of possibilities. Should you hang around the waiting room for a full year, for example, waiting for the crowd that you know will be the largest you will see?[1] Data collection by direct observation is painfully laborious and inefficient, and so cumbersome that analyzing any single workflow problem will become a major project.

Direct observation has another serious drawback, a phenomenon known by all, but rarely ever acknowledged: The presence of an observer may distort the process while also introducing a subtle subjectivity. When we are observed, we tend to change our work patterns [2], and when we function as the observer, we may bend the reality to meet our expectations [3]. As a result, observations may reflect our preconceptions more than objective reality. "Man sees only what he already knows and understands," as Goethe put it.

Keep It Real!

Nothing alarms hospital staff more than the unexpected appearance of *an observer*. Clearly an outsider, with his fancy notepad—or any pad—in hand; the observer may be younger, more formally dressed, and obsessively focused on issues other than the usual procedures. The appearance of an observer suggests impending layoffs or other loathsome management-driven interventions. Lame explanations ("no worries, we are only looking into optimizing our workflow") only make it worse: "Optimizing" has always been Aesopian for "times are tough; layoffs are coming." For those occasions when direct observations must be made, we have found it useful to fabricate a lexicon of less threatening reasons for observation. Even so, our observed work patterns are sometimes very different from the unobserved baseline.

Fortunately for those of us who measure processes, the whole approach to observation started to change in the late 1990s, when healthcare slowly but surely went digital. Digital standards, such as DICOM and HL7, began to capture and store more data than even a thousand notepads ever could [4–6]. Interestingly enough,

---

[1] Note that the task can be even more complex. One would also need to be aware of the risks of overestimation and underestimation, as well as any physical constraints that might make it impossible for the room to exceed a certain maximum size, thus rendering the analysis useless beyond a certain point.

most of this new data was created for a one-time use, to manage a single interaction: For example, patient arrival times were recorded only to know that the patient had checked in and was available to be seen. But software applications had to hold on to the data in order to survive reboots, crashes, upgrades, etc. As a result, digital systems ended up collecting this information over the long term, in files and databases. Thus, tiny drops of data, created for transient reasons, accumulated into lakes and oceans of historical records. Days and years passed, and this finally led to the *Big Data* phenomenon: huge data warehouses filled with petabytes of information waiting to be mined.

Know Your Tools

DICOM and HL7 are two major digital standards that are omnipresent in contemporary radiology. Originating in the late 1980s, the standards were developed by different groups for entirely different purposes. HL7 ("Health Level 7," www.hl7.org) [7] was built to exchange textual data between various medical devices and applications. This data might include patient arrival and transfer updates, clinical reports and observations, billing information, prescriptions, lab results, and virtually anything else that can be communicated by way of text messages [8]. In essence, HL7 has become the main messaging tool in modern digital medicine. Hospital and Radiology Information Systems (HIS and RIS) are driven by HL7 messages. Collecting these messages into HIS/RIS databases creates large historical records of virtually all processing steps occurring in radiology.

DICOM ("**D**igital **I**maging and **CO**mmunications in **M**edicine," dicom. nema.org) was designed strictly for digital imaging, which makes it particularly important for radiology. DICOM governs the entire medical imaging workflow: It interfaces with medical imaging devices; creates digital imaging files; supports imaging networking, storage, and exchange; and ensures high standards of digital image quality [8]. Unlike common multimedia imaging, DICOM images store a tremendous number of additional data items (around 3000 standard fields) relevant to each image acquisition. Typical fields include patient information (often acquired from HL7), image acquisition parameters (slice thickness, orientation, timestamps, calibration, and many more), hospital and physician information, scanning protocols, and so on. This makes DICOM images extremely data rich, leading to countless data processing applications, from 3D image analysis to machine learning. DICOM runs picture archiving and communication systems (PACS), which are responsible for all image storage, and viewing, completely replacing the printed films of the old days.

Radiology was not exempt from this digital metamorphosis. In the modern radiology department, every critical step of every encounter generates new digital data (Figs. 2.1 and 2.2). The data collection process usually begins when a physician orders an examination for a patient, providing the information required by the

```
MSH|^~\&|SENDING_APP| SENDING_FACILITY|RCVAPP|RCVFAC|201810021226||ORU^R01|DCGTORD.2.79|P|2.4|
PID|1|89300043|||SAMPLE^JOHN||19600507|M|||||||||1259801|999-00-
888|||ZPI|1|N|N|N|N|""|""|""|""|""| | | | |""|N|0|0|0|0|0|0
PV1|1|2|||||||| ||||||N|| ||
ORC|RE||2060059||||^^^201807061707^^ ||201807051013|DIONA |||""|||1007
OBR|||2060059|999991^Knee MRI WO| |201807061707|201807061621|201807061707||||""|""|||
DGC|APRV^APPROVED|201807090801|||||||||||0|0|0|0|N|N|N|N|""|""|""|""|""||EOK
OBX|1|TX|||PROCEDURE: MRI OF THE LEFT KNEE WITHOUT CONTRAST~ ~HISTORY: Right knee pain for three months...~
~TECHNIQUE: MRI of the left knee was performed on the 1.5 Tesla magnet operating at ECIC. Images were obtained in
multiple planes and with varying pulse sequences. ~FINDINGS: ~IMPRESSIONS:
```

Fig. 2.1 Sample HL7 message with radiology report. You can see that the message consists of separate segments, identified by three-character segment names (for instance, the second line begins with a segment named PID because it contains patient information; the OBX segment, observations and reports; and so on). Each segment, in turn, contains individual data fields, separated by vertical lines (|) known as "pipes." You can read and understand most of the message even if you do not know its format. Patient names, reports, and timestamps are all quite visible. For instance, the PID segment in the example above contains patient name (SAMPLE^JOHN) followed by patient date of birth (19600507—May 07, 1960), patient sex (M for male), etc. Note that empty fields still keep their pipes, so fragments like ||||| correspond to sequences of empty fields

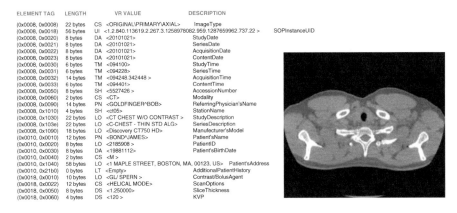

Fig. 2.2 DICOM image, aka DICOM "information object," and some of the information it contains in addition to the image data. Instead of the segment names used in HL7, DICOM data elements are identified by element tag numbers, and instead of HL7 "pipes," DICOM fields are separated according to their data lengths. For example, data element (0×0010, 0×0030) contains the patient's birth date (in our case, November 12, 1988). When extracted and processed properly, these DICOM data elements support a broad spectrum of fascinating and indispensable radiology applications—from routine reconstruction to complex imaging analysis or workflow management

order-entry process. The order is then sent to the radiology department, where it must be scheduled and subsequently performed as an imaging study. The study is then interpreted by radiologists. This step yields the imaging report, the final product, which is delivered back to the ordering physician.

This sequence may appear simple and straightforward but, upon closer inspection, it is anything but. In fact, it is not even a sequence, but rather a branching network of interdependent events and decisions, where each major step leads to several smaller sub-processes, each with its own meaning and value. For instance, examination scheduling requires allocation of specific devices, rooms, and other resources, which could in turn impact allocation of other devices, rooms, and schedules. As a result, not only will each examination point to its own data (ordering and performing physicians, technologist, scanner, exam type, and so on), it will also connect to a mountain of other records. Data will therefore be coming from a multiplicity of sources. Some of the data are entered manually: patient notes, reports, and examination descriptions. The acquisition devices will collect more: timestamps, image counts, and radiation doses. Data may also come from freestanding post-processing systems and physician scheduling software. Even power injectors and computerized supply cabinets can become sources of useful data.

Know Your Tools

It is very common for software systems to record some of their state data in various logs. For instance, in addition to its main database of medical images, any PACS would also keep an error log file (sometimes as a separate database table), recording system failures and warnings. Albeit less structured, and far less standardized than DICOM or HL7, those error logs could be your best friends in investigating patterns of failures, or other exceptional conditions that might arise in your work.

Another typical data companion is an audit log, required in any HIPAA-compliant software. Audit logs indicate who accessed clinical data, when this occurred, and sometimes what was done. This becomes indispensable in analyzing productivity patterns.

As a result, our workflow serves us with a thick data soup, into which new, heretofore-unknown ingredients might be dropped at any minute. This begs the question: With so much information captured and recorded, what data should you actually be looking for?

Let us outline a few of the principal types:

- *Timestamps.* These are the real bread and butter of any operations management project. Simple to generate, timestamps can be found in virtually any system. The information system used for daily operations captures most of the workflow timing. The RIS and/or HIS captures patient arrival, examination begin and complete times, resources and personnel allocated to the procedure, etc. (Fig. 2.3). The PACS receives timestamps from the imaging devices (image acquisition times) but captures much additional information such as radiation dose, identity of individuals logged on, as well as times of log-on and log-off. The digital dictation system (DDS) keeps track of the times of preliminary and final reports, and often keeps an audit log of changes made to reports. Error and audit logs found within each of these systems note the time of errors and data access.

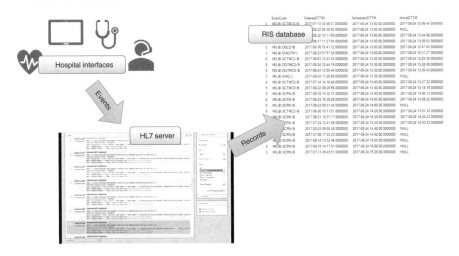

Fig. 2.3 Clinical interfaces send HL7 messages about various workflow events, including patient arrivals, examination begin/end times, and reports. These events are captured by a radiology information system (RIS) and then logged in to a RIS database. From there, the events can be sent to the other interfaces, exchanged with other systems (such as PACS), or mined for informative data patterns

While much of this data is captured automatically, many important timestamps still come from manual entry, so their accuracy may be questionable. Nonetheless, they will be much more reliable than manual observations, and even errors in the manual entry could reveal significant hidden trends (recall our example of MRI examination timing).

- *Process owners*. Who is responsible? This includes the radiologist who is responsible for the report, the technologist who performed the examination, and even the names of the transporter responsible for patient movement. It also includes the divisions and departments responsible for particular aspects of the hospital workload. Capturing process owners is essential for identifying all real actors and their roles. Moreover, improving the processes will be impossible if you do not know the individuals responsible for them.
- *Resources*. What does it take? This type of data encompasses imaging devices, staff, software systems, and anything else involved in operations. Analyzing resource use can help reveal bottlenecks in resource allocation and in resource utilization, whether caused by humans or machines. Such analysis is also imperative in assessing your resource utilization. Any large discrepancies in the productivity of identical scanners or between radiologists demand an explanation as well.
- *Locations*. Where does it happen? Locations include examination and recovery rooms, waiting areas, floors, and facilities. They are similar to resources but they also literally put your workflow on the map. Transporting a patient from a nearby room is very different than transporting one from another building. Once you know the timestamps and locations of each event, you can see the entire healthcare "assembly line" in action.

- *Workflow parameters*. How can we make it work? Examination codes, device settings, image acquisition protocols, patient types, conditions, and the like belong to this very broad type. The richness of parametric data makes it possible to differentiate between various branches of the same process. Sometimes seemingly minor distinctions can be critical, creating unique patterns and turbulences that seriously disrupt the standard workflow. Managing these patterns is one of the most essential tasks in operations improvements.
- *Data formats*. How is it recorded? For example, do you capture your timestamps with minute-to-minute precision? Are your physician names entered as free, "type whatever you want," text, or are they taken from a fixed, well-structured list? The answers to these and other, similar questions will affect the data quality and, consequently, your ability to make sense of it. If you think that the data format used is not data in itself, you are setting yourself up for trouble.

These essential types of data, as incomplete and noisy as they may be, provide us with a range of metrics and allow us to make rational decisions. Quite frequently, they set the limits of our data projects as well. For example, it is pointless to even start an improvement project without knowing who owns different segments of its execution chain. It is still possible, but very painful and time consuming, to trace patient records based on free-text patient name entries, instead of standardized, robust medical record numbers (MRNs). Is "Joe Sample" indeed the same person as "Sample J."? It is painfully difficult to maintain your data-driven improvements if the source of the data itself is unreliable. A brief example in the next section illustrates this point.

2.1.1   Example: Tracking Process Owners

As noted above, capturing information about process owners and their many activities is important: This is how we can determine who is responsible for doing something either wrong or right. If the process owner is required to log in to an information system, this information will likely be captured automatically. For instance, a radiologist will almost certainly be logged in to the dictation system to create a report and will therefore be identified by the system. Otherwise, the comings and goings of process owners need to be recorded manually. For example, when performing an intervention, the radiologist will probably not be logged in to either the RIS or the EHR. The technologist who assisted with the procedure will be identified, but the radiologist could easily remain anonymous until the report is created—an obvious point of vulnerability for process improvement.

One day we realized that some of the interventional cases performed at our hospital were not being reported on time—at least not within the time window we encourage and are trying to enforce. As is typically the case, this did not come as a tremendous surprise. Usually, by the time a formal investigation is initiated, a good manager will have suspected a problem for quite a while. To address the shortcoming, we wanted to use an approach that had proved successful in other, similar settings: implementing a paging system to remind our radiologists to complete their delayed reports. But in trying to do so, we ran into an unexpected but serious obstacle: the name of the interventional radiologist was not recorded anywhere when the procedure was completed. To put it simply: We had no idea to whom we should send the reminder.

To recap: The technologist was logged in to the RIS to begin and complete the examination. The nurse was logged in to the HIS to document medication and patient condition. Yet the performing radiologist was not recorded anywhere until the report was created.

We decided to require the technologist to enter the physician name. We recognized that this would be a manual and therefore imperfect process. However, once the process was in place, at least in the majority of instances we knew whom to page. The effect was obvious, as can be seen in Fig. 2.4. Here, we show percentages of moderately (beyond 3 days) and significantly (7 or more days) delayed reports. There was an abrupt decline in both categories following implementation.

But our initial success was short lived. Somewhere around March 2018 (Fig. 2.4), our physician-tracking database started to break down as a result of technical issues. To address this deteriorating situation, the database was gradually migrated to a new server and the old server was retired. In the meantime, though, as the database on the old server grew increasingly outdated, our ability to track radiologists' names declined. This "system failure" led to our losing most of the gains we had achieved with the new process, but it also provided us with a natural experiment.

Switching to the new fully functional database resolved the issues associated with the system failure. As you can see in Fig. 2.4, this led to an immediate drop in the most delayed reports and a gradual reduction in moderately delayed reports. Our performance improved still further and, this time, we were able to sustain the advances. This underscores another important lesson we learned from the system failure: Data-driven improvements must be maintained for a substantial period of time before they become "baked in" to operational culture. Do not expect instant miracles. Even if you are lucky enough to experience one, you still need to stay on top of your data if you want the benefits to endure.

2.1.2 Obstacles to Data Retrieval

Having described the huge quantity of data that every radiology department produces and almost certainly saves, the question remains: Can you get access to this data?

The short answer is: Yes. The slightly longer answer is that you can, but chances are you will run into one or more of several common obstacles along the way:

– *System design:* Some vendors do not see data sharing as a priority. In some cases, they may even actively try to conceal data—for example, by storing key data elements in proprietary or otherwise unavailable ways. For this reason,

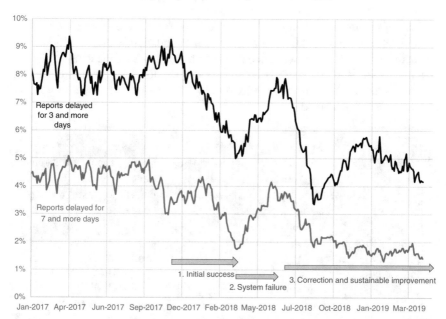

Fig. 2.4 Frequency of delayed reports for interventional (IR) cases. A paging system was implemented in late 2017 after a system to identify the process owner (radiologist) was created. Technical difficulties with the system in spring 2018 led to an immediate increase in delayed reports, which was then addressed by technical improvements

when shopping for software, hardware, or service, we recommend moving data completeness and accessibility to the top of your list of required features. Stay away from organizations or so-called solutions that seek to make *your* data *their* secret.

– *Lack of technical support:* Some organizations do not understand the value of being able to extract and analyze their own data, and therefore will not set aside funds to fill this technical support role. Happily, this type of retrograde thinking is falling out of vogue as healthcare providers are devoting more time and resources to documenting the value of their services. If you have the misfortune of working in a department that still subscribes to this antiquated notion, you can always point out that, without data, there is no real management.

– *Territoriality:* In some instances, access to data is rigidly controlled by information technology (IT) or by clinical departments. The departments might offer one or more of several possible reasons for this. They may be concerned about patient confidentiality, for example, or they may be afraid that "outsiders" looking into their systems will cause system failures for which they—the departments—will be held responsible. Whatever the rationale, we believe that a clear and forceful appeal to institutional leaders emphasizing the importance of access will convince the leaders to loosen their grip on the data.

– *Lack of management vision:* In our experience, this is the most prevalent and intractable of the obstacles you may encounter. Individuals tasked with managing the department may not understand how best to evaluate the data—or how to make use of it at all. There is no simple solution for this problem, other than education. To those who are not sure how or why to avail themselves of the data, we say: Read this book!

Know Your Tools

Inefficient data access puts a severe performance penalty on many radiology systems. Imagine you want to query your PACS database to count all of the images your scanners have produced over the past year. If the database stores this information in a single, concise table, the query could be completed in a fraction of a second. If this is not the case, though—if the data is broken into several poorly linked tables, if the study counts are not kept, and if the system therefore has to *recount* all of the image records from scratch—the same query could take hours. If it does, its execution will require significant processing effort, slowing your PACS and the other jobs it runs. Worse still, we have seen cases in which major departmental systems—including PACS, RIS, and dictation—were either completely frozen or outright broken by data queries they could not digest. Needless to say, this will wreak havoc on any radiology workflow. Let us be very clear, though. You cannot blame the query for annihilating a poorly designed data system. Instead, blame the poorly designed data system that made the failure possible.

2.2   Data Quality

Figure 2.4 gives a good picture of the potential impact of insufficient and low-quality data on daily clinical operations. With this in mind, once you have gained access to all the databases and records, be sure that they are actually good enough to be used. The data contained in them should be:

– *Original.* That is, it should come from the process in question, capturing the processes' original characteristics. It should not be subject to any filtering, cleansing, or "curation." As noted earlier, these steps can and often must be done in the context of particular problems or analyses, but never before.
– *Sufficient.* One of the questions typically asked at the beginning of any operational analysis is: "How much of the data do we need to include?" Should you look at 1 day, 1 month, or 1 year? Many opt for 1 month, thinking this will provide a sufficient overview of the operations in question. Ask yourself, though:

Does your workflow look the same in February as in August? Most likely it does not. So, with only a month of data, you might be missing important seasonal variations. Here is another example: Poor performance at one MRI scanner (maybe one located in some forgotten corner of your institution or network) could lead to unmanageable bottlenecks in other scanners and facilities. In a scenario such as this, studying one function without considering the others would be essentially pointless. Because processes in the real world tend to be interconnected, we offer here a simple rule of thumb: Capture and study as many parameters as you can think of, over a period of time long enough to encompass relevant variations.

- *Structured*. Ideally, all data should be stored in a database with well-normalized, clearly defined fields. Oftentimes, though, "well normalized" and "clearly defined" are the exception rather than the rule. At one of our sites, for example, imaging protocols were kept as *PowerPoint slides*. Wonder why? Because it was easier to use slides for technologist training—which, in fact, makes some sense! But mining data from slides, PDFs, free-text entries, and "files in that shared folder" is not simply inefficient—it is error prone as well. Working with poorly structured information can add processing mix-ups to any inaccuracies already present in the data. Store your data in databases, where it can live happily ever after in the most organized and most complete form possible. And give each information item its own field, with its own type. Any other means of presentation—slides, reports, and dashboards—should be derived from this structured storage, never used as its substitute.

All three of the above rules are geared toward a single, principal goal: Make sure that your data adequately and accurately represents the process from which it comes. Think of data quality as the fidelity of its process representation, which must also include intelligibility. One of the great misconceptions of our time is that computers should interpret big data. Nope. Understanding data is always the responsibility of a manager, who, ideally, will not have a problem making sense of it. Also bear in mind that understanding of the data typically consumes some 90% of an operational analysis. Further, unless the data is available in such a way that it can be readily transformed into recognizable operational metrics whose validity can be checked against real-life experience, this percentage could easily reach 99.9%. For example, if all patient arrival times, schedule times, and examination begin times are stored properly, it should be straightforward to create a metric such as patient waiting time, which has meaning to a manager. If your data incudes an examination record that suggests a patient has been waiting for 100 h, *think!* Undoubtedly, this is an error, but what caused it (Fig. 2.5)? Sloppy timestamp entry? Offset scanner clock? Some accidental action (modality work list synchronization, random button push) that created an incorrect timestamp? Look at *what* and *how* you are collecting, and be sure that you can read the story behind the numbers (Table 2.1).

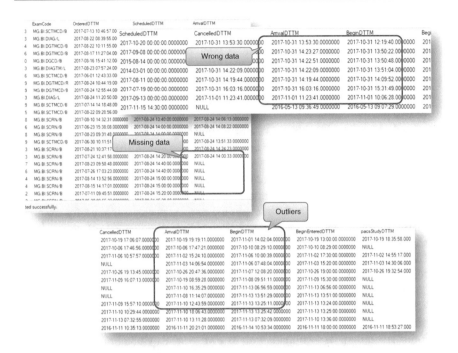

Fig. 2.5 Data problems in radiology: missing records, incorrect records (patient examination begin time occurring before patient arrival time), outliers (patient examination starting several hours or days after patient arrival)

Table 2.1 Methods of data collection: Adapted from Towbin, AJ, "Collecting Data to Facilitate Change" [9]

Manual concentrated collection	A single individual or a small group of individuals manually collects data. This is best for short-term, limited-size data
Manual distributed data collection	A large group of people is involved. Training is required. Detail expected must be very limited
Electronic data collection with manual extraction	Someone generates a report from an electronic repository
Electronic data collection with partially automated extraction	This is uncommon. Data extraction can be automatic, but each occurrence must be initiated or scheduled
Electronic data collection with fully automated extraction and analysis	This is a highly sophisticated approach. It works best for stable processes, not those that are in the process of being improved
Fully automated data collection, extraction, and evaluation	This type of process is in its infancy. Machine learning makes it possible for evaluations to proceed using new data. Early successes include prediction of "no-shows" and patient waits

2.3   Processes

The main value of data has always been in representing the processes that generate it, and number crunching alone cannot untangle what is happening in those processes. Decisions and actions should be driven by procedural interpretation of the data, not by the numbers themselves.

Therefore, in addition to what can be discerned from the numbers, you should always examine the process itself. If you consider yourself a data guru, here is when you have to leave your cozy data bubble and descend into the trenches of the routine operations, swarmed by flies of skepticism and entangled in barbed wire of denial. Try to ignore all of this and focus on the following:

- *Is there a method behind the madness?* For instance, is there a plan to handle an add-on patient who shows up unexpectedly in a busy CT facility? Or is it entirely ad hoc, the sole goal being to never turn anyone away? Most medical facilities seem to operate in this way, making decisions for seemingly random or erratic reasons (and their data will show this clearly). The rationale behind existing processes, whether formal or informal, sustained or disrupted, must be understood before planning any interventions.
- *What are the constraints?* Constraints can be understood as the boundaries that make our ideas fit reality. If analysis of your MRI operation reveals that you need one more MRI scanner but you cannot afford another scanner or would not have anywhere to put it, then the analysis was, simply put, unnecessary (you probably knew this going into it). Pragmatic optimization analyses generally should be limited to feasible scenarios, making use of the tools and resources you have at your disposal.

Keep It Real!
Sometimes operational analyses are done even when they are destined to fail. For example, there can be value in knowing that improved throughput or decreased waits can only be achieved by purchasing another scanner even if the money and space are not available. Perhaps this knowledge will lead to more realistic productivity expectations, or maybe even the money or space will be found!

- *What are the acceptable margins of errors?* Can you complete all of your MRI scans in exactly 30 min? Will your patients show up exactly on time? The answer to these and other questions is clearly no. Real life is filled with random deviations from the expected. Unfortunately, most of us try to ignore the deviations, hoping they will somehow cancel each other out. This may be possible or even likely in theory. In reality, though, unpredictable events come at a very high cost, disrupting your workflow and spurring operational tsunamis throughout the organization.

Keep It Real!
Sometimes even the most carefully laid plans can be sabotaged by unexpected events.

In one of our projects, we were asked to develop an optimized schedule for a large interventional facility that received frequent complaints from patients experiencing delays. After a substantial amount of data processing, personnel training, and dealing with internal politics, we devised and piloted an optimized schedule for the facility, demonstrating the potential to cut patient wait times by half an hour.

Having shown this was possible, we were ready for the big rollout. At the last minute, though, a senior radiologist decided to establish educational morning rounds, delaying the start of all scheduled examinations by half an hour.

The senior radiologist had no idea of the operational implications of his decision. A half-hour delay sounds like a minimal change but this decision necessitated our redoing all the calculations, and in the end the 30-min delay resulted in a 10% reduction in potential procedure volume.

In short, the combination of workflow logic and constraints renders many operational steps far less trivial than they might seem at a first glance. This is particularly true for sequential processes, where each step both sets and constrains the next. Consider a simple example: For unforeseen reasons, patient A has to stay in a recovery room for an extra 20 min. This may not sound like a significant delay but what if the recovery room is completely full? If it is, then it will not be able to accept the next patient (patient B) from the procedure room. Consequently, patient B will have to stay in the procedure room for an extra 30 min (20 min for patient A to leave the recovery room plus 10 min to communicate this update and prepare the recovery bed for patient B). Consequently, patient C, who is currently waiting to have his procedure done, will be delayed by 40 min (30 to get patient B to recovery plus 10 to communicate, get the procedure room ready, and transport patient C into the procedure room).

You get the idea: By the time you get to the next letters of your workflow alphabet, a few minutes of initial delay will be amplified into hours. Real-life constraints often produce cascading effects. This is why we so often find ourselves stuck in airports, traffic jams, and coffee shop lines. Even if some steps can be completed ahead of schedule, they are not likely to cancel out the negative effects of the original disruption. Failures should not be "averaged" with successes. Failures should be eliminated.

For all these reasons, the workflow logic (or, if you do not consider workflows logical, "workflow practices" or "procedures") should be the real target of data mining. Most likely, though, you will not be able to derive this from the data alone. You will have to study the process, and you will need to acquire sufficient domain knowledge.

Finally, be prepared to face the illogical, because reality is overrun with it. The illogical will exist both in your operational practices (as "exceptions to the rules") and in your workflow (as all kinds of random errors and events). This is why you absolutely must plan for the unplanned. Your workflow should be robust enough to withstand these disruptions; it should not completely fall apart as a result of a 20-min delay. To safeguard against this, you need to study the magnitude of the random shocks and then allocate enough of extra time or resources to absorb them.

Keep It Real!

Most clinical processes are sequential: The next step is possible only after the previous one has been completed. You have to boil water before you brew the tea. This is exactly how a bottleneck in a single step can disrupt an entire process.

To devise a more robust process, think if there are any steps you can do in parallel. For instance, if one of your scanners is overloaded, can your patients be moved to another one? If one of your physicians calls in sick, can the work be offloaded to someone else? Parallel, distributed processing networks are much more stable than traditional sequential chains. We will return to this concept later, when we discuss gaining efficiency from our equipment.

2.4 Data Presentations

Metrics, reports, dashboards—can we ever have enough? They are the fast food of current medical management: prepared from unknown ingredients, ill digested—a prime cause of "data obesity."

Shortly after our department purchased its first business intelligence (BI) system, we ended up with some 3000 reports, only a few dozens of which we actually used. The rest was "metric junk," which nonetheless still had to be maintained by several full-time employees. How does this make sense?

Well, one might argue, *we all want to keep informed. And scientific management is the flavor of the day.* This is certainly true. But …

Stop.

Step back for a moment.

If all of your dashboards and all of your pie charts disappeared tomorrow, what would change?

Anything important at all?

Data seems to have three different uses:

– *Impress others with what a good job we have been doing.* We want to decorate our presentations with handsome pie charts and mesmerizing data tables. For visual appeal, these must be condensed, simplified, and selectively chosen to illustrate a predetermined point. Ultimately, most of these presentation decks and the talks that accompany them wind up in the recycle bin, or the "circular file" (if you still use paper). They are useless for management.

– *Understand our operation.* Analysis and presentation of data can focus on virtually anything, even if we do not have the will or the ability to change what we see. We regard this type of analysis as "data appreciation." For example: Many quality assurance studies have sought to determine whether clinical information provided on imaging requests is adequate. Studies have consistently shown that it is not. Okay, fine. We accept that. But what are you going to do about it? This is not something that most radiology departments can change, and therefore the effort spent in studying it is largely wasted.

– *Manage our operation.* To serve as a useful management tool, any report drawn from data must satisfy several criteria: (1) The report needs to have a clearly understood purpose. (2) It must be assigned to an individual who is responsible for understanding its content and taking action based on the findings. (3) The manager must *need* the information in the report to do his or her job. An especially revealing test of the importance of the report is to ask the manager what he or she is willing to pay for it. In addition to the above, there must be a means of determining the effectiveness (if any) of actions taken in response to the report.

In recent years, dashboards have become particularly fashionable among managers of healthcare facilities. Dashboards can be decidedly useful in a variety of contexts. If they display key performance indicators (KPIs), they may serve to focus the institution's attention on certain important metrics. When designed by talented graphic artists, they may provide impressive representations of just how good the hospital (or other facility) is, and/or how much it has improved in a particular area. Unfortunately, these two ends often compete with one another for primacy. There are so many important and/or useful metrics that the displays can easily become cluttered, to the extent that important information is easily overlooked. As a general rule, we have addressed this conundrum by creating different dashboards for different purposes. For marketing and for senior management, simple dashboards elegantly displaying KPIs in glorious color are provided. For those who are expected to manage a complex operation with numerous metrics, we define an expected range for each metric we regard as being "in control" or falling within the natural process limits. The dashboard displays only those metrics that fall outside this range—or better yet, actively alerts a responsible individual of a deviant value, by page or by email.

Anyone who has attempted to work with dashboards knows that they are like the "screening" examinations of business intelligence. They can point out issues worthy of investigation, but they seldom provide enough detail to diagnose the problems. Also, most dashboards are retrospective, displaying a snapshot of data from the past. The time window can be wide or narrow, but the data is very seldom current. Finally, most of us are not good about performing regular data checks. Even if your dashboard is updated daily, you may only be looking at it once a month, rendering it outdated from a functional perspective.

A working dashboard should be more than a simple data display. This leads us to the following, fundamental question.

2.5   What Is Your Problem?

In this book we are interested in management and not so much in decorative metrics.

Take a look at Fig. 2.6. Then think about your current data projects, viewed through this lens. How many of them began with an actual, clearly defined problem?

Information becomes important only when it addresses a real-world problem. Indeed, we believe that metrics should be defined as the distance between "now" and "success." Only after you have established this distance can you begin to tackle the problem. Thus, identifying a clear, important, objectively measured problem is the first major step in achieving a solution.

A simple example illustrates this point. Most quality improvement projects originate either with an index event (such as a patient complaint) or with a subjective observation by a manager or other responsible individual. Let us assume that, in response to the event or observation, you decide you need to reduce patient wait time in your imaging facilities by implementing some kind of active alerting system, texting your staff about any patient whose appointment has been delayed for more than 20 min. Problem solved, right?

Not so fast. First, look at Fig. 2.6 and ask yourself once more—"what in fact is my problem?" The only way to answer this question pragmatically is to pull several months of RIS records and determine the patient wait times, defined as the difference between the scheduled start and the actual begin times. Once you have done so, you can plot the distributions of these wait times, as we did for one of our projects, as shown in Fig. 2.7.

In reviewing the distributions, you note that, if your wait times look like those for facility A, you probably do not have a major problem. The vast majority of your patients wait far less than 20 min, which, as we will see later in the book, is usually acceptable. If you ever do experience long wait times, they are most likely due to rare, random events (staff forgetfulness, assorted patient issues, occasional processing errors) that would not be considered systemic issues. You could still choose to implement the alerts but you would probably be better served by turning your attention to other projects with more critical problems.

In contrast, if your distribution looks anything like that for facility B, you are definitely facing a wait-time fiasco. In this case, 60% of your patients wait longer than 20 min, which tells you (at least) two things:

- You must have systematic failures in your operations: dysfunctional scheduling, insufficient resources or staff, or some other issue. This calls for a more detailed investigation, including a deeper dive into your data.
- The original plan to text your staff about 20-min patient waits will most likely fail, because some six in ten patients will trigger this alert. The staff will be overwhelmed and annoyed by the endless stream of paging alerts and yet the underlying systematic problems will persist.

Attempting to enforce a maximum 20-min wait for facility B by using alerts— similar to forcing 45-min MRI scans in Fig. 2.6—is a good example of choosing a solution before you have properly identified the problem. Imagine that a deeper

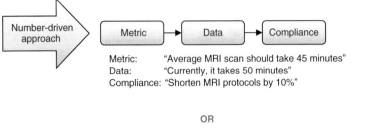

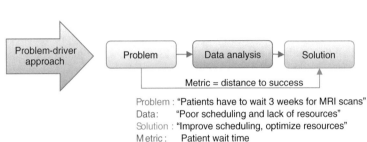

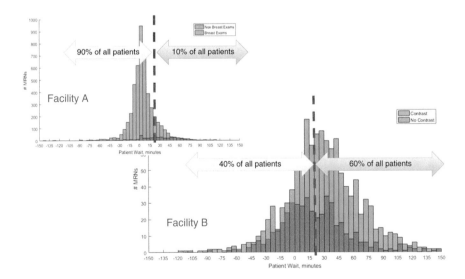

Fig. 2.6 Are you driven by problems or by numbers? In the example given, the actual problem is a lack of available MRI appointments, not the duration of the scans. Forcing conclusions based on numbers is a common approach, but it may not address your fundamental problem. Starting from the problem, and identifying the best metric to determine what needs to be done to achieve success, is ultimately the way to go

Fig. 2.7 Patient wait time distribution for two radiology facilities: facility A with breast imaging and facility B with PET scanning (note that two different patient subgroups were considered in each case). The vertical dashed line corresponds to the 20-min threshold

data dive confirmed that the observed delays were the result of dysfunctional scheduling—that is, allocating less examination time than is actually required. In that case work should focus on scheduling and starting examinations on time—not on the waits. A careful analysis of the data displayed in Fig. 2.7 would save hours of guesswork and days of failed pilots.

Avoiding poorly formulated or nonexistent problems is imperative for rational operations management. Next time you consider dedicating the next month of your life to yet another pilot or number crunching exercise, please ask yourself first:

- Is this an important and well-characterized problem?
- Is there someone who needs these results and will use them?
- Will any actions be taken based on the analysis?
- Will near-term implementation of these results be possible?
- Are there enough resources to do this project?

If the answer to at least one of those questions is "no," do not even start. You will be wasting your time—and the time of others. Needless project overload—just like information overload with too much to display, or implementation overload with too many alerts or too much to click or write about—is a sign of poor planning. Similarly, guessing the right answers—instead of deriving them from an objective data analysis—is an ineffective approach, at best. Few of us have the time to spend on dead ends such as these.

The problem-driven approach should save you from some of the more predictable pointless outcomes. The main part of the book you are about to delve into will be devoted to the data analyses applied both to identify problems and to measure their scope and impact. We will walk you through all major workflow steps, looking at the most meaningful ways to control and improve productivity, improve the quality of outcomes and job satisfaction, and make optimal use of resources. Please remain critical as you read this book, and always project our suggestions onto your own workflow, problems, and goals.

Okay, let us get started.

References

1. Ai J, Oglevee C, Pianykh OS. Determining waiting room occupancy at an outpatient clinic using simulated observations and probability-duration curves. J Am Coll Radiol. 2016;13(6):620–7.
2. Hawthorne effect. [Online]. https://en.wikipedia.org/wiki/Hawthorne_effect. Accessed 1 Jan 2018.
3. Observer-expectancy effect. Wikipedia. [Online]. https://en.wikipedia.org/wiki/Observer-expectancy_effect. Accessed 1 Jan 2018.
4. Pianykh OS. Digital Imaging and Communications in Medicine (DICOM): a practical introduction and survival guide. New York: Springer; 2012.

5. Bhagat R. HL7 for busy professionals: your no sweat guide to understanding HL7. Anchiove; 2015.

6. Trotter F, Uhlman D. Hacking healthcare: a guide to standards, workflows, and meaningful use. O'Reilly Media; 2011.

7. H. L. S. International. HL7 International. [Online]. www.hl7.org.

8. NEMA/MITA. DICOM Digital Imaging and Communications in Medicine. [Online]. dicom. nema.org.

9. Towbin AJ. Collecting data to facilitate change. J Am Coll Radiol. 2019;16(9 Pt B):1248–9.

Part II

Radiology Seriatim

Ordering

3

"The orders ordain events, change the face of the world"

Antoine de Saint-Exupéry, "Flight to Arras"

Contents

Things That Happen
- The clinician determines the need for an imaging examination.
- An order is created using an order-entry form (historically paper, but now usually electronic).
- Information related to the order is collected.
- A priority is selected.
- The order is communicated to the radiology department.

Things to Measure
- When do orders arrive?
- When do walk-in patients arrive?

© Springer Nature Switzerland AG 2021
D. Rosenthal, O. Pianykh, *Efficient Radiology*,
https://doi.org/10.1007/978-3-030-53610-7_3

- Who is sending you orders?
  - ... and who is not?
- Quantity of each order priority:
  - Volume of STAT orders.
- How easy is it to place an order at your facility compared to competitors?
- How often do orders not get scheduled?

3.1   Setting the Rhythm

The order is one of the two major ways in which clinicians interact with the radiology department.[1] The pace, rhythm, and quality of the ordering process drive the downstream effects of radiology operations echo throughout many of its day-to-day decisions.

Coming from the outside, orders are not controlled by radiologists. Instead, the rhythm of ordering is governed by a multitude of external factors—schedules and activities of the local physician practices, administrative work patterns, snow days, traffic jams and bus schedules, and human activity cycles in general. We cannot change most of them, just as we cannot change tomorrow's weather forecast.

It is worth taking time to visualize a few of these patterns. If you are curious enough, you can always do this with a bit of data science, exploring ordering time-stamps commonly recorded in RIS databases. Figure 3.1 illustrates the rhythm of ordering with a characteristic curve that, as it happens, is ubiquitous even outside the hospital. In this case, the curve represents the volume of orders for radiology imaging services as a function of the time of day but, as the inlay suggests, its "twin peaks" shape is omnipresent in all human activities. Note that there are two maxima here—one at about 10 AM, and the other at 2 PM.

You can see that although the charts in Fig. 3.1 refer to different facilities (and different imaging modality types), their trends look strikingly similar. This is true because they all reflect the same human activity pattern: peaking at around 10 o'clock in the morning, slowing at lunchtime (12:00), and reemerging in the early afternoon (sometimes a third peak can be found after dinnertime, if the facility is still fully active). We can call this the *human activity pattern* (HAP) as it is followed by most humans. This pattern is a major driving force of ordering volumes in healthcare.

Why would this matter for a radiology department? The timing of orders is a major factor behind expectation of service. The nature of the expectation can vary considerably (depending upon whether the order relates to a walk-in service, a scheduled appointment, or a test on an inpatient) but in each case the order results in some kind of expectation. The peaks and valleys of the workflow have obvious implications for processing times and customer satisfaction.

---

[1] The other being receipt of finalized diagnostic information, which can include formal written reports or any number of means of communication: from formal consultations to curbside consults, emails, and text messages.

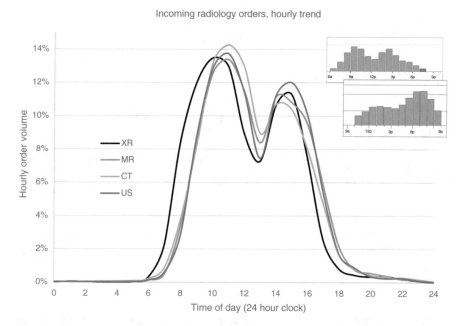

Fig. 3.1 Classical example of a diurnal human activity pattern (HAP), peaking at around 10 o'clock in the morning, slowing at around lunch (12:00–13:00), and peaking again in the early afternoon. Although this particular example shows the number of radiology orders issued for different outpatient facilities, the same curve pattern repeats itself in virtually all workflow metrics. Inlay—popular times at our favorite coffee shop and the Boston Museum of Fine Arts, showing the same trend

- For outpatients who will be scheduled to return a later date, the expectation is for timely creation of an acceptable appointment. This scheduling step might be decentralized and performed by the office that originates the request, or it might be performed by the radiology department itself. In the latter case, the time of the request determines the need for scheduling support, such as the use of call centers.
- For inpatients and patients in an emergency department, the time of the request carries an expectation for performance of the study within a predictable interval. Similarly, for walk-in procedures (and for urgent or unplanned additions to the schedule), the time of the request will determine the arrival time of patients.

Thus, the Asian camel of HAP drives the radiology workflow.[2] This phenomenon is evident in Fig. 3.2, which shows how the ordering pattern propagates through the ensuing workflow steps (patient arrival and exam begin and complete times) for a large walk-in X-ray facility.

---

[2] Unless you have read "The Little Prince" and perceive this chart as "a boa constrictor digesting an elephant."

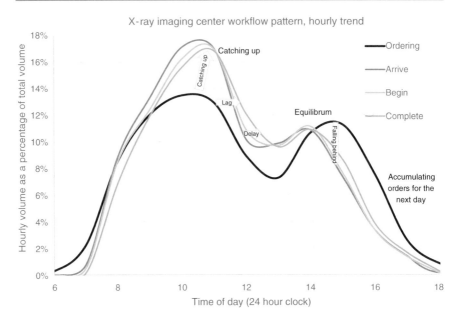

Fig. 3.2 Ordering pattern driving daily walk-in workflow, extracted from RIS data for a large radiology outpatient X-ray facility. Observe how patient arrival and exam beginning and completion rates reflect the original ordering pattern. This is a walk-in facility; therefore the scheduling curve (not shown) will also correspond to the patient arrival curve

In this case, the orders originated from physician practices located nearby (in fact, virtually next door), so the pace of ordering translated directly and almost immediately into the tempo of patient arrivals. As Fig. 3.2 demonstrates, orders start to arrive first thing in the morning, shortly after 6:00, and continue to pile up until the facility opens at around 7:00 and begins processing its patients. The facility already has a backlog of orders when it opens its doors each day (including some late orders left from the previous afternoon). As a result, the peak times for patient arrival, examination begin time, and examination complete time run to the right of the ordering trend (lagging behind), although the performance peaks are higher than the ordering peaks as the facility attempts to "catch up" in processing the orders. This race continues until 14:00 (2:00 p.m.), when the various trends finally meet. Completions outnumber arrivals until the facility has finally caught up with most of its daily work. However, note that while patient arrivals drop after 14:00, generation of orders continues at an increased pace, peaking at 15:00 before finally falling. These late-afternoon orders will most likely arrive at the facility the next morning, at which point the same, frenetic pattern begins again.

Practical Advice

Note that we can derive the facility work hours from its HAP pattern alone. We do not even need to ask about the work schedule—it is clearly evident in the data in Fig. 3.2, where examination begin and complete curves start at exactly 7:00 in the morning and end at exactly 6:00 PM (18:00). You can use this simple data science to corroborate the timing of your operations. This should not be necessary, but sometimes it is. Not everything works exactly as expected, as we will see later in this book.

This is how the universal human activity pattern drives the pattern of ordering pulses, which, in turn, defines the pattern of patient arrivals. Making everything even more interesting, these patterns interact with one another, producing subtle but important effects. Look at Fig. 3.1 once more. You can see that generation of orders for X-ray examinations occurs over much of the 24-h day (from 6:00 to nearly midnight). Yet the X-ray imaging facility in Fig. 3.2 works only from 7:00 to 18:00. Consequently, while X-ray exam processing curves (arrival, begin, and complete) have a narrower shape, they are higher because of the need to handle the volume of orders in a shorter time than the orders were generated.[3] This is why the processing curves approach 18% in the morning but the ordering curve peaks at only 14%.

You can also see that the peak of the ordering volume, when the facility is getting slammed by demands for service, occurs at 10:00. One in three patients walks in during a relatively short 2-h period between 10:00 and 12:00, and one in four orders is issued during this time. When the workload surges to its highest volume, it can easily overwhelm the facility's resources. This daily occurrence, a classic case of demand exceeding supply, results in daily delays, as can be seen in Fig. 3.2 in the offset of the "Complete" curve from the "Arrive" curve. As might be expected, the delays are most severe during and shortly after the peak patient arrival period (8:00–11:00). The facility then has an opportunity to catch up but the delays return between 12 and 1 PM, during a period when orders are down. Could this reflect technologist staffing patterns over the lunch hour? Possibly. In any event, the facility recovers relatively quickly: by 2 PM the gap has once again closed.

Try building similar charts from your facility data. You may uncover important patterns that change the way you think about your operation.

3.1.1   Linear Thinking

The facility represented in Fig. 3.2 operates in a reasonably controlled fashion. However, as we will see in a later example, not all imaging sites run as smoothly. If a facility cannot handle its demand, it can easily descend into operational chaos. We

---

[3]The daily volume corresponds to the sum of all hourly volumes—or, simply, to the area under the curve.

will examine this type of occurrence more closely in the next section. For now, let us stop for a second and think about what drives the phenomenon. We flatter ourselves if we believe that chaos arises from circumstances no one could possibly anticipate. As we have just seen, a handful of simple analytics can tell a fairly detailed story of what is happening—we do not need to spend hours on workflow observations and interviews to reach this understanding. So what prevents us from foreseeing the unforeseen?

There are two unrealistic habits of thought that can be disastrous when they take hold in the context of operations management. Both stem from poor understanding of data, and an inability (or unwillingness) to recognize the true causes of performance issues.

The first bad habit is *linear thinking*. From the time we learn the multiplication tables in our early school years, we are programmed to think linearly. If $2 \times 3 = 6$, then $4 \times 3 = 12$, right? Or, to put it in radiology terms: If the capacity of a room is four patients per hour and the facility is open for 8 h, why would you have any problem accommodating 30 patients a day?

This is how the consultants like to calculate capacity. Real operations rarely run in a linear fashion, though, and for this reason linear projections often fail. The HAP curves demonstrate this fact brilliantly. Neither the generation of orders nor the radiology workflow occurs in a linear fashion. So, if you (and/or your organization) are planning your resources linearly, dividing the total daily workload by the total number of work hours and the capacity of each imaging device, you are paving a road to operational chaos. In reality, a significant portion of the daily workload may fall during a brief time window. Such surges in activity can wreak havoc, creating stress for the staff and breakdowns in customer relations.

The second bad habit is *elastic thinking*: "If we try really hard, we can do everything." Everyone knows that we can get more done when we are moving faster; all managers have observed that their facilities are sometimes more productive than during other periods, generally when the staff is operating in high gear. Why can't we apply these lessons indefinitely? Didn't Albert Einstein teach us that time dilates—the faster we move, the more it slows down, allowing us to get ever-more done?

Bad news! This does not apply to radiology operations.

Do not get us wrong—there is certainly some "elasticity" to the workday, as affirmed by the old saw "work expands to fill the available time." But what if you create a workflow assuming maximal effort on the part of your staff and the work suddenly doubles, or equipment fails, or your staff gets sick or goes on vacation? If you can still accomplish the same tasks in the same time when any of these happens, then you, so unlike most of us, must be blessed with abundant resources! In the real world, when workload greatly exceeds our elasticity, corners get cut, errors ensue, and tempers fray [1].

Real workflows are highly nonlinear and may have conflicting goals, and therefore should be "tuned" to produce a specific expected result—be it optimum staff and equipment use, or rapid turnaround, or limited waiting time. *Do not guess, and do not make unrealistic promises. Study your real data.*

3.1.2 Ordering Disasters

What happens when the stream of incoming orders overwhelms radiology resources?

We will cover this topic in more detail when we talk about patient arrivals and waiting times but it is worth examining it briefly in this chapter, looking at the same walk-in facility we studied with Fig. 3.2. The charts there gave us a year-averaged display of ordering and workflow rhythms. These averaged data made sense and were followed pretty closely on most days.

Figure 3.3 provides a different look at these same data, with the average order rate shown in a solid black line and the average patient wait displayed as a dotted black line. Here, though, we have superimposed upon the annual performance events that occurred on one of the worst days of the year.

One day in the facility, things changed drastically when the referring physician group ordered a much-larger-than-usual number of exams (red solid curve in Fig. 3.3). Instead of adhering to the gradually increasing HAP pattern, the morning started with a burst of 25 orders at around 8:00—some 2.5 times greater than the expected number. The waiting-patient count started to climb out of control, and the facility had to mobilize all of its resources to deal with the ensuing chaos, with only partial success. The number of patients still waiting started to drop at 10:00, but the pressure had only begun to lift when a second burst of orders followed at 11:00,

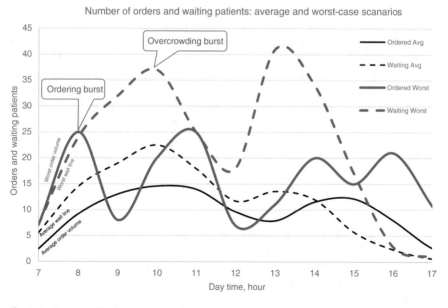

Fig. 3.3 Average ("business as usual") and worst-case days at an outpatient XR facility. Solid curves show the number of orders generated each hour and the dashed lines show the number of patients waiting for their exam. The solid black curve is the HAP curve we discussed previously. The red "worst case" corresponds to a single day when a busy new practice was abruptly introduced, resulting in many more orders than usual

resulting in a crush of patients in the waiting room at around 13:00. Two more ordering bursts hit the facility, at 2 and 4 o'clock in the afternoon, making the day completely miserable for all involved. The patients were complaining, the staff was exhausted, and the referring physicians were bombarding the managers with angry "why the hell does it take so long?" phone calls.

A year later every detail of this nightmare remained burned in the memory of the facility's managers. Why did this happen? As it turned out, a very busy orthopedic practice had begun seeing patients that day, without considering the likely consequences of introducing an influx of patients into the clinical workflow. Lacking all understanding of radiology capabilities, the clinical services were guilty of elastic, wishful thinking. They knew there would be a huge increase in the amount of work but the only preparation and help they offered was a "We hope you can handle it"! Needless to say, the imaging facility could not "handle" it, and rapid adjustment was required. The managers of the orthopedic practice were chastened for a time, but this sort of thing will presumably happen again when a new group of managers has forgotten the lessons of the past.

We have been talking about problems relevant to walk-in services, where the generation of an order leads directly to patient arrival. However, surges in demand can cause other types of problems. For sites where scheduling requires a telephone call to radiology, orderly management of telephone queues is necessary to avoid bottlenecks in scheduling [2]. Failure to manage the telephone queues properly can cause significant delays.

For example: one center experienced a bottleneck due to an inability to match demand for service with the availability of resources in large part because it attempted to obtain protocols prior to scheduling [3]. There was sound reasoning for this decision: namely that the protocol determined the examination duration and therefore scheduling would be improved if the protocol was known. Following assignment of the protocol, the technologists would estimate the time required and scheduling could proceed. In this case, though, assignment of protocols required the participation of the radiologists and, because clinics batched their order entry to the end of the day (a perfect example of nonlinearity in workflows), a large percentage of orders arrived between 4 PM and 6 PM. So, by the time the order was entered, the radiologists had left for the day and the orders were not protocoled until the following morning, leaving the schedulers underutilized between 4 and 8 PM, when they finished their shifts. Furthermore, in this institution, the cases were scheduled into individually timed appointments based on known times needed for specific sequences, in 5-min increments. Thus, an examination might be scheduled for 30, 35, 40 min, etc., based upon the technologists' understanding of the selected protocol. This is an extremely labor-intensive way to schedule cases, and it ate up an additional 7 h from when the protocol was selected. As you might expect, the combination of these two requirements led to staff members being alternately underutilized and overcommitted, ultimately creating massive delays.

How can you avoid these types of problems? We would recommend several approaches:

- *Study your HAP curve* and its surge patterns. Try to have a plan for handling peak loads.

- *Do not rely on averages*—Study the worst cases since these are the ones that will generate a disproportionate number of complaints and a huge amount of stress.
- *Adjust your service guarantees and expectations* using the real data. If a facility is starved for resources (either human or equipment), it may be because those responsible for planning are guilty of linear or elastic thinking. Be prepared to show what will happen when capacity is exceeded even temporarily.

Given the complexity of healthcare, some problems are likely inevitable. But knowing the magnitude and frequency of these problems will put you in a much better position to manage them when they arise. We will have more to say about unavoidably unsatisfactory service when we discuss patient arrivals in the following chapters.

3.2   Order Priorities

Assigning priorities is a time-honored way of dealing with overloads. In radiology, identifying a priority class for either image acquisition or examination interpretation is a classic form of subdividing a queue. As such, while it may improve performance for a specific category of examinations, it cannot improve overall performance: as you might recall from the pages above, someone has to be below the average.

The priority assigned to image acquisition can be either the same or different from that which is assigned to interpretation. For example, a patient from out of state may need to have an imaging study done before returning home, but the interpretation could be routine. An inpatient may require an urgent imaging study to document successful completion of a procedure (such as a line placement) but the images might be viewed by the proceduralist, thus removing the pressure to obtain a rapid formal interpretation.[4]

There is an infinite number of possibilities when it comes to order priorities and priority combinations. Similarly, what the priority means can be both variable and vague. Indeed, a "priority" might be nothing more than a relative assignation—for example, priority #3 will be addressed more quickly than priority #4, with no implication of a service guarantee. Are there more precise and practical ways to define priorities? We can see one in the simple example of a grocery store, where shoppers purchasing "8 items or less" get to use the express line. (We all know that customers with 9 or 10 items will sometimes sneak into the express line, but this is not because there is any ambiguity in the definition of "8 items or less.") In healthcare, though, coming up with a clear definition of what belongs in each priority group can be difficult. In one study of inpatient imaging, the authors described a four-point priority score for image acquisition and included brief examples of what can be included in each priority category (Table 3.1) [4].

---

[4]This of course introduces the issue of potentially discrepant interpretations between the clinician and the radiologist—but that is beyond the scope of this chapter.

Table 3.1 Order of inpatient imaging acquisition times, achieved with four-level prioritization, study by [4]

Priority	Description	Mean, observed time (order-to-acquisition), h	STD, observed time (order-to-acquisition), h
1	Critical/alert: Absolute most urgent studies (such as stroke alerts)	1.18	1.92
2	Emergent/inpatient spine clearance (such as non-alerted traumas)	1.51	2.43
3	Urgent/discharge pending	4.23	6.32
4	ASAP/most inpatients (performed ASAP *after* more urgent exams)	5.66	7.55

Here, as one hopes would be the case, the fastest times were reported for the highest priorities across imaging modalities. However, though the mean values were distinct, there was significant overlap among the categories, suggesting that a "service guarantee" would not be possible (note the high standard deviations in Table 3.1). Perhaps the most useful result was that the number of "routine" examinations (priority 4) increased from 6 to 39% after this system was implemented. By providing a clear definition of a relatively small number of categories, the authors were able to reduce the problem of assigning priorities to manageable dimensions. We can mention in passing that a similar study of interpretation (rather than acquisition) allowed for a larger number of priorities and yielded a less definitive result [5]. In this case, technologists were given the definitions for nine "read" priorities and asked to assign a priority number at the completion of each case. After implementation, turnaround was more or less in the order of priority but the differences in performance for the lower priorities were minimal.

Of course, the concept of relative priority described above does not address certain types of priority requests commonly seen in medical facilities—including requests like "in 2 hours" or "in the AM." Nor would it be especially satisfactory to referring clinicians who want some assurance of when an "urgent" examination will actually get done.

Two priorities are found virtually everywhere: "routine" and "STAT." STAT is a special case. Hospitals are expected to have policies covering the handling of so-called STAT examinations (although not, as far as we are aware, specific performance expectations). "STAT" is a time-honored term that is usually interpreted as indicating medical urgency, and that may carry medicolegal implications. In thinking about the appropriate use of the STAT designation, we can easily encounter uncertainty as it is quite possible to imagine circumstances that require equally expeditious handling without implying life-or-death consequences: for example, an instrument count in an operating room. In devising a program that does justice to the literal meaning of STAT ("statim"—Latin for "immediately"), it is almost certainly necessary to create an "interruptive" workflow that causes the technologist (and possibly the radiologist) to stop what they are doing and deal with the "STAT" case.

3.2.1   How Many Priorities Can a Radiology Department Support?

How many priority categories should there be beyond STAT and routine? Should inpatients receive priority over outpatients? Patients awaiting discharge and patients in intensive care units over other inpatients? When a doctor is awaiting a report, should that report be prioritized? Should patients on their way to a clinical visit be prioritized over those who will receive their results at home?

The answer to the question of how many priorities are supportable depends entirely on whether you believe a particular priority should be linked to a particular service expectation. If all you are looking to do is perform services in the order of priority, then a very large number is feasible. In our opinion, though, such an approach would be pointless. Clinicians do not care if their order is handled faster or slower than others. The only thing that matters is *how long* it takes from the time of the order to the time of the imaging study and the report. Therefore, if the goal is to provide service expectations (as we think it should be), the number and timing of each priority must depend upon the means available to respond to the request (remembering that the department's ability to comply may be very different on evenings, weekends, and holidays, for example). Our experience suggests that only a small number of priorities can result in predictably different outcomes.

> **Keep It Real!**
> There is another practical limit in expanding your priority list: How many of the priorities can you remember? When we recently pulled a list of all priorities implemented in our PACS, we could not interpret some of them. Priority implementation involves training, learning curves, and implementation plans. Worse, as your list of priorities grows, you may find that some overlap and/or conflict with one another, making the list impossible to manage. Keep it short to keep it real.

Let us begin by examining the issue of interpretation priority. We consider this to be less complex to implement than performance priority because, in most instances, the radiologist's worklists are structured by computer—driven either by PACS or by RIS, depending on the system.

Like people everywhere, radiologists have essentially three major ways of working: interruptive, prioritized, and routine.

The interruptive mode means "topmost priority" and requires the radiologist to stop what he or she is currently doing and attend to a case. This mode of delivering service is expensive because it disrupts the radiologist's workflow and almost certainly decreases overall productivity. In addition, it typically requires the services of trained support staff to be aware of the need for an interpretation and to alert the radiologist to that need. We attempted to automate this process some years ago when we introduced an interruptive "pop-up" that would appear on the radiologist's workstation announcing the need to stop what he or she was doing and turn to something else. The radiologists called the pop-up windows "NagMe" screens, giving you an idea of how popular they were! (See Fig. 3.4.)

How well did the "NagMe" system work? It reduced the time needed to generate a preliminary report by approximately 35% for staff reports and by 44% for reports generated by trainees (Fig. 3.5). However, the system did not work at all if an appropriate radiologist was not sitting at a workstation when the "NagMe" screen appeared. We have since abandoned it in favor of having a human coordinator manage the cases. Note also that although the "NagMe" system worked for reports created by residents and for those created by staff, turnaround was much faster when no trainees were involved.

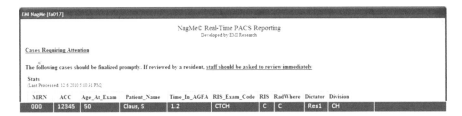

Fig. 3.4 A pop-up window that appeared automatically on the workstation of the appropriate radiologist (in this case a chest radiologist) when an examination with an "interruptive" priority was received by PACS

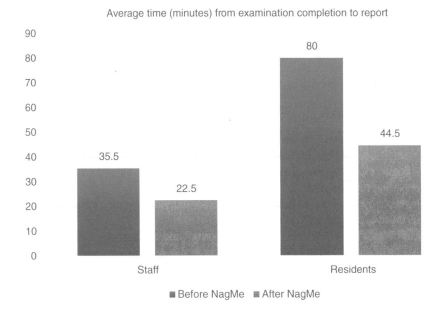

Fig. 3.5 The effect of an electronic "interruption" on report creation. A "NagMe" pop-up screen (see Fig. 3.4) appeared on the workstation of the radiologist telling him to stop what he is doing and attend to an urgent case. This improved the turnaround time considerably

If the radiologist is not going to be interrupted, the approach is for the radiologist to read each case in order of priority. A high priority can accelerate the interpretation of a case, but the actual performance will vary depending upon the relative number of studies accorded equal or higher priority. For example, if your department wants to contract with an urgent care center and offers them a priority "just below an intensive care unit," the interpretation will be faster or slower depending upon how many patients are in the intensive care units that day. The more levels of priority there are, the less predictable the number of cases with equal or greater priority becomes. Therefore, we believe that multiple levels of priority will quickly become unmanageable and that any "service guarantees" should not claim a better level of performance than can be achieved with the lowest prioritized case (i.e., immediately above routine). This information can be readily obtained by review of historical performance.

The situation is somewhat more complex for image acquisition since the technologists' workflow is not so readily managed by a computer. Prioritizing walk-in patients is usually not a problem and can be done "on the fly." However, prioritization becomes more difficult for scheduled outpatients. What happens, for example, if an examination that is usually scheduled in advance must be done before the first appointment is available? To deal with this problem, we have created an "urgent imaging" program which attempts to fit such patients into full schedules while doing as little harm as possible to already scheduled appointments. This interruptive process is handled manually by a manager, and as a result is relatively costly to maintain. The process begins with a telephone call, following which the manager identifies the resource and time that best fit the urgency of the request and that cause the least disruption to the schedule. The first question asked during the process is whether an urgent report is required. If it is, staff are assigned to alert the appropriate radiologist of the pending examination.

Inpatient priorities come with their own set of requirements. In our institution, a day's work is organized by a manager or supervisor who reviews inpatient examination orders and decides on a sensible sequence. Despite the best of intentions, though, and even using the most sophisticated of tools, this sequence is subject to a host of factors that are simply impossible to control: among them, the availability of transport, the location of the patients (for portable examinations), and other conflicting appointments the patient may have. What tools are available to manage this mélange of moving parts? In reality, there are very few. Inpatient priorities are generally managed using a simple sorted list—whether electronic or on paper—that may or may not be re-sorted during the course of the day.

Finally, providing radiology reports within a defined time limit should be regarded as a distinct radiology "product." Clearly, faster turnaround is more expensive to maintain than slower turnaround (because it requires excess capacity, or more manual interventions, especially in the interruptive workflows). Yet compensation is the same regardless of urgency. Therefore, demands for faster turnaround must be kept within sustainable bounds. What causes clinicians to designate an order as high priority? One might assume that the decision is based on medical urgency but experience suggests that this is often not the case. Any practicing radiologist can tell you that many of the "urgent" requests he or she receives are not urgent in any medical sense. The urgency may be tied to an administrative issue, such as the requesting clinician leaving for vacation. Or it might simply be a matter of trying to control one's environment—like the useless door-close buttons on elevators, nonfunctional office thermostats, and buttons that claim to operate crosswalks but probably are not actually connected to anything [6]. Ultimately, urgency is all about perception. One study showed that the longer the perceived access time, the greater the number of high-priority requests [7].

3.3 Should Orders Expire?

How quickly do we expect an order to be added to the schedule once it is written? In our institution, we expect scheduling to happen rapidly because it can be done both before protocols are assigned and before pre-authorization. Also, scheduling is decentralized, and the clinical offices that create the orders often schedule the examination concurrently to placing the order.

Based on the ordering data for our hospital, Fig. 3.6 and Table 3.2 demonstrate this rapid order processing trend. Here, the majority of all orders are processed—i.e., put on the schedule—within a few days of being created. Walk-in

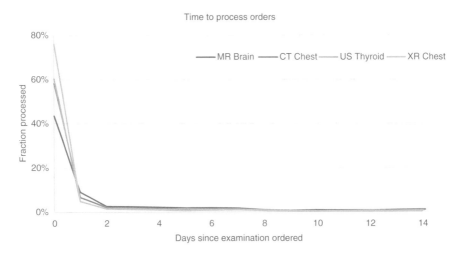

Fig. 3.6 Number of days required to process (schedule) an order

Table 3.2 Order processing metrics for different radiology modalities

Modality	Orders processed during the first …				Days required to process …			
	1 day (%)	1 week (%)	1 month (%)	3 months (%)	50%	75%	90%	95%
XR	75.9	85.7	93.3	96.3	1	1	15	48
CT	58.2	72.9	84.5	93.6	1	8	59	111
US	60.3	72.0	82.7	89.5	1	10	98	111
MR	43.5	63.3	79.5	90.8	2	21	85	159

facilities (such as XR, in our case) usually show the highest rates of order process-ing because walk-in patients are typically examined relatively soon after they arrive. Scheduling for facilities such as MR, CT, or US imaging centers can be done at a somewhat more leisurely pace since there is no expectation of the patient immedi-ately undergoing examination. In such cases, many additional factors—such as patient scheduling preferences—can impact and even delay scheduling. Nonetheless, the fact that all of the curves in Fig. 3.6 share the same fast-decaying pattern sug-gests that the chances of an order actually being scheduled decrease significantly with time.

It is important to understand these behaviors, because if an order is placed but not scheduled within the expected time, something may have gone wrong. Not may the unscheduled order become clinically irrelevant, there is also a risk of a provider selecting the wrong order for a patient who has multiple orders on file. Moreover, aging orders clutter the system with "dirty" data, which cannot be used or analyzed. As a result, orders placed in the system but never activated (scheduled) should expire after a predetermined amount of time. What should this amount of time be? Our experience (Fig. 3.6) suggests that most unscheduled orders could expire after a few weeks, but a conservative estimate might place the number between 3 and 6 months.

3.3.1   Case Study: Patterns of Order Aging

What patterns can be found in aging orders? Figure 3.7, based on a year of our out-patient brain MRI examinations, uncovers several. Each order on this chart is repre-sented by a separate dot; the horizontal axis measures the number of days it took to process the order (that is, to put it on the schedule), the vertical, and the number of days it took to perform the examination ordered once it was scheduled.

As expected, the vast majority of the orders are clustered in the bottom-left cor-ner, showing that they took only a few days to schedule and then only a few days to perform, as suggested by Fig. 3.6. But the remaining orders either are scattered randomly or form interesting linear patterns. The scattered orders are understand-able; they could arise from any number of order processing inconsistencies. But what accounts for the perfect lines?

Delving more deeply into this unusual result, we have seen that a number of our referring clinicians place orders for examinations at periodic intervals (such as 1 or 2 years) and that these orders may be scheduled at any time between when the order is placed and the expected date of performance. Mathematically, the "1-year follow-up" means that:

$$\left(\text{Time to schedule the order}\right) + \left(\text{Time to perform a scheduled exam}\right)$$
$$= \left(\text{Time to perform the order}\right) = 365\,\text{days}$$

This clearly corresponds to a diagonal line in Fig. 3.7, representing the orders performed 1 year after they were placed. Similar distinct linear patterns are also seen at 18 months, 2 years, and even 183 days (6 months).

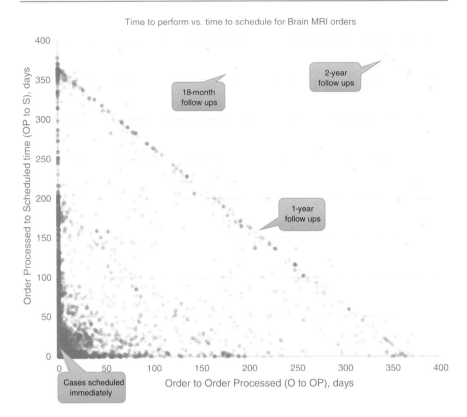

Fig. 3.7 Graphic display of the relationship between ordering, scheduling, and performance. The horizontal axis represents the interval between ordering and scheduling (time to process an order). The vertical axis, the interval between scheduling and performance (time to perform the ordered examination)

These patterns indicate that, for examinations intended to be performed at some future date, clinical offices may delay scheduling until almost any point prior to the required performance (most likely to coordinate patient and physician schedules). We do not know what triggers the scheduling event, or how often this approach does not work as it should, making it necessary to request a higher priority in order to meet a calendar deadline. However, since radiology departments are unlikely to stop the practice of deliberately delayed scheduling, some allowance for the practice must be made—for example, delaying expiration of an order until well after the "expected performance" date (Fig. 3.8).

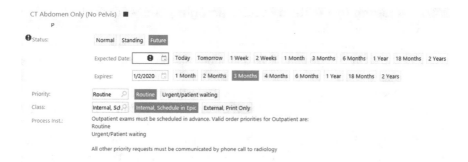

Fig. 3.8 Screenshot from our information system showing the "expected performance date." This can be used to manage the expiration of the order

3.4   Who May Place an Order?

The answer to this seemingly straightforward question is neither simple nor straightforward. The legal answer is the most clear-cut: licensed physicians, including osteopaths, chiropractors, and physician surrogates (physician assistants and nurse practitioners). However, whether a radiology department will be reimbursed for filling the order depends on a bizarre and internally inconsistent amalgam of rules derived from state licensure, hospital privileges, and a host of different insurance payment policies. Given the number of payers, plans, guidelines, and local, state, and federal regulations, simplifying the rules would be challenging at best—unless one were to adopt an overly conservative stance. At least in the United States, this type of complexity and ambiguity is one of the major reasons for the high administrative costs of healthcare.

Since the federal Medicare program (run by CMS, the Center for Medicare and Medicaid Services) is the largest provider of coverage in the United States, its policies carry the greatest weight. It is important to recognize, though, that the policies represent payment *rules*, not *laws*. Violation of the rules could be regarded as billing fraud but there would not be any consequences if no bill were rendered. Different sets of Medicare rules govern diagnostic test ordering depending upon whether the examination is to be performed in a diagnostic testing center (defined by Medicare as a physician, a group of physicians, or an independent diagnostic testing facility) or a hospital, and whether the patient is an inpatient or an outpatient. The "Ordering of Diagnostic Tests Rule" covers imaging tests performed in a testing facility, and the "Conditions of Participation: Radiology Service Rules" cover hospital inpatients and outpatients. Despite efforts by CMS to clarify these distinctions, some facilities still operate in a gray area.

Let us consider a few examples of radiology ordering in different types of medical facilities.

3.4.1   Imaging in a Testing Facility (Imaging Center or Office)

For imaging performed in an imaging center or office, Medicare requires that *the orders be placed by* "the treating physician or practitioner." Orders placed by nurses and physician assistants are permitted by Medicare. The same is not always true with insurance companies, though, and even if it is, the companies differ on whether the case should be billed using the name of the advanced practitioner or the covering physician.

Surprisingly, Medicare rules do not require a signed order. A telephone call or an email is permitted. However, if an order is communicated by telephone, both the treating physician and the testing site must document the telephone call in their respective copies of the patient's medical record by means of a signed note. Of course, the chances of the radiology department actually confirming that the appropriate documentation is present before providing the service seem remote.

These definitions clearly exclude diagnostic radiologists from placing orders in testing facilities. This leads to a somewhat odd situation in which a radiologist may decline to do a test as ordered but cannot change the order—except in certain, very limited circumstances, as described below—as doing so would constitute creation of a new order. This rule does not apply to interventional radiologists, who are considered treating physicians and thus can order tests related to the condition associated with the intervention.

The limited changes a radiologist is permitted to make to an order include protocol selection, modification of an order with clear and obvious errors (e.g., an X-ray of the wrong foot was ordered), and cancellation of the order if the patient's physical condition will not allow performance of the test.

There is a catch, though. While Medicare rules allow the radiologist to specify whether contrast is to be used during imaging, appropriately regarding such use as part of the protocol, this permission only applies if the requesting clinician has not specified use of contrast as part of the order. If the original order requests the use of contrast and the radiologist does not think it is needed, the radiologist may not simply change it; a new order is required. Furthermore, because the addition or removal of contrast necessitates the use of a different procedure code, some insurance companies will consider the order to have changed. Such modification might be viewed as invalidating the precertification process and thus become grounds for payment denial.

Precertification (pre-authorization) introduces yet another layer of complexity. Precertification was originally conceived of as the responsibility of the requesting clinician or his or her nurse, presuming that only those individuals really knew the purpose of the request. An exception can be made, though, when the referring clinician and the imaging facility are part of the same organization and share a common medical record. In these cases, pre-authorization may be obtained by the imaging facility itself [8]. Precertification is everywhere considered an onerous burden, so radiology practices that can handle precertification for their referring clinicians have a competitive advantage in receiving their referrals.

Sometimes an abnormality found on an imaging study will lead to a request for additional examinations. The radiologist may perform the additional testing, but only in limited circumstances. In most cases, it is necessary to obtain an additional order from the clinician before doing so. The radiologist can generate the order, without contacting the referring physician, but only if he or she is unable to reach the referring physician and all the following criteria are met:

– The diagnostic test originally ordered by the treating physician/practitioner has been performed.
– The radiologist determines that an additional diagnostic test is medically necessary due to abnormal results of the first diagnostic test.
– A delay in additional testing would have an "adverse effect" on the patient.
– The treating physician is notified of the results of the test and uses the results in the treatment of the patient.
– The radiologist documents why the additional testing was necessary. (It is critical to document the reason in the reports of the original test and the additional test.)

"Conditional" orders are permitted under specific circumstances. For example, an order that reads "diagnostic mammogram of right breast with ultrasound if mass identified" is acceptable if it applies to a single patient. Not acceptable is a standing order for all patients of a given requesting physician: e.g., "if gallbladder ultrasound for Dr. Smith is negative, do UGI."

Mammography is a special case, in several ways. Under the Mammography Quality Standards Act, a specific order is not required for screening mammograms, or for diagnostic mammograms performed to evaluate an abnormality seen on screening mammograms. Computer-aided detection in conjunction with mammography is yet another special case. Here, the radiologist can determine whether the procedure should be performed, without a written order from the treating physician.

With the exceptions above, CMS does not allow radiologists to change the originally ordered test or perform additional tests (including 3D reformations). The organization reasons that the radiologist may not know the true intent of the order or of studies performed on the patient prior to the request. In these cases, written or verbal communication must occur prior to the change in order to obtain a new or revised order.

3.4.2 Ordering Services Performed in a Hospital, Including Hospital Outpatient Facilities

As if that were not complicated enough, there are different rules for imaging performed in hospital facilities!

For these facilities, the CMS rules state, "Radiologic services must be provided only on the order of practitioners with clinical privileges or, consistent with state law, of other practitioners authorized by the medical staff and the governing body to order the services." This rule applies to both inpatients and outpatients. Since radiologists generally meet the above qualifications, they can be the source of the orders as far as Medicare is concerned (though this is not necessarily true for private payers).

The upshot? If a single radiology group's practice encompasses both hospital-based and freestanding imaging centers, it is likely the group will need to follow multiple sets of rules.

3.5   Making Sense of Orders

In the "old days," paper requests for imaging studies were often completely unstructured ….

We initially began this section with those words, but then we realized that we are still very much in the "old days." Radiology orders are, even now, often done on paper (Fig. 3.9). This, it should go without saying, is the least efficient and least structured possible approach. A paper order form might request certain specific information, for example, even though there is little or no way to enforce completion. As a result, the radiology department has limited control over the information it receives. Also, unstructured requests frequently lack essential information, such as appropriate indications. Even a complete absence of indications is not rare [9].

3.5.1   Required vs. Optional Information

With electronic order entry, it is possible to require answers to particular questions, and to establish how the answers are entered. Options include "free text" entry (similar to a paper request) or structured entry using multiple-choice drop-downs or "pick lists." When specific information is necessary, the latter, forced-choice

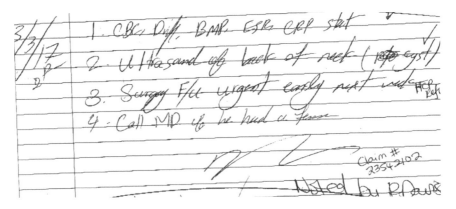

Fig. 3.9 A recent example of a paper imaging request. The request is difficult to read, it is buried among several other orders (#2 out of 4), and the "indication" is cryptic at best ("cyst")

approach is better. Free text can still be allowed, but it should be used to enhance or support the forced choice, not replace it.

How much information should be required to complete an order? While it is true that a great deal of information can be collected by requiring answers to specific questions, such demands can prove irritating for referring offices and may lead to dissatisfaction and even to loss of referrals. Since referrals are the life blood of a radiology practice, the wise manager will make ordering as easy as possible. This means that thoughtful design of the ordering form is a key tool for marketing as well as for operations. Simplicity should rule! Indeed, whenever possible, the wise manager will resist the temptation to include "optional" questions on the order form. Why? Well, if the answer is optional, then either the information is not really necessary or there are other ways to obtain it. In our practice, optional questions are routinely ignored by clinicians, and by encouraging the practice of ignoring portions of the form we devalue the entire process. In any event, reducing this clutter reduces the work of ordering. We believe in the rule of the Kingdom of the Ants: "Everything Not Forbidden Is Compulsory" [10]. However, our efforts to follow this principle are sometimes met with internal opposition from department members who see the potential value of obtaining additional information but are not sensitive to the burden this imposes on the referring clinicians.

> **Keep It Real!**
> Anything that makes the order placing process longer will be seen by the ordering clinicians as an obstacle, an impediment, and an incentive to send the patient elsewhere. Even attempts to be helpful—such as providing decision support for orders—run the risk of driving away business. If they are carefully designed, requests for additional information might be accepted [11], but radiology departments need to be constantly alert to the need to lighten the administrative burden by limiting such requests, and where possible taking on some of the burden themselves (for example, in obtaining pre-authorizations, where permitted).

As we can see, achieving the proper balance between information and effort is complicated and can have any number of unintended consequences.

The question is, then, what information should we require?

3.5.2 Minimum Information Requirements

Here is the information we absolutely must have to perform an examination:

- The name (or other ID) of the patient
- The examination requested
- The name of the individual who requested it
- The side, when appropriate
- Clinical information that is sufficient to generate an ICD10 code

Some (hopefully most) of this data can be harvested digitally. Electronic health records (EHR) and radiology information systems (RIS) often collect essential pieces of information using dictionary-driven data entry. For example, the name of the ordering physician (and the examination) is very likely to be selected from a prepopulated list rather than entered as free text. If a physician is not on the list, either that physician will not be able to order a test or manual processes must be implemented to add his or her name. Radiology departments often receive orders for patients who are not otherwise being seen in their institution. The institution certainly wants to be able to accept these patients, and this provides motivation to make the physician dictionary as inclusive as possible. Still, as the list of names in the dictionary grows, so too does the risk of error.

Consider this quite common scenario: There are three physicians with the same name in the dictionary, so it is necessary to use a second identifier (ID number, office address, etc.) to avoid choosing the wrong one. However, if two of them have not previously ordered imaging studies, they are likely not the source of the request. The same could hold true for very infrequently selected indications. Ideally, information systems should be able to inform users if they are selecting something out of the ordinary, just as bank's website tells you if you are about to make a transaction that is significantly different than transactions you have made in the past. Unfortunately, healthcare IT is primitive and we are not aware of any systems that do this.

Radiology information systems increasingly are being absorbed into hospital EHRs. This has certain benefits, but it also results in a loss of flexibility. If possible, within the context of your EHR, you should try to establish a regular schedule to "clean" system data that is relevant to radiology to reduce the risk of error. Indications that are rarely or never used should be considered for deletion. Clinicians who have not placed orders within a reasonable time frame should be deleted, or otherwise inactivated as the system allows. Questions regularly ignored should be eliminated. This will make life easier in a variety of ways: in terms of tidiness, efficiency, marketing, and patient safety.

You may want to include other types of information in addition to the essential five types listed above, for any number of reasons. Remember, though, that each additional request for information may be viewed by the referring physician as an imposition. Even worse, if the information is not readily available to the individual placing the order, or if he or she does not understand perfectly the request you are making, the response may prove nothing more than an unreliable attempt to work around the system. So, think carefully before you request other types of information.

Information associated with orders can be problematic in other ways as well. Consider one of the more serious issues you may encounter: the name of the requesting physician is inaccurate (due to someone misreading a handwritten request, or mistranscribing a verbal order, or due to interface errors between electronic systems). Sometimes, the name of the physician who placed the order *is* correct (hurray!) but, due to a change of service or change of shift, for example, he or she might not be the appropriate person to send the result. The history could also be wrong, whether due to a sloppy selection from "pick lists" or due to standing orders [12].

The best way to obtain the highest quality information for both billing and diagnostic purposes is for the radiologist to interview each patient individually but this solution is probably not practical in a large-scale operation [13].

Keep It Real!

(The Parable of the "Wise Manager")

Some years ago, our technologists at an outpatient facility were bothered by the occasional unheralded arrival of a patient from a *skilled nursing facility* (nursing home or "SNF"). So they requested that a question be added to our order entry form: "Is this patient from a skilled nursing facility?"

This did nothing to stop the problem. Nursing home patients still arrived at outpatient facilities. In most cases, the question was not answered but sometimes it was and the answer was "No." Why was this? Was the user simply too lazy to answer a question? Too distracted to notice it? Was it a deliberate attempt to mislead, thinking the patient would have greater access to imaging if the outpatient facility did not know he or she was coming from an SNF? Did the individual placing the order not know that the patient was in a nursing home? Or is it possible that, at the time the order was placed, the patient was actually not at a SNF?

Whatever the case, the technologists requested that the question be made mandatory. We objected on the grounds that it would add work (admittedly a small increment) to the process of ordering thousands of imaging studies each day. Instead the question was removed entirely. You may ask, "Why remove it? Wouldn't it be better to leave it on the form for the occasional referral that did it correctly?" The wise manager does not think so. Even if the answer is not required (or perhaps *especially* if the answer is not required) there is a "cost" to including low-value items on order screens. The user becomes accustomed to bypassing parts of the process and the probability of overlooking more important information increases.

3.5.3 Other Helpful Information

1. *Protocol selection.* Should the clinician be asked to select the protocol? This may work well when the order originates from a specialist who understands well the capabilities of the imaging modality. It is probably unreasonable to expect that all clinicians will have this level of expertise, though, and the radiology department that demands this level of specificity at the time of ordering will almost certainly receive a barrage of questions from baffled clinicians. We will have more to say about this approach when we discuss Chap. 5.

   Alternatively, one could require that all of the information needed to specify the protocol be included with the order. This is not usually a good idea as the types of information that qualify as necessary can be quite variable and unpredictable.

Most places place the burden for correctly specifying the examination on the radiologist (or, in some instances, an experienced technologist). This seems appropriate, and can be made to work with reasonable efficiency, especially in the context of a modern EHR, which permits convenient access to information.

Practical Advice

If you decide to allow the clinician to specify particular protocols, we believe it is important to be transparent about two critical issues:

1. Whether or not the protocol selected requires the use of intravenous contrast: This fact should be explicit in the name chosen for the protocol. It is important to avoid the contradictory (and dangerous) scenario in which a clinician requests a protocol that requires contrast and then specifies that contrast should not be used because of allergy or renal function.
2. Whether the selected protocol will result in an additional charge, as with, for example, protocols that scan multiple body parts or require 3D processing.

2. *Duration.* This brings us to one of the "Achilles heels" of radiology. Because the duration of the imaging examination can be altered by the specific protocol, it may not be possible to know how much time is required when the order is placed. This is especially true with orders tailored to the specific patient. In general, *the more highly customized the examination, the less predictable the duration.*

As a compromise, we require certain types of information that help us estimate how much time will be needed. These include the examination itself as well as any factors that could (or would not) result in the use of contrast. For example, most lumbar spine MR scans do not require the use of contrast. But if the examination is done for infection or tumor, or if the patient has relatively recently had spine surgery, contrast may be indicated. Therefore, answers to questions about these issues are required.

3. *Billing information that can be used to assign an ICD10 (International Classification of Diseases version 10) code.* If an examination results in abnormal findings, then the findings can be used to assign an ICD code. But what if the examination is normal? An ICD10 code is required in order to submit a bill. So, while it is possible to perform and even interpret most examinations without this information, it is reasonable to require that every order be accompanied by an indication that can be translated into an ICD code. Methods for doing this will vary with the capabilities of the EHR and order entry system.

As clinicians and radiology departments have grown accustomed to the ICD requirement, including an indication for an examination has come to seem almost natural. But it is not! For one thing, the system used can be absurdly detailed. A senior pulmonologist has complained bitterly to us that he is no longer able to order imaging studies for the diagnosis of "pneumonia" because he can never find it among the long list of specific types of pneumonia. The partial list of ICD10 pneumonia codes in Fig. 3.10 will give you an idea as to why!

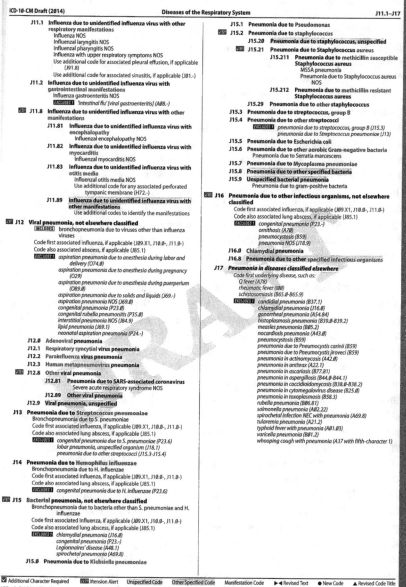

Fig. 3.10 Partial list of pneumonia billing codes

Also, ICD coding by definition requires the ordering physician to state what is wrong with the patient (disease or symptom), but it *does not* address what the clinician wishes to learn from the examination. Thus, if a patient has fallen down a flight of stairs and has a swollen ankle, the clinician might want to know whether there is a fracture. Here, the code for "swollen ankle" is an appropriate ICD10 indication, but the question of fracture ("rule out fracture") is not. The involvement of the stairs is irrelevant.

Why is this? If a test is ordered to "rule out" a specific condition (in the absence of documented signs or symptoms), it is regarded as a screening exam, and in nearly all cases will not be covered by insurance. This way of thinking does not come naturally to most doctors. It is like being told you cannot ask whether it will rain today but rather must state, with nary a hint of uncertainty, "There are storm clouds in the sky!" [14]. Also, the indication is not the same as the patient's "diagnosis." For example, a patient may be in the hospital for a diagnosis of diverticulitis. An MRI of the knee may be requested, but certainly not because of diverticulitis. Similarly, in the previous example, the examination is not ordered because the patient tripped on the stairs, but rather because of the "indication" of a painful and swollen knee.

These subtleties have proven remarkably difficult to explain to doctors. For this reason, the order entry system should require selection of at least one indication from a predefined list, to ensure that at least some useful information is provided. Allowing only free text as the indication will likely result in a significant number of un-codable examinations [9].

Still, we recognize that the ICD10 indication does not provide any opportunity for the clinician to indicate what he or she is attempting to learn. We use a compromise between structured and unstructured input to address this limitation. The user is obligated to choose from a predefined list for certain purposes (such as appropriate ICD10 indications) and offered the option of supplementing (but not replacing) these choices with free text.

With electronic order entry, it is possible to include the entire ICD10 dictionary within the drop-down list. This list of options can be daunting, and in some cases ludicrous [15]. We believe that the indications list should be as large as necessary, but as small as possible. The indications should be appropriate to the examination requested. In the example above, "diverticulitis" should not appear among the potential indications for a knee MRI. Fortunately, the ICD10 code is laid out as a branching tree, with higher order terms serving as headers for more specific indications. While indications should be coded to the highest possible level of specificity, greater specificity is usually available after the imaging study is completed.

3.6   Convenience vs. Safety

In the (admittedly imaginary) best of all worlds, the information needed to perform an examination safely would be collected well enough in advance to make all necessary preparations. Unfortunately, the time it takes to collect this information can vary significantly. For example, if it turns out that the patient has an allergy to the contrast material, a prophylactic regimen might have to be started 48 h in advance. On the other hand, a positive response to a question about whether the patient might be pregnant can be resolved within an hour. If the patient has implants (thus impacting MRI safety), it might take days to research the necessary preparations, whereas a positive response to a question about the risk of falling might not require any advance preparation at all.

Since this is a book about management, we will ignore the specifics of *how* each of these medical issues should be handled and focus on the information itself.

In our institution, information about allergies, implants, and possible pregnancy is extracted from the medical record using a semiautomated method and reviewed with the patient either upon arrival or shortly in advance. This information is not required as part of the order. That said, for those places that absolutely believe this information must be collected as part of the order, we recommend keeping the questions simple, easily understood by individuals without a medical degree and crafted in such a way as to flag items for future investigation, but not necessarily to provide final answers.

> **Know Your Tools**
>
> Pre-screening patients for contraindications is one of the areas where AI can help. Patient records can be quite complex, spread over different systems and formats (from structured text to very unstructured imaging). Manually looking for a needle in this haystack of data, on a regular basis, becomes a Herculean task with very high probability of error. Intelligent data processing systems, capable of natural language processing (NLP) and image interpretation, can do this much faster—at least to identify the most suspicious candidates.

Although there is a prevailing belief that redundancy equates safety, we think it is to omit questions that are unnecessary, that are duplicated by a subsequent process, or whose answers may not be reliable. Safety is the responsibility of the individual performing the test, and this responsibility cannot be passed on to others. Absolutely no amount of data collection at the time of ordering can remove the need for safety checks at the time of the procedure. In short, more is not necessarily better.

And there you have it. The order entry system should require information necessary to specify and report the examination (name of the examination; side, where appropriate; and name of the individual(s) who should receive the report). It should also require either an ICD10 code or language that easily translates into such a code. It might in some instances require information that determines the length of the examination. It should permit free-text entries but only as supplements, not replacements for other elements. Nothing else should be required, and "optional" data fields should be discouraged whenever possible.

References

1. Rhea JT, St Germain RP. The relationship of patient waiting time to capacity and utilization in emergency room radiology. Radiology. 1979;637(41):130–3.
2. Scott M, Waldron A. Improved scheduling operations in diagnostic imaging. Radiol Manag. 2013;35(1):30–5.
3. Wessman BV, Moriarity AK, Ametlli V, Kastan DJ. Reducing barriers to timely MR imaging scheduling. Radiographics. 2014;34(7):2064–70.
4. McWey RP, Hanshew MD, Patrie JT, Boatman DM, Gaskin CM. Impact of a four-point order-priority score on imaging examination performance times. J Am Coll Radiol. 2016;13(3):286–95.
5. Gaskin CMP, Hanshew MD, Boatman DM, McWey RP. Impact of a reading priority scoring system on the prioritization of examination interpretations. Am J Roentgenol. 2016;206(5):1031–9.
6. Mele C. Pushing that crosswalk button may make you feel better, but …. New York Times; 27 October 2016.
7. van Sambeek JR, Joustra PE, Das SF, Bakker PJ, Maas M. Reducing MRI access times by tackling the appointment-scheduling strategy. BMJ Qual Saf. 2011;20(12):1075–80.
8. Mulaik MW. Orders: to do or not to do? that is the question. Radiol Today. 2013;14(8):30.
9. Schneider E, Franz W, Spitznagel R, Bascom DA, Obuchowski NA. Effect of computerized physician order entry on radiologic examination order indication quality. Arch Intern Med. 2011;13:1036–8.
10. White T. The sword in the stone. New York: G.P. Putnam's Sons; 1938.
11. Prabhakar A, Harvey H, Misono A, Erwin A, Jones N, Heffernan J, Rosenthal D. Imaging decision support does not drive out-of-network leakage of referred imaging. J Am Coll Radiol. 2016;13:606–10.
12. Cohen MD. Accuracy of information on imaging requisitions: does it matter? J Am Coll Radiol. 2007;4(9):617–21.
13. Davis D, Mulligan M. Patient-centered care in diagnostic radiology: lessons learned from patient interviews prior to musculoskeletal magnetic resonance imaging. Qual Manag Health Care. 2015;24(1):38–44.
14. Buck S. Follow the rules of diagnostic test orders for radiology. In: Healthcare business monthly. 2017. p. 42–45.
15. Skievaski N. Struck by Orca: ICD-10 Illustrated. 2013, 0615955053, 9780615955056.

Scheduling

4

"There cannot be a crisis next week. My schedule is already full!"

Henry Kissinger, American politician

Contents

Things That Happen
- A scheduling template is created.
- Order information and protocol information are used to determine examination requirements.
- Examinations are put on the schedule either:
  - By a call center
  - By referring offices
- Some examinations require rescheduling.

Things to Measure
- Actual examination duration compared to scheduled duration
- Call center metrics (if applicable):
  - Time to answer
  - Time on hold
  - Dropped calls
- Availability (next available appointment)

4.1   The Art of Scheduling

A few years ago, a Norwegian plane carrying 40 passengers turned around and returned to an airport hundreds of kilometers away—despite having already started its descent—just so the crew would not have to work overtime. The crew's working time regulations were so strict that it was decided to make a full U-turn only to avoid extra working hours. All the time already spent on this flight, all the fuel burnt, and all the priorities and schedules of the 40 passengers aboard were sacrificed to comply with the crew schedule.

Welcome to the sometimes-strange world of scheduling—the art of assigning tasks to resources to make performance predictable. You can do it intuitively, but you probably want to play it smart and try to minimize some "cost function" (such as overtime in the case of that airline). For example, you may want to build your schedule to maximize utilization of the most expensive resources, or to minimize expenses, or even—and this happens as well—to give yourself as little work as possible while forcing others to pick up the slack (cost equated to your work time).

The "cost optimization" part, as you might easily imagine, has led to many cunning strategies and has been practiced for centuries, probably since the invention of sundials. Countless theses and papers have been published, dissecting every aspect of scheduling, and healthcare scheduling in particular [1, 2]. If any of them had been fully implemented, the world would be a much better place, with hospitals actually running on time. It is not.

This results in an interesting conundrum. Industry has introduced a wealth of advanced algorithms that can do smart scheduling [3], but healthcare continues to operate late, and inefficiently, using the most archaic scheduling tools, often with a "one-size-fits-all" mentality.

Why is this the case? We think that it is often a matter of inattentiveness or assigning a low priority to timeliness. Sometimes it may be due to lack of clarity about which aspect of performance is being optimized. There is no simple magic scheduling trick to fix this, but if you are aware of your scheduling problems, there is a chance that you might be able to ameliorate them.

4.2   Scheduling in Radiology

Scheduling in radiology refers to the process of assigning a patient examination to a particular device, physician, room, and other related resources, at a particular time. The requesting clinician may do it at the time of ordering (distributed scheduling), in which case the selection of time, place, and device is most likely (and hopefully) guided by an algorithm that has been built into the order-entry system. It can also be done by a group of specialized individuals who have (or should have) expert knowledge of the requirements of the examination (centralized scheduling). Finally, scheduling of "walk-in" service may be a "pro forma" function that acknowledges the arrival of a patient and schedules the examination for the current time and place.

There are pros and cons to each approach, and many places may use a blend of the three.

Distributed scheduling means that the examination is scheduled by the clinician's office at the time that the order is placed, and the appointment can be selected in the presence of the patient, helping to satisfy the patient's time preferences, and making it more likely that the appointment will be coordinated with return visits and other patient appointments. Patient "self-scheduling" is a form of distributed scheduling. It is used by some facilities, especially for scheduling annual mammograms that do not require an order. For distributed scheduling to work, the scheduling software must be sophisticated, robust, and very easy to use. It must not require knowledge of radiology operations—which means that the software should be clever enough to translate various requests and guesses into a good scheduling roster. To minimize errors, it is desirable to simplify the scheduling process as much as possible, forcing all cases to fit into a limited number of possibilities. Finally, it requires that the radiology department "open" its schedule, so that referring offices can conveniently view the available appointments.

Centralized scheduling, on the other hand, removes the burden of scheduling from the clinician's office. If done by properly trained individuals it should decrease the possibility of a scheduling error. Centralized scheduling functions are usually managed by a call center. Modern communications technology makes it possible for the functions of the call center to be performed at multiple locations simultaneously (a sort of distributed central scheduling). This has the advantage of permitting schedulers to perform other tasks such as reception. However, it is difficult to maintain the necessary levels of service quality with such arrangements. Radiology call centers require a well-trained workforce, adequate telephone access, appropriate staffing coverage, and convenient hours of operation. They are difficult to manage and can be a significant source of complaints. Fortunately, modern telephone systems provide a great deal of data that facilities can use to ascertain whether performance is up to par. Telephone call abandonment rates should probably not exceed the national benchmark rates of 2–3%, with 80% of calls answered in 20–30 s [4]. Bear in mind, though, that your competition is local, and therefore the benchmarks to meet or exceed are local, not national.

If a central scheduling call center is used, someone must inform the patient about the proposed appointment or negotiate any necessary changes. This someone can be a staff member at the scheduling center. If it is, though, the referring office will need to be kept in the loop as to the outcomes of the scheduling conversation. Many facilities deal with this issue by having the referring office select the appointment in cooperation with the call center, and then inform the patient about it. From the clinicians' point of view, central scheduling lifts one administrative burden from the office, only to replace it with another. One interesting paper reported the use of an automated calling system to notify the patients of the appointment. This effort proved ineffectual, presumably because patients thought that they were unsolicited robocalls, and hung up on them! [5]

"Pro forma" scheduling. This approach can be used for "walk-in" examinations. The examination is arbitrarily scheduled for the date and time of the patient arrival without regard for the actual capacity of the facility. There is no real appointment. The scheduled time simply reflects the arrival time (Fig. 4.1).

Inpatient scheduling is often a form of "pro forma" scheduling. Unfortunately, inpatients are often viewed as the quintessential "captive audience" and consequently they may be managed by means of a queue, rather than a defined appointment. The radiology department may act as though it can call for the inpatient whenever it has time. This approach, which has little basis in reality, creates numerous problems due to the fact that inpatients are not necessarily always available.

Finally, *rescheduling* (changing the time, date, or equipment) presents its own set of challenges. Although often overlooked, the rescheduling function is not inconsequential. There are many reasons that an examination may need to be rescheduled, most being patient issues: Patients may call to say that they cannot keep an existing appointment, or they may miss the appointment because they arrive late. Some simply forget about their appointments, resulting in a "no-show." Other reasons for rescheduling can be internal to radiology: For instance, the radiologist may decide

	ExamCode	TimeOrdered	TimeArrived	TimeScheduled
1	XR.MS.LSSPN	2019-08-06 15:39:36...	2019-08-07 11:56:20....	2019-08-07 11:57:...
2	XR.MS.SHD2/L	2019-08-07 11:09:45...	2019-08-07 11:10:17....	2019-08-07 11:17:...
3	XR.MS.LSSPN4	2019-08-06 15:33:04...	2019-08-07 10:36:16....	2019-08-07 10:37:...
4	XR.MS.FT3/L	2019-08-06 11:52:01...	2019-08-07 10:17:48....	2019-08-07 10:22:...
5	XR.MS.FT3/R	2019-08-06 11:52:01...	2019-08-07 10:17:21....	2019-08-07 10:17:...
6	XR.MS.PELHIP4/L	2019-08-06 16:28:03...	2019-08-07 10:10:58....	2019-08-07 10:12:...
7	XR.MS.PELHIP4/R	2019-08-06 16:25:32...	2019-08-07 09:36:49....	2019-08-07 09:37:...
8	XR.MS.ANK3/L	2019-08-06 11:40:44...	2019-08-07 09:18:47....	2019-08-07 09:27:...
9	XR.MS.FT3/L	2019-08-06 11:40:44...	2019-08-07 09:18:21....	2019-08-07 09:22:...
10	XR.MS.ANK3/L	2019-08-06 11:38:44...	2019-08-07 08:55:25....	2019-08-07 09:07:...

Fig. 4.1 A snapshot from a walk-in facility scheduling record. Scheduling time needs to be filled in, but as you can see, it is commonly entered right after the actual patient arrival time. In this case, the field contains no valuable information and acts as a simple data placeholder

that the patient would be better evaluated using a different device (e.g., 1.5 T vs. 3 T MRI), or that the examination would be better done with or without contrast. Some of those changes might be completely unpredictable, but others can be foreseen and avoided with a "more intelligent" scheduling system.

We were surprised to discover that in our institution rescheduled examinations outnumber examinations that have not been rescheduled, or, in other words, there is a greater than 50% chance that any given examination will be rescheduled at least once!

4.3 Designing a Schedule

A good schedule optimizes the time of the most "important" component of the imaging supply chain, while, at the same time, minimizing (to the extent possible) the wasted time and inconveniences that result for others. This probably sounds rather cryptic, so let us look at a few extreme examples:

(a) *Patient-optimal strategy (extreme):* If only one patient were scheduled each day, the patient would arrive at an empty waiting room and find staff and equipment waiting to provide services for as long as necessary, having nothing else to do. While certainly satisfactory for the patient, this is not something your CFO would appreciate!
(b) *Department-optimal strategy (extreme):* All patients are scheduled for 7:00 in the morning, a few minutes before the department opens its doors, so that there will be a guaranteed supply of patients for the entire day: As soon as one is finished, the next will be called from the huge waiting line outside. This will ensure that radiology equipment and manpower are always fully used. However, every patient would spend hours waiting. Even within this strategic goal there are alternative approaches: optimize the use of equipment or optimize the use of manpower. *They are not the same!* In Chap. 7 we will discuss how "overstaffing" can lead to greater profitability through more intensive equipment use.
(c) *Institutional-optimal strategy (extreme)*: Schedule patients to optimize the function of the costliest (or most profitable) activities of the institution (for instance, operating rooms). An example of this type of optimization is given in Chap. 7, where we discuss the optimization of emergency ward use.

These strategies frequently collide, and any of the three parties involved (patients, departments, institutions) can spoil the plans of the others.

And there is another wrinkle to consider. Influential fourth parties (major referrers, contracting organizations) can make demands that the prudent radiology facility will want to meet, thus undermining all attempts at rational schedule design!

Assuming (hoping!) that your department does not schedule all patients for 7 AM, you will want to have clear definitions of when the procedure is considered to have begun, and what it means to be "on time," topics that we will consider in more detail in Chap. 6.

4.4   Dealing with Variability

Before any scheduling can be done, the schedule template must be created. In order to do this, one must know the anticipated duration and equipment requirements for every possible imaging procedure. The template has to be fairly simple—so different examination durations are often rounded to one or two of the most common durations (such as 45 and 60 min in MRI), making it pretty easy to manage, and "universal" for accommodating different examination types.

However, as the famous physicist Wolfgang Pauli put it many years ago, "For quite a while I have set for myself the rule: if a theoretician says 'universal,' it just means pure nonsense." These words apply to scheduling as much as they do to anything else. With scheduling, "nonuniversal" variabilities can wreak havoc in any operation.

Why is this? Let us begin by considering the components of the examination that may vary. First of all, we may have a spectrum of "predictable deviations," such as unavoidable differences in the time required to create images. MRI almost always requires more time than CT because image formation is inherently slower. An individual plain radiograph can be faster than CT, although changes in patient position can make the overall examination as long as a CT examination. Nuclear studies have to allow time for pharmaceutical injection and sometimes for metabolic distribution.

Variability also stems from the fact that different conditions are being evaluated. For example, evaluation of condition "X" may require more images than that of condition "Y," thus influencing the protocol selection. This can be classified as a predictable source of variability only if the protocol is known at the time of scheduling.

In addition, there is predictable variation in the necessity for pre-procedure activities associated with imaging (safety screening for MRI, nursing evaluation for interventions) and post-procedure activities (image processing, room turnaround).

Finally, truly unpredictable variability may also occur. Causes of unpredictable variability can include late patient arrival (for both inpatients and outpatients) and untoward events that might occur during the procedure such as contrast reactions or extravasations and claustrophobia.

The entire art of scheduling can be defined as the *reduction of variability wherever possible*. But how can one reduce something that is changeable and unpredictable?

One cannot. But it is important to attempt to understand the sources and magnitude of predictable variation before designing the schedule template. The choices that are made will either magnify or reduce the probability that procedures will occur as planned—a feature that is critical to the serenity of the workday. It is not possible to anticipate the unpredictable, but it is possible to understand its frequency and to create sufficient redundancy to withstand the random shocks due to untoward events.

In the following sections, we will consider the range of durations that the schedule must accommodate. We will also look at the most common scheduling disruptors, and will try to see how their affects can be minimized.

4.5   Designing the Schedule Template

All radiology examinations consist of three components (Table 4.1):

1. Necessary preliminaries
2. Actual imaging
3. Necessary post-procedure activities

Each of the above has its own moving parts contributing to the overall uncertainty. Necessary preliminaries, for example, include the "checking-in" step so that the staff can confidently identify both the patient and the examination to be performed. Other preliminary steps can vary with the type of procedure and might include changing into a gown, performing safety screening, starting intravenous lines, obtaining informed consent, drinking oral contrast media, and/or evaluating a patient for sedation. Pre- and post-procedure activities are often thought of as "room turnover." As such they are necessary but do not make use of the actual imaging capacity of the resource and are therefore suitable for performing in parallel.

Some of these steps are expected to be straightforward and relatively quick. Yet even the most ordinary of them might run into unpredictable delays. For example, simple patient identification at check-in (providing date of birth or a photo ID to the radiology receptionist) is a brief matter *unless* there is a language problem, or the facility is very busy, or the receptionist is engaged in some other activity when the patient arrives, or *something else happens*. Similarly, changing into a gown may require 5 min for a young vigorous patient, but 15 min for someone frail or elderly. A safety screening procedure (for example, MRI) can be brief if the patient

Table 4.1   Pre- and post-examination activities in radiology

Necessary preliminaries	Necessary post-procedure activities
– Patient and procedure identification	– Help the patient from the imaging room
– Completing safety evaluation	– "Complete" the examination in the
– Completing a "risk of falls" questionnaire	information system
– Chart review, obtaining consent (for	– Perform any required post-processing (e.g.,
interventions)	3D, reformats)
– Starting an IV for those patients who	– Make certain measurements (primarily
would require a contrast injection	ultrasound)
– Administering oral contrast for those	– In some settings, split a single continuous
patients who need it	acquisition into multiple examinations
– Setting up coils, phantoms, or other	– Forward the examination to PACS
required devices	

understands the questions and if no safety issues are encountered, but much more protracted otherwise. To complicate the matters further, the pre- and post-examination steps are typically not captured in RIS or HIS records. As a result, these steps are hidden from any analysis.

In the course of our ongoing operational surveillance we have evaluated the pre-procedure functions in two areas that were problematic—MRI and interventional procedures. Because the pre-procedure activities are not captured as timestamps in our data systems, this evaluation required observation and manual data collection.

In the case of MRI, we discovered that pre-procedure activities require a mean of 11 min *even before the patient meets the technologist!* These activities include secure identification, changing out of street clothes, and completing a safety screening form. The technologist then reviews the information, and brings the patient into the room. The total time required for all pre-procedure activities is almost 28 min.

As Table 4.2 demonstrates, interventional procedures require even more time—a mean of 26 min for a nurse (standard deviation of 12 min), plus an additional 12 min for the radiologist (standard deviation of 8 min).

To someone who is familiar with radiology operations, these numbers may appear self-evident. Yet they lead to a nontrivial conclusion that is easily overlooked. Notice that the standard deviation for the time required is large as a percentage of the mean (half or more). Therefore, *in order to have 85% confidence of staying on schedule*, it is necessary to add one standard deviation to the mean in planning the interaction. In this illustration, the patient and the nurse must be available fully 38 min earlier if the MD interaction is not to be delayed, assuming that these activities are sequential.

Bottom line: Pre-procedure activities are likely to differ from one institution to another, but as these examples show, they can be significantly time consuming. As we will discuss later, these activities can sometimes be performed in parallel with the actual imaging or intervention. However, it is advantageous to keep them as short as possible, because it can be challenging to get patients to arrive in advance of their appointment, and because, as we will shortly show, the longer the process, the less predictable it becomes. Regardless of length, it is essential to plan on having enough resources available to perform the pre-procedure activities so that the procedure itself is not delayed.

Table 4.2 Pre-procedure activity times for interventional cases

	Mean duration, min	StdDev, min	Median duration, min	Mean plus StdDev, min
Chart preparation	8	4	8	12
Workup	18	8	17	26
MD/patient interaction	12	8	10	20

4.6   Variability Due to the Duration of Imaging

Unlike the pre- and post-examination activities, the actual in-room examination duration is captured by the information using the examination "begin" and "end" ("complete") timestamps. These timestamps make the imaging workflow much more amenable to analysis—for example, the timestamps were the source of data that we used to illustrate the variability of MRI durations in Part 1, Chap. 1.

In most cases, these timestamps are entered manually, which, as we know by now, is an imperfect way of collecting data (or the best way to fake it, if you prefer to be positive). But despite the noisy source data, it can still teach us a few important lessons.

Figure 4.2 illustrates one of these. Here we see the *variation* of examination duration as a function of the average *duration* for different types of MRI scans performed at our hospital. Each blob corresponds to a different type of MRI examination, sized proportionally to the relative volume of this examination, so that larger circles represent more frequent scans. Despite the noisy data, the pattern is clear. There is a linear relationship between exam duration (on the horizontal axis) and variability (on the vertical axis).

The major takeaway from this figure is as follows: The longer an examination takes generally, the less predictable its duration becomes. This striking relation is

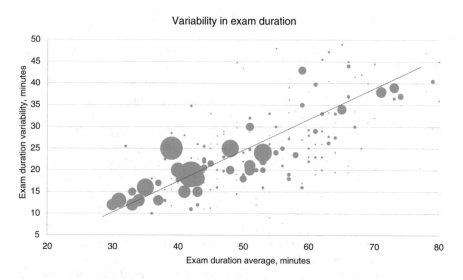

Fig. 4.2 MRI exam duration variability as a function of the average exam duration. The data was taken from 372 different types of MRI examinations. The size of each blob is proportional to the examination frequency. Variability was computed as the difference between the 75th and 25th percentiles of exam duration. There is a clear linear trend

intuitively plausible: More events occur during a longer period of time, each with its own variability, adding up to higher deviation from the expected timeline. (The infamous "if anything can go wrong, it will" law is instructive here.) MRI scans and interventional procedures provide the best illustration of this principle, due to their relatively long durations, but the same pattern can be observed with the other types of radiology examinations—and with any time-consuming task in general.

Know Your Tools

If you are a fan of statistics and you looked at the distributions of the examination duration times we provided earlier in this book, you might have observed that they follow the gamma distribution shape: a wave with a rapid increase and long right-hand decay [6]. The probability density function for gamma is defined as

$$\mathrm{PDF}_\gamma = \frac{1}{\Gamma(k)\theta^k} x^{k-1} \mathrm{e}^{-\frac{x}{\theta}}$$

and therefore is controlled by two parameters, k and θ. It turns out to be that the standard deviation of the gamma distribution is θ times its average, which nicely reflects the trend we observed in Fig. 4.2: deviation is proportional to the mean. This makes the gamma distribution particularly handy for modeling operational data.

Recognizing this "variability linearity" alone can drive some nontrivial decision-making, which would not be possible without an understanding of this phenomenon. For instance, given such a spread between the average duration times (look at the horizontal axis), which examination would you schedule to be the first in the morning—a short or a long one? Without looking at Fig. 4.2, this question sounds irrational: why would I care if I have to do both of them during the day anyway? Figure 4.2, however, suggests a more nuanced answer: Starting with a long exam means starting with a less predictable one, very likely disrupting the rest of your daily schedule. Starting with a short examination will help keep your day on track. You can still schedule the less predictable long exams at the end of the day, and in doing so inconvenience fewer patients.

Clearly, the duration-dependent variability is accompanied by other variability types, most of them adhering to the same "the more, the worse" principle. Interventional procedures can be particularly problematic, for example, introducing variability related to the performance of both radiologist and nurse. In general, the more "moving parts" a task involves, the less predictable its duration becomes. Let us consider a couple of major sources of examination variability in more detail.

4.6.1 Variability Due to Protocol Selection

To a substantial degree, the length of an imaging examination depends upon the "protocol" selected, usually by the radiologist. Although the word "protocol" typically refers to either MRI or CT, analogous considerations also affect plain-film imaging, ultrasound, and nuclear imaging. The protocol determines:

1. How many images and image series are required
2. How much time is required to generate the necessary images
3. How many changes of patient position are required

We will have more to say about protocols later in the book. For now, let us review some basics. First, while the protocol can be selected either before or after the examination is scheduled, doing so in advance can improve the scheduling process. It can also aid in obtaining insurance pre-authorizations, which often specify whether the use of contrast material is authorized, or indeed whether the examination will be covered at all. In addition, knowing before the examination is scheduled whether contrast will be used can also help ensure that the necessary laboratory work is done [5].

Not knowing the protocol in advance of scheduling introduces a major unknown. The significance of this unknown will vary depending on the portion of the patient visit dedicated to image acquisition (e.g., high for MRI, relatively low for CT).

Even if the protocol is available at the time of scheduling, the examination length will not be entirely predictable because compliance with standard protocols can vary considerably. In theory (here we go again, using the T-word), protocols should define the examination. In practice, though, any number of factors can gum up the works. These include myriad possible alterations, device-specific tweaking, and countless "exceptions" such as physician demands—basically, anything that can go wrong during scanning.

Recently, we took one of the most frequently performed MRI examinations—brain MRI—and counted how many different images, pulse sequences, or combinations of sequences were performed under this rubric over a period of 6 months.

The series noted in Table 4.3 are combined to form a complete examination. How many combinations might one expect? We counted 1200. The same examination, as protocoled by various radiologists, performed by various technologists and applied to different patients on different scanners, resulted in 1200 different combinations of images, series, and series names. Does this mean that our institution recognizes 1200 different methods of scanning the brain? Certainly not!

In reality 90% of the scans fell into a limited number of variations, but there were numerous exceptions, often with different names for the same sequence type, or

Table 4.3 Brain MRI series (sequence) names used in a busy MRI facility during a period of 10 months, in order of their usage frequency

MRI series description	Number of times used in 10 months	Image count, minimum	Image count, maximum
Screen Save	16,755	1	272
Localizer	16,454	1	99
Ax FLAIR T2	7230	10	62
DWI	4748	14	868
Average DC	4606	1	68
Fractional Aniso.	4601	1	68
EXP	4578	14	80
ADC	4575	14	80
Isotropic image	4575	12	68
FA	4528	6	80
Post Ax T2	4485	14	56
Sag T1	4233	1	69
3D COW	4041	36	46
ZERO-B	3637	14	68
FA (color)	3587	14	68
Ax T2	3466	12	106
Apparent diffusion coefficient (mm^2/s)	3340	13	103
NULL	3250	1	341
Ax DIFF check swap look at images	3165	56	6052
Ax 3D BRAVO Post	3045	54	234

The table shows the top 20 most frequent series names; the total list includes 60,488 names (!)

different sequences (Fig. 4.3). This variability might result from alterations made by radiologists in the interest of "tailoring" the examination, variations in naming that are proprietary to manufacturers or which may vary with hardware and software generation, inclusion of pulse sequences that were difficult to perform and frequently repeated (such as "breath-hold" sequences) protocols that are ambiguously defined, or technologists who were poorly trained.

Even when pulse sequences on two different devices are medically comparable, they may vary in duration, and require individual development, testing, and technologist training.

Reducing protocol complexity and variability is by far the most efficient way to achieve a reliable schedule. It not only makes the scan times more predictable, but also diminishes technologist uncertainty. The most important step in controlling protocol duration is standardization. The idea of a "tailored" examination has a seductive appeal, suggesting that a particular examination has been done for the unique benefit of an individual patient. However, the more variability that is permitted, the greater the potential for error, and the less predictable the duration. Think of the imaging examination not as a "handmade" item but rather as a factory product with a limited number of options. Henry Ford was onto something when he said: "Any customer can have a car painted any color that he wants so long as it is black."

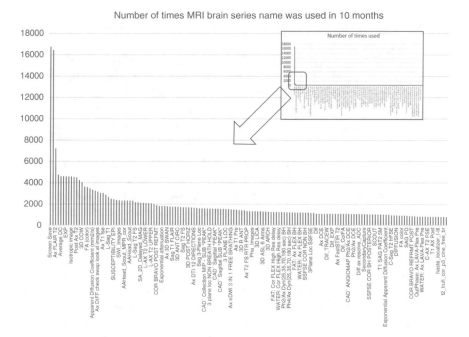

Fig. 4.3 Brain MRI series (sequence) names, used in a busy MRI facility during a period of 10 months: The vertical axis shows the frequency of the 150 most frequent series names. Series are listed in the order of frequency. Note the "hockey stick" pattern: The first few series names are much more frequent than the rest. The total list includes 60,488 names (see the smaller chart), but some 4600 of them were used only once (!)

4.6.2   Variability Due to Equipment

In order to create a radiology schedule that will direct examinations to the correct imaging device at the correct time, you need to know the capabilities of those devices, and their hours of operation. In addition, for each examination you have to know not only that the equipment is capable of doing the examination, but also what additional support might be necessary.

Unfortunately, real-life facilities vary widely with respect to age and competence of their equipment. It would be naïve to assume that all your devices and scanners came from the same vendor and were purchased at the same time. And even if they did, this ideal state would not last long. A combination of complexity, cost, and an "if it ain't broke, don't fix it" management philosophy will make it difficult to maintain a rigorous replacement schedule. All of which brings us to another major source of variability: radiology equipment.

Know Your Tools

You might have heard this question at some point: "Are you still running this crappy old scanner?" The age of your device can significantly affect its throughput, and as a result its ability to keep you on schedule. Take the admittedly extreme case of early CT: In 1971, when computed tomography was invented, it took 5 min to make a single low-resolution CT image. Today it takes a fraction of a second, with much superior quality. When we recently ran a throughput analysis, we found that, in our institution, some MRIs were producing 1.8 exams per hour while others, due to their venerable age, were barely eking out 1.2 exams. This means that any patient arriving to our MRI facility can be facing a 50% variation in examination duration.

The problem of equipment variability is probably most severe with MRI, where different devices might have different field strengths, different coil availability, different software generations, different pulse sequence availability, different bore sizes, etc. However, similar considerations apply to CT, where some scanners may be substantially faster than others, may be equipped with the latest dose reduction techniques, or may have dual-energy capability. Ultrasound may require different transducers, or 3D capability, Doppler, or elastography. Even plain radiographic rooms differ in that some have slit scanning capabilities, whole-body upright imaging, and specialized positioning devices while others do not. The situation is complicated further still if an examination needs to be supervised (monitored) by a radiologist, since this introduces the needs to coordinate with the physician's schedule and to allow for any variations in the examination that might result.

With all of these factors in play, equipment variability can produce multiple ripple effects in scheduling. It fragments the patient population (when only certain scanners can be used to schedule certain patients), and thus fragments the scheduling. It also fragments scanning protocols, when the same protocol should be edited and versioned to run on different hardware.[1]

In most cases, there is nothing you can do to make your equipment more uniform. The best way to deal with the variability—maybe the only way—is to acknowledge that it is a problem and incorporate this understanding into your scheduling system. One common means of doing this is to batch examinations by the types of examinations supported on specific devices and schedule them accordingly.

4.6.3 Controlling the Controllable

Even apart from the protocols and equipment, there are many other moving parts that, while predictable, can still affect exam durations. Just think about all the different technologists, physicians, departmental policies, seasonal and daily trends, and more that come into play with examinations. They all can be known, but the

---

[1]The protocol maintenance problem has been haunting radiology departments for years and is largely ignored by the medical device vendors.

sheer multitude of factors here can overwhelm any scheduling process. So, you have to manage them. Fortunately, there are a few rules that can help:

- Whenever possible, eliminate anything optional for the examination. For example, make your physicians agree on the essential protocol sequences and remove everything else.
- Assign unique, unambiguous, and consistent names to all elements of your examination chain: unique exam codes, unique scanning sequence names, and unique scheduling time slots (for example, 30, 45, and 90 min for MRI).
- Train your staff to adhere to these standard conventions.
- Reduce the allowable frequency of protocol modifications and updates—once a quarter or, better still, no more than twice a year.
- Reduce the number of people who have the ability to update and modify protocols.

As demonstrated in Figs. 4.2 and 4.4, scheduling standardization depends heavily on the analysis of examination durations. That is, for each examination code, you will have to compute the *average duration* and the *standard deviation* from it.

The standard deviation, the measure of uncertainty, will tell you how much each examination's length can deviate from its average. You may have an exam that takes 45 min but, if it is 45 "plus/minus 20," there will be times when the schedule does not work. When the "plus 20" happens and the examination takes 65 min instead of the average 45, the schedule will collapse. When it does, please do not jump to the conclusion that the collapse was due to "random events"! Instead, ask yourself, why does this examination have such a variable duration? Could it be the result of physicians returning late from their lunch? The result of frequent problems in the pre- or post-examination steps—such as last-minute discoveries of unreported implants? Or maybe the result of poor protocoling, with extra imaging sequences added seemingly at whim? You may not be able to address all of these problems completely, but you should be able to determine their origins and then ameliorate them as much as possible.

4.7 Unpredictable Sources of Variation: Have We Not Had Those Patients ...

Oleg's father, a university professor, used to say that he would have gotten much more work done had he not had to deal with students all the time. Many physicians probably feel the same way, blaming their inefficiency on the patients.

Schedules are regularly disrupted by unanticipated events, occurring before, during, or even after procedures. Pre-procedure delays may stem from late patient arrivals or from underestimating or having inadequate resources to perform the necessary preliminaries. Post-procedure delays are often the result of patient disposition: inadequate recovery rooms (in the case of procedures) or an unexpected finding that leads to a change in plans for patient disposition.

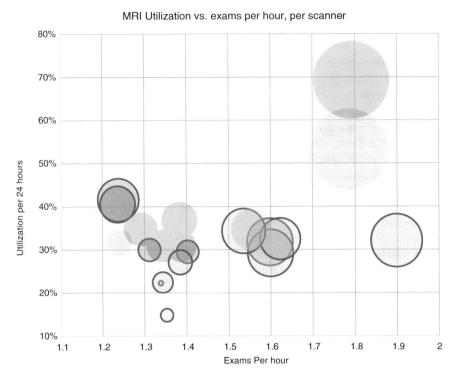

Fig. 4.4 Comparing MRI scanner utilization (the amount of time each scanner is open during a 24-h day) to scanner throughput (the number of exams per hour during the hours of active work). The data was taken in 2018 from two major hospitals in the Boston metro area (with blue and green corresponding to the two hospitals' scanners), and the size of each circle corresponds to the relative number of examinations performed on each scanner. Outpatient scanners are shown with dark borders. Although there is a good amount of clustering, indicating consistency in scanner use, one can still see significant variability in scanner operational time and throughput within each hospital. In general, the faster scanners receive more use (as shown by their larger circles), but this is not invariably true. In cases where it is not, there is opportunity for improvement. The two largest circles, in the right top corner, correspond to the emergency MRIs—the busiest scanners in most radiology departments

As you might expect from Fig. 4.2, unanticipated delays can be a problem particularly for longer procedures such as MRI and complex interventions. In one study, unanticipated events occurred during almost 17% of MRI scans. These were grouped into the following categories: (1) problems with orders and scheduling including protocols (1.9%); (2) scan delays other than those due to orders and scheduling, such as late arrival and transportation delay (3.3%); (3) unanticipated foreign bodies (0.5%); (4) non-contrast-related patient events (such as patient motion, discomfort, claustrophobia, need for sedation) (10.4%); (5) contrast-related patient events (1.3%); and (6) technical acquisition issues (1.5%). Categories involving delay were more prominent in university hospitals (18.5%) than in community hospitals (5.2%). The numbers were even higher when inpatient scans were included as well as outpatients (21.5% compared to 16.2%) [7].

Some "unanticipated" events might in fact be anticipatable if more attention were given to collecting information prior to the encounter. In one interesting study, for example, researchers showed that having "child-life specialists" coach children through their MRI scans could greatly reduce the need for anesthesia in children between the ages of 5 and 10. Perhaps a similar approach could be attempted for adults with either known or suspected claustrophobia [8].

> **Keep It Real!**
> Building simulation models is a popular way to study workflows. We have built quite a few of these ourselves. This works well when you have a well-contained and very logical process. However, if your MRI or CT workflow model consists of some 20 processing steps (which is not uncommon), each with its own conditions, exceptions, duration, and variability, you tend to arrive at a rather desperate conclusion: With small tweaks here and there, *any model complex enough can produce virtually any output.*

As if this were not enough, most radiology departments add to their scheduling difficulties by creating a host of special scheduling situations, such as reserving certain times for special use. For example, certain times may be withheld from general scheduling for "urgent" cases. Others may be set aside for the use of influential doctors or practices (the "brain tumor clinic," Dr. X's cases, etc.). Still others might be reserved so particular radiologists can be involved, or in order to coordinate activities with other devices (MRI and a fluoroscope for arthrography, for instance) or specific needs (general anesthesia, electrophysiology, etc., etc.).

Reserved times may or may not revert to general scheduling if they are unscheduled by a certain date. Despite this, it is extremely difficult to match the number of reserved times with the clinical demand. In our experience, clinicians plan their activities without considering such arrangements. For example, Dr. X may not have any cases scheduled because he is on vacation, and yet radiology still has time reserved for him.

These types of arrangements tend to proliferate when there are competing demands for insufficient equipment or personnel. And as we have seen, dividing one queue into many tends to exacerbate, not improve, overall delays.

4.8 Managing the Unpredictable

4.8.1 Organizing the Schedule to Minimize Disruption

Variability is evil, but knowledge is power.

Knowing not only the mean duration of each examination but also the variability to which it is subject can help us order the examinations in such a way as to minimize variability in the daily schedule. Figure 4.5 comes from one of our recent machine learning studies: It shows a daily MRI schedule with the same set of 20

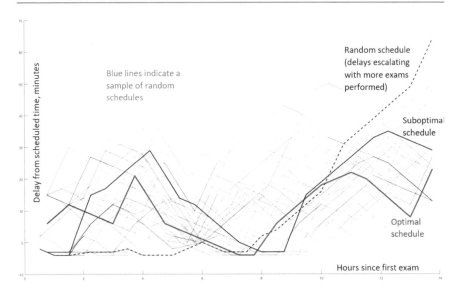

Fig. 4.5 Machine learning algorithm discovering the most stable schedules. All sequences consist of the same mix of 20 examinations, but put into different order. The horizontal line shows hours of operations (starting from the beginning of the first examination), the vertical, delays from the scheduled begin time, and each schedule corresponds to a single chart. You can see that the optimal scheduling sequence reduces delays to 23 min at most, balancing them throughout the day. The other schedules may have delays as high as 1 h, frequently accumulating toward the end of the day

examinations randomly arranged in different orders (blue lines, status quo in radiology scheduling). You can see each schedule as a sequence of delays, and each polygonal line chart represents a single choice of scheduling sequencing. Notice that the delays can be very substantial. They can also be "explosive"—especially when several more variable exams follow and the delays pile up, usually toward the end of the day (black dashed line).

But when we ran a search for the optimal exam sequencing, the algorithm produced the least delayed schedule, shown with the red line. This schedule contains the same exams, with the same unavoidable variation. It simply puts the exams into the most "balanced" order. The gain is obvious. First, the maximum delay is reduced to some 23 min instead of the 40–60 min seen in the blue lines. Second, with the optimal schedule, delays are distributed evenly throughout the day, making the day much less stressful.

We do not know how practical it would be to implement this in real life. It could probably be done for inpatients in which the timing of the examination is (in theory) under the control of the radiology department. But it would be more complicated for outpatients, because the day would be divided into multiple queues for the purposes of scheduling. Nonetheless, this machine learning study extends the lesson we learned from Fig. 4.2: The order in which examinations are performed matters, and one should not start the day with the most variable tasks.

4.8.2   Managing Patient Arrivals

How do radiology facilities determine how much time is needed to complete other activities—for instance, how long before imaging begins does the patient need to arrive? The answer is simple, and somewhat embarrassing: In most cases, they simply guess. If they underestimate, imaging is delayed, and productivity suffers. If they overestimate, the patient waits. As mentioned earlier in this chapter, we conducted an observational study of one of our MRI facilities to quantify pre-procedure activities. The goal of the study was to schedule patients' arrivals closer to the time they actually needed to be there. Prior to this initiative, all patients were told to arrive 45 min before their appointment. Our hypothesis was that this was longer than was necessary, that a patient who did not require injection of contrast prior to imaging could arrive later than one who did.

Here is what we found:

- The necessary time of arrival was in fact closer to the appointment than we had been telling patients.
- The difference in preparation time between patients who required contrast and those who did not was much less than expected.
- Patients did not arrive when they were told to arrive.

By telling patients to arrive earlier than is necessary, we are subtly (or not so subtly) encouraging noncompliance, since patients come to recognize that they do not have to arrive when they were told. Late patient arrival is a common problem everywhere. In fact, one study from Germany concluded that implementing a sophisticated scheduling system was pointless because patient punctuality was so poor (in Germany!) [9]. Our own experience has not been quite as discouraging. Late patient arrival is more complicated than it might initially appear. Obviously, a patient is late who arrives for an 11 AM appointment at 11:15. However, if pre-procedure activities require 28 min, that patient is also late who arrives any time after 10:30. In the interest of being respectful of patients' time, and because we cannot necessarily control when patients arrive, it is useful to minimize the time required for pre-procedure work. We have drastically reduced the amount of time needed for pre-procedure information gathering, making it possible for patients to arrive later and still not delay their scan. Also, when we ask patients to arrive ahead of their appointment, we tell them specifically why we have done so (e.g., safety screening, preparation for contrast), hoping that this knowledge will encourage compliance. Others have tried to reduce the amount of time needed for pre-procedure work by decoupling it from patient arrival, through the use of an online check-in and screening process, resulting in a shorter and more accurate evaluation once the patient arrives [10].

In short, you cannot, and should not, expect the patients to fit perfectly into your scheduling plan—they have other priorities apart from making you happy. Instead, optimize your workflow, making it more resistant to patient arrival disruptions.

4.9 Fitting the Spectrum of Examinations to the Schedule

4.9.1 "Exact" Scheduling

Exact scheduling means scheduling each examination type for the amount of time it takes (and only for the amount of time it takes).

Assuming we understand exactly how much time each examination will require (and recognizing that we could never actually know this), how closely should we attempt to fit the expected duration to the schedule? In other words, if we know that one examination will require 40 min, and another will require 45 min, should we schedule these examinations for different durations?

Trying to fit the exact examination duration to the schedule will always involve some amount of approximation due to the many uncontrollable sources of variation we have described. Pursuing this ideal will add complexity to the scheduling process. In extreme cases, it can complicate things so much that the process of scheduling becomes a bottleneck. In Chap. 3, we described the experience of a center that tried to provide individually timed appointments based upon the time requirements of the protocol itself. The complexity of this approach inevitably led to long delays. Once the center realized what was happening, it arbitrarily set all MR imaging intervals to either 45 or 90 min, as determined by radiologists during the protocoling process (which was still done in advance of scheduling) [11]. This was an improvement but, obviously, fitting a spectrum of examination durations into arbitrary 45- or 90-min intervals is an approximation at best. Some examinations will run longer than the assigned interval and others, shorter.

Clearly, there is no simple way to perfectly match the scheduled amount of time to the anticipated duration of the examination, partly because of the difficulty in determining how much time is needed, and partly because doing so would result in oddly configured blocks of time between examinations that would not be useful for anything. For example, if we somehow were able to determine that a particular examination required 22 min, would we create appointment blocks of 22 min? If we did, would we limit 22-min examinations to only those appointment blocks? And then, how would we ensure that the blocks were not wasted if not enough 22-min examinations were scheduled?

One possible answer would be to perform examinations consecutively on a device. Then you could have a 22-min examination follow a 1-h examination, followed by an examination of X, Y, or Z length, so you could begin each examination immediately upon completion of the one before. This would work if all patients were immediately available when their slots started. How realistic is this? It might be possible with inpatients, but even here the vagaries of transport and patient and nursing availability would make planning very, very difficult. Outpatients, on the other hand, must be offered a defined time in advance and therefore it is essential to be able to predict the duration of the preceding studies. If we overestimate this time, the equipment and the technologist will end up waiting for the patient. If we underestimate it, the patient waits.

What else can we do?

4.9.2 "Block" Scheduling

Most departments try to overcome the challenges of exact scheduling with different approaches to examination "blocking." Typically, this amounts to one of the following two options:

- Creating less customized scheduling slots to accommodate more generic exam groupings: For example, you might limit your entire MRI exam scheduling to either 30- or 45-min durations.
- Assigning long intervals of time ("blocks") to groups of similar exams: For instance, you might allocate Monday mornings to MRI prostate cases only.

With the first approach, you avoid the rigidity of exact scheduling: Two or three examination types are much more interchangeable, and easier to manage, than a dozen. However, forcing a variety of examination types into a few standard durations virtually guarantees that some exams will be too long and others too short for the scheduled time. As one example of the problems you can encounter: In a report from an institution in which MRI was arbitrarily scheduled in slots of either 1 or 2 h, fewer than half of examinations actually used the scheduled amount of time [9].

Fragmentation and subsequent lack of interchangeability were also apparent. If appointments are assigned to one of two or more time windows, there may be too many shorter appointments and too few longer ones, or vice versa. This type of imbalance will give the appearance of inadequate availability for certain types of examinations, resulting in long "third next" or "OAS" scores (see discussion of appointment availability below).

> **Keep It Real!**
> Some problems become obvious only when you attempt to work with your data.
>
> Suppose you want to use only two time slots, such as "short" for 40-min MRIs and "long" for 60-min ones. And then, when you look at the distribution of your examination types, you see that you have an average of 7.27 short and 4.62 long examinations per day. Do you see any problem with these numbers?
>
> Yes: *sregetni ton era yeht* (printing this backwards to give you some time to think). So, with 4.62 long examinations per day, do you include 4 or 5 of them on your scheduling template? With 4, you underestimate, jamming your workflow with an extra-long exam 62% of the time. With 5, you overestimate, leaving yourself with an idle time gap.
>
> One possible solution: using different schedules for different weekdays. Then you can have four long exams on three weekdays and five on the remaining two. This will give you an average number of exams much closer to the expected 4.6.

Facilities that operate multiple co-located scanners can take advantage of a possible workaround here. If they can allow some flexibility as to which patient goes to which scanner, and if this decision can be made "on the fly," they can, essentially, make one queue out of many. Here, the benefits of the averaging effect are substantial. If an examination on one device is taking more time than expected, perhaps an exam on another will take less, allowing the overall schedule to proceed on time [9].

The second type of blocking—allocating longer time intervals to a sequence of similar exams—presents another means of mapping actual workloads onto the available scheduling slots. In this case, one would use longer time intervals (a few hours or half a day, corresponding to several consecutive schedule slots) to accommodate a group of examinations that have something in common. The definition of "common" will likely vary with facility, but the most typical examples are:

- Examinations of the same nature ("interventional," "research," etc.)
- Examinations requiring the same scanner settings (such as using the same MRI coil)
- Examinations performed for, or by, specific physician practices ("orthopedic") or divisions (e.g., "abdominal," "chest")
- Any other features that can be clustered into broader exam archetypes

In this way, blocking essentially divides your schedule into several sub-schedules, which may prove easier to manage and perform due to the similar examination types within each. For example, our data indicates that running several MRI brain exams one after the other (in a block) decreases scan time for each exam by a few minutes. This makes sense because coils do not need to be changed, or the technologists are familiar with all of the steps, etc. Thus, blocking several similar examinations into the same cluster helps reduce scanning and scheduling variability—the fewer scheduling "queues," the greater the overall efficiency (at least in theory). However, there are clear limits to this approach, which can involve the same sort of access issues mentioned above. In one study, the MRI schedule was divided into 15 different blocks determined by examination type, and 2 by urgency. As a result, the facility suffered from long delays in getting access to appointments. But by reducing the number of categories, they were able to reduce significantly the access time. The schedule they ultimately decided on recognized only four blocks (regular, stereotactic, cardiology, and anesthesia). The elimination of block time scheduling (such as "neuro," "body," "MSK") led to a precipitous decline in access times and an increased rate of equipment utilization [12].

4.9.3 The Odds Are …

Obviously, variable examination lengths are a huge management problem. There are, in fact, ways to address the problem, but you will need a good data scientist to implement them (Oleg could not resist inserting this line). Several well-known scheduling algorithms are available to give you a highly optimized scheduling template. But before considering the state of the art, let us take a look at the root of the problem.

Suppose we take an overall average amount of time per appointment for a large class of similar examinations—for example, the average length of an MRI appointment—and based on this allocate the same time slot (say, 45 min) for all instances of the exams. Since this is an average examination duration, one might expect the length of the appointments to "even out" over the course of the day. However, even allowing for the inherent difficulties of determining what constitutes an "average" appointment, this approach is unlikely to be even remotely successful.

There are two reasons for this. One is statistical. It is intuitively obvious that, given a sufficiently large number of examinations, the time required to perform each of them would be somewhere in the vicinity of the overall average duration. This is known as the law of regression toward the mean. However, on any given day the schedule will include a relatively small number of patients (perhaps a dozen for MRI) drawn from the universe of all possible examinations. What are the chances that the exams on such a schedule will have durations equal to the overall mean?

Figure 4.6 answers this question. Using thousands of MR and CT examination records from our radiology department, we ran simulations using randomly selected sequences of 12 MR exams, corresponding to a 9-h scanning day (our MR scans take 45 min on average). We then compared the average lengths of the 12-exam sequences, expressed as a percentage of the 9-h workday (horizontal axis), and found the cumulative probability of this distribution. The MR curve in Fig. 4.7 shows the probability that a set of any 12 exams drawn from the all-MR universe will have a mean that does not exceed the mean for the entire MRI group. We repeated the same simulation for CT exams (these take 15 min per exam on average, so we considered random sequences of 36 exams to fill the same 9 h of work).

Both CT and MR curves turned out to have very similar shapes. The most interesting point on these curves corresponds to the 100% mark on the horizontal axis, meaning that a randomly chosen daily sequence of exams will end on time or before. In the case of MR, one can see that the overall probability of this happy "we got all our work done" day actually occurring is only 55% (point A on the chart). Which is to say that, if schedule slots are each equal to the average examination duration, then 45% of the time it will take us longer than 9 h to process what should take 9 h on average. This does not look good—nearly every second workday will take longer than scheduled! If we want to ensure that the examinations fit into the scheduled time with 90% certainty, we need to select a scheduling interval that is 120% of the mean duration—meaning adding the average of 20% idling to our average exam length (point B on the chart). This observation applies to the entirety of the examination duration, not just the actual imaging time or pulse sequence duration!

But that is not all. If even a single examination finishes late, the following exam will likely be delayed. However, if an examination finishes early, it is *unlikely* that the next exam will begin early—not unless all of the day's patients miraculously make this possible by regularly arriving earlier than their scheduled appointment times. Thus, while an early finish can help correct delays, you can almost never

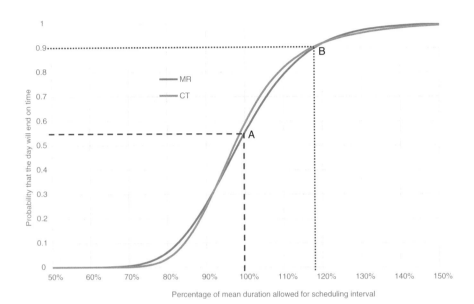

Fig. 4.6 Staying on time with a randomly chosen schedule. This curve was built from 10,000 random samples of MR and CT examination instances, randomly selected to simulate a full day's schedule (12 MRI, 36 CT). We expressed the summated time for each combination as a percentage of the expected 9-h length—that is, we divided the total examination duration of each 12-exam sequence by our total MRI workday duration (9 h). In this case, 100% on the horizontal axis corresponds to a 12-exam day finishing on time (taking 9 h or less)

actually get ahead. This is how, as we will see in the section dealing with "on-time" performance, delays pile up over the course of the day.

At this point, it is worth revisiting Fig. 4.5 and comparing it with Fig. 4.6. Though they represent different projects with different examination duration distributions, they tell us two sides of the same story. The random schedules in Fig. 4.6 correspond to the blue charts in Fig. 4.5: scheduling sequences built without any sort of systematic design, a more or less accurate reflection of how most of us approach scheduling in reality. As both analyses demonstrate, these sequences will almost certainly result in delays. This, of course, will prove stressful to your staff, and dissatisfying to your patients.

4.10 Determining Availability

4.10.1 Outpatients

Outpatients put greater demands on the schedule than inpatients do, both because their time is less flexible and because they have the option of choosing another imaging provider. If you cannot offer an outpatient a timely and convenient appointment, he or she may well go elsewhere.

Outpatient scheduling systems often assume that all outpatient examinations are elective, and that all appointment times are equal. This is a convenient fiction, as any radiology manager will tell you. If you are to meet demand for outpatient services with any degree of success, you need to consider the fact that not all patients are the same, and that not all appointment times are equally desirable. For example:

– Elderly patients might not want to come to a nighttime appointment.
– Working patients might not want to take off time from work.
– Patients might want to coordinate an appointment for imaging with another medical visit.
– Patients who are traveling a considerable distance might not want to make an additional trip.

We would love to have a metric that indicates whether radiology availability is "adequate." Looking at the "next available appointment" is generally not sufficient. It is possible, for example, that even with a tightly packed schedule the next opening might be within days or even hours due to a last-minute cancellation. This would certainly be a happy circumstance for the patient who is offered that slot. But it does not tell us anything about the general availability of the resource.

For these reasons, some have advocated the use of the "third next available" appointment as less susceptible to chance occurrences [13]. The theory here is that, while the schedule may be full in the immediate future, if you look far enough ahead you will reach a point at which the schedule "opens up" and many options are available to the patient. And indeed, this is generally true. But since we would like to identify a middle ground between "packed" and "generally available," the third next seems to be a reasonable compromise. Figure 4.7 illustrates this idea.

SUN	MON	TUES	WEDS	THURS	FRI	SAT
-	0	0	0	0	1	0
-	1	0	4	8	12	6
-	14	16	16	18	20	14
-	20	20	20	20	20	14

Fig. 4.7 A hypothetical schedule for an outpatient imaging facility (any modality) that is open 6 days a week. The numbers indicate the available appointments for each day. Note that the first available appointment is on Friday, but availability is basically negligible until the following Wednesday, which would be the "third next" appointment. This type of pattern is largely typical of outpatient schedules

Although such an approach has merit, it has at least two practical limitations:

- It does not tell you how many patients the facility will be able to absorb at the "third next available" time.
- It uses a single-number metric ("third next"), which, while better than the "next available," is still subject to random exam cancellations.

For this reason, we believe that aggregate statistics work better. We prefer to use a measurement we call the outpatient availability score (OAS) [14]. This score represents the percentage of total appointments available daily when looking ahead on the schedule. For a busy facility, this percentage will likely be low in the immediate future, but it will eventually increase to 100% as you look further into the future.

Using this score, we have created a metric that we call 4-6-8, representing the number of days into the future when the score crosses the 40, 60, and 80% thresholds (Fig. 4.8).

In our experience, when availability is less than 40%, patients complain about the lack of satisfactory appointment times. This metric is valuable for tracking changes in demand and determining whether availability is adequate. However, since demand is likely to be highly site and time specific, it needs some refinement before we can draw inferences about the need for additional capacity. For example, if a manager notes that the 40% point is 15 days out, it might be necessary to increase

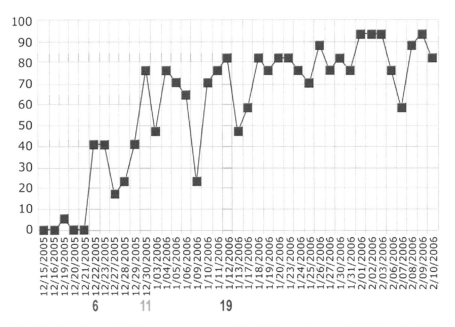

Fig. 4.8 Outpatient availability score: percentage of available appointments by business day. OAS graph for nuclear medicine with 40, 60, and 80% appointment availability highlighted

capacity by adding a night shift. That will immediately shorten the time to 40% availability but it still might not have any effect on patient satisfaction.

The reason for this is that appointments vary in their desirability. Our experience suggests that daytime appointments on our "main campus" are more desirable for outpatients than evening or weekend appointments and that they are more desirable than appointments at the outlying imaging centers despite the fact that the equipment and radiologists are the same. Late evening and nighttime appointments are generally undesirable everywhere (though some patients may appreciate not having to contend with traffic jams and waiting lines). As an illustration of this point, please see Fig. 4.9, which shows the number of days in which individual appointments are booked ahead. Note that late-morning appointments are more desirable than early-morning ones, and much more desirable than late-afternoon and evening ones (note also the similarity to the "Asian camel" human activity curve discussed in Chap. 3).

Whether you use the "third next" or the OAS approach, the metric must be made granular enough to account for differences in appointment desirability. We will return to this topic later, when we discuss service guarantees.

Failing to meet your outpatient preferences will result in patient "leakage"—that is, patients seeking care outside of your healthcare system. The amount of leakage can be high: Referral leakage is commonly reported as in the range of 20–30%. In our own system, imaging leakage is approximately 30% [15]. Note that scheduling problems may not be the only cause of this. For example, some insurance plans have

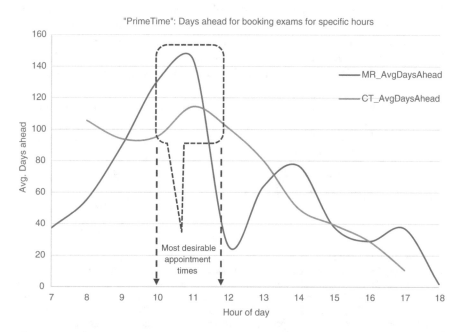

Fig. 4.9 Average number of days ahead for booking MR and CT appointments at Massachusetts General Hospital. As both curves indicate, morning hours are taken first, while late hours are increasingly unpopular

preferred contracts with certain imaging providers. Co-pays may be higher if the patient selects a facility without a preferred status. In some cases, a patient may see a clinician who has ties to a different imaging provider. Here, there may be little that a radiology department can do to prevent leakage. Still, ease of access is an important determinant [16], and appointment availability is one measure of ease of access. Another measure is the convenience for the ordering clinician's office, which is one reason that we emphasized the importance of simplicity and brevity in the ordering process (as we have already discussed in the previous chapter).

4.10.2 Inpatients

As we have mentioned, inpatients are often perceived as readily available. They tend to be displaced to the less desirable evening hours, when outpatient demand is low (Fig. 4.10, left). While economically advantageous, this approach is less than optimal in terms of customer service. Also, it is a fallacy to think that inpatients are available at all times. They can have any number of other demands and priorities that might conflict with an imaging appointment (additional testing procedures, physician visits, and so on). It is true that these types of activities are less frequent during the evening and nighttime hours. But even if an inpatient is available, necessary support such as nursing and transport may not be. This conflict between perceived and actual inpatient availability produces a rather ironic outcome: Inpatient-specific scheduling is less predictable than outpatient scheduling; Fig. 4.10 (right) demonstrates this (note the greater percentage of delayed examinations as well as the wider spread (higher variability) of the delay pattern). Finally, there is one other aspect to inpatient scheduling that may not be obvious from all of the charts and tables. Inpatient scheduling is often abused, with schedulers entering

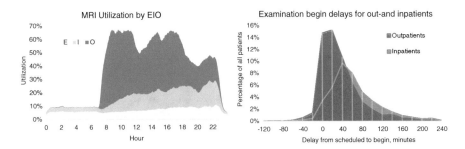

Fig. 4.10 Left: Stacked ratios of in-, out-, and emergency patient contributions to overall utilization of a major MRI facility. You can see how outpatient volume (O) decreases in the late afternoon (as well as during lunch and dinner times), while inpatient volume (I) tends to increase during the late hours. Right: Delay between the scheduled examination time and the actual examination begin time for a pair of collocated MRI scanners. Clearly, the delays in inpatient arrivals are much more spread out, which may at first seem paradoxical (inpatients are already in the hospital; why can't they arrive on time?). The explanation for this is simple: The incorrect assumption of inpatient availability ("we can get them anytime") collides with real availability problems, delayed transportation, and processing bottlenecks

incorrect or imaginary appointments simply as placeholders ("let's schedule them all for 10 PM; we can figure out the actual order later").

In our opinion, individual inpatient schedules, including imaging appointments, other testing, and consults, should be coordinated by someone who is familiar with the full picture, such as the patient's nurse—though we acknowledge that this is rarely actually done.

There is another compelling reason why inpatient scheduling should be tightly coordinated with scheduling for other patient types: resource sharing. All patient groups depend on the same radiology resources, on the same staff, physicians, rooms, and scanners. Running different scheduling strategies—"timely" for outpatients, and "opportunistic" for inpatients—can lead to operational chaos. This is evident in Fig. 4.10 (right), which was derived for a pair of collocated MRI scanners running a mix of in- and outpatients (40% and 60%, respectively). The chart shows the distribution of delays in examination start times: that is, how late the examinations begin relative to their scheduled start times. For outpatients, the most frequent delays happen in the 0–20-min range, while for inpatients a 40-min delay appears to be business as usual. As a result, an increased variability in one patient type makes it impossible to manage the other, creating a perfect recipe for a broken workflow. This is one reason some experts believe it is important to keep inpatient and outpatient workflow and devices separate [17].

Inpatient imaging represents a cost to the hospital (because the payment system is based on diagnosis groups) whereas outpatient imaging is profitable. However, efficient performance of inpatient and emergency department studies is economically important because it can affect the patients' length of stay (LOS)—the metric all hospitals want to minimize. We should have a goal of imaging never delaying transit through the facility, whether the impact is on time spent in the emergency department or on the length of hospitalization. Unfortunately, whether or not such delays are occurring is difficult to determine. As a result, somewhat arbitrary goals are often set. Our goal is to be able to offer a routine inpatient appointment (not urgent or STAT) within 6 h of when the order is placed. For an emergency room patient, the target is 1 h. Of course, not all examinations can be completed within this time frame. Certain types of studies are uncommon and may require specialized expertise or equipment or pharmaceuticals that are not freely available. Furthermore, there can be unforeseen delays due to patient schedule conflicts or safety issues that require investigation.

4.10.3   Walk-In Patients

Scheduling walk-in patients may sound absurd. But before you scoff, remember the definition of scheduling we laid out at the beginning of this chapter: it does not exclude walk-in examinations at all. All resource allocation, and all workflow orchestration, still must be done, despite not knowing if and when patients are going to arrive at the facility. In this sense, walk-ins present the extreme case of scheduling variability that we need to manage in radiology.

How do we do this?

We do it using the same two strategies outlined above: by studying trends and by reducing variability. In the case of walk-ins, the main trend is the pattern of patient arrivals. We touched on this subject earlier, when we looked at HAP curves: Arrival patterns are extremely uneven during the daytime, and generally high in the late morning and during the "back-from-lunch" early afternoon. If you are to remain on time, your resource allocation should match this trend. You can achieve this using one of several approaches:

- *Dynamic staff allocation*, when only a few staff members arrive early and stay late but most are available during the peak times: To allocate staff in this way, you need to create several daily shifts, ensuring that they overlap during the most critical times, when you need most of your staff.
- *Dynamic resource allocation*, that is, creating an escape valve to help relieve pressure that you can call into use during the peak times: This is particularly important when you have to share your resources with other workflows. To manage backup workflows such as this, you need a carefully designed resource scheduling template to avoid collisions. We will describe one such system in our Chap. 6.

Identifying the main sources of walk-ins is an important step. The sources may be many and varied, and in some cases you will not be able to control them at all—for instance, if patient arrivals are impacted by traffic congestion, holidays, or weather. But in other cases you can. In our hospital, a classical example includes our orthopedic physicians sending their patients to our X-ray imaging floor. In these cases, the physicians' schedules become the main driver for the walk-in volume: when most orthopedic visits take place, most patients arrive for X-rays. Working with the orthopedics group to distribute visits could result in a more balanced walk-in flow.

This may be completely obvious, but achieving it has been elusive, in our experience. Doctor's office hours are subject to a host of other factors that may not be within their control, such as assigned operating room time. Consequently, our most successful strategy has been to study the patterns and react rather than to attempt to change the rate at which patients arrive.

1. Using your RIS/HIS data, make an export of all patient arrival times for your walk-in facility, for a few months.
2. Compute the number of patients arriving at each hour of each day.

We suggest that the mean number is not sufficient for planning purposes. You should also add the 90th percentile as the "worst-case" scenario. This will result in yet another HAP curve, like the one shown in Fig. 4.11, illustrating patients arriving per hour at different times of the day in our outpatient walk-in facility. As an example, it clearly demonstrates that on our "busy days" (90th percentile, more than a month per year) we face twice as many patients as during our "average" days—a

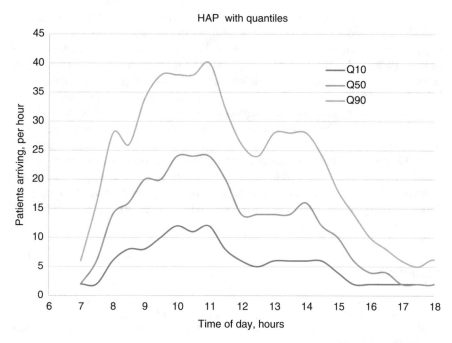

Fig. 4.11 Number of walk-in patients arriving each hour in our walk-in X-ray facility. This time, instead of the average per hour, we show three quantiles: Q10, corresponding to the lowest 10%; Q50, to the median (50%); and Q90, to the 90th percentile. One year of data was used. The average number is not shown, but in this case it is very close to the median

considerable change in demand to be met! Create these plots for each day of the week, and you will see some weekday-specific patterns as well. This very simple exercise often results in unexpected discoveries: "Wow, this is what we are dealing with?"

4.11   What Is the Cost of Saving Money?

We began this chapter by saying that schedules are usually designed to minimize some "cost" function. Creating availability costs money. It might mean purchasing equipment and/or hiring personnel. Sometimes the cost that is being minimized is external to radiology. For example, the goal in an emergency department may be to ensure that imaging is performed shortly after an order is placed, to minimize transit time through the facility. If this is the case, you will need to have "excess" equipment and personnel available in times of low demand so the high demand can be met at other times.

Some years ago, a member of our department ran a numerical analysis that allowed him to make a prediction: In order to satisfy the requirement that the maximum waiting time in our emergency department be no more than 30 min, devices could only be used approximately 40% of the time [18]. Ensuring this type of access virtually guarantees that equipment is utilized to considerably less than its full capacity. However, isn't it true that idle technologists and idle equipment waste money? Perhaps, but the costs of the unused equipment and technologist time must be balanced against becoming a "bottleneck" in ED operations, and possibly slowing the rate of hospital admissions coming from the emergency department.

In Chap. 3, we noted that the perception of a lack of availability leads to an increase in demands for higher priority service. In this chapter it becomes clear that higher percentages of utilization result in a "fragile" schedule in which late additions either are impossible to accommodate or ensure delays and dissatisfaction. We will have more to say about this in Chap. 7, when we discuss image acquisition. Therefore, measures of availability must be evaluated within the context of the need for prompt service, and costs must be calculated in a framework that extends beyond radiology.

References

1. Ernst AT, Jiang H, Krishnamoorthy M, Sier D. Staff scheduling and rostering: a review of applications, methods and models. Eur J Oper Res. 2004;153(1):3–27.
2. Cayirli T, Veal E. Outpatient scheduling in health care: a review of literature. Prod Oper Manag. 2003;12(4):519–49.
3. Pinedo ML. Scheduling: theory, algorithms, and systems. New York: Springer; 2016.
4. Waldron M, Scott K. Improved scheduling operations in diagnostic imaging. Radiol Manag. 2013;35(1):36–7.
5. DiRoberto C, et al. Prioritizing the protocol: improving the process of scheduling imaging examinations in a radiology department with partially integrated IT systems. J Am Coll Radiol. 2017;14(3):444–8.
6. Wikipedia. Gamma distribution. Wikipedia. [Online]. https://en.wikipedia.org/wiki/Gamma_distribution.
7. Sadigh G, et al. Prevalence of unanticipated events associated with MRI examinations: a benchmark for MRI quality, safety, and patient experience. J Am Coll Radiol. 2017;14(6):765–72.
8. Durand D, et al. Mandatory child life consultation and its impact on pediatric MRI workflow in an academic medical center. J Am Coll Radiol. 2015;12(6):594–8.
9. Nickel S, Schmidt U. Process improvement in hospitals: a case study in a radiology department. Qual Manag Health Care. 2009;18(4):326–38.
10. Pirasteh A, et al. Implementation of an online screening and check-in process to optimize patient workflow before outpatient MRI studies. J Am Coll Radiol. 2016;13(8):956–9.
11. Wessman B, et al. Reducing barriers to timely MR imaging scheduling. Radiographics. 2014;34(7):2064–70.
12. van Sambeek J, et al. Reducing MRI access times by tackling the appointment-scheduling strategy. BMJ Qual Saf. 2011;20(12):1075–80.
13. Institute for Healthcare Improvement. Third next available appointment. [Online]. http://www.ihi.org/resources/Pages/Measures/ThirdNextAvailableAppointment.aspx.
14. Asfaw BA, Nagtegaal B-J, Rabiner P, Thrall J. The outpatient availability score: an alternative approach to measuring demand. J Am Coll Radiol. 2007;4(3):171–7.
15. Prabhakar AM, Harvey HB, Misono AS, Erwin AE, Jones N, Heffernan J, Rosenthal DI, Brink JA, Saini S. Imaging decision support does not drive out-of-network leakage of referred imaging. J Am Coll Radiol. 2016;13(6):606–10.

16. Becker's Hospital Review. [Online]. www.beckershospitalreview.com/finance/referral-net-works-stopping-leakage-and-technology-investments-5-top-revenue-generation-strategies-for-cfos.html.
17. Boland GW, Duszak R. Modality access: strategies for optimizing throughput. J Am Coll Radiol. 2015;12(10):1073–5.
18. Rhea JT, Bauman RA, Jeffrey P. Determination of needed radiographic room capacity to serve an emergency department. Emerg Radiol. 1994;1(3):133–7.

Examinations, Protocols, and "Auto" Protocols

5

"When I use a word," Humpty Dumpty said, in rather a scornful tone, "it means just what I choose it to mean—neither more nor less." [1]

Contents

Things That Happen

- The order is converted to an examination that can be performed.
- The views and series are specified.
- The use of contrast material is specified.

Things to Measure

- The number of possible variations on each order:
  - "Sanctioned" protocols
  - Variations
- Examination components that are frequently repeated
- The effect of variability on scheduling accuracy and timeliness

© Springer Nature Switzerland AG 2021
D. Rosenthal, O. Pianykh, *Efficient Radiology*,
https://doi.org/10.1007/978-3-030-53610-7_5

5.1   Creating an Imaging Examination

This chapter is about how a clinician's thinking is translated into a specific imaging study. It is also about the never-ending struggle between standardization and customization in patient care. Standardization makes things less expensive, decreases the risk of error, and makes the operation more predictable. Customization tailors the examination to the radiologist's understanding of the patient's condition and the clinician's questions. Depending upon the accuracy of the available information, it could yield an examination better suited to the patient's needs. Because it gives the radiologist a sense of having made a unique contribution to the care of the patient, customization can also be professionally gratifying. The benefits can be difficult to quantify, but the adverse effects on the operation, in terms of examination length and lack of predictability, are all too obvious.

To understand the essence of this challenge, we need to start with definitions. We have talked a great deal about examinations in this book. But what exactly constitutes an "examination"? This seemingly simple question is made exceedingly complicated by the conflicting demands arising from healthcare, information technology, healthcare insurance, and politics. Five overlapping terms are used to describe different aspects of the examination (Fig. 5.1):

1. The *order*
2. The *procedure name* (institution or department specific)
3. The applicable *CPT* (Current Procedural Terminology) code

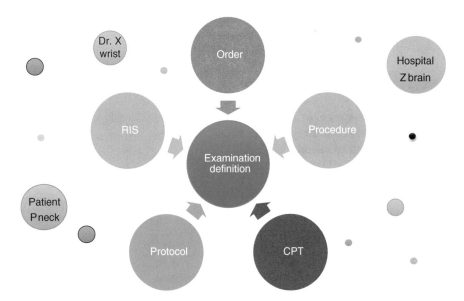

Fig. 5.1   Different practical, yet often inconsistent, ways to define radiology examinations

4. The imaging *protocol*
5. *Vendor-specific* definitions used by your radiology information system (such as the "performable," a term used by Epic®)

The boundaries between these terms and the concepts they represent can be elusive.

An examination usually originates with an order placed by a clinician. The order should be specific enough that it can be identified with a study offered by the radiology department. The components of the examination may be standardized, or the clinician may individually specify them, or they may be prescribed by a radiologist.

Regardless of how the examination is performed, it must match the description of one or more CPT codes to be billable. As noted above, CPT stands for Current Procedural Terminology [2]. In the United States, this is a coding system used for identifying and billing all medical procedures—not just radiology. Assignment of a CPT code is essential for billing as well as for insurance "pre-authorization" if it is required. Pre-authorization is common for outpatient imaging studies but not so much for inpatient imaging.

Within the constraints of CPT, a radiology department may choose to offer an infinite variety of examinations, consisting of different combinations of views, acquisitions, pulse sequences, series, etc. It may also assign any name it wants to the examination. However, regardless of what the department calls its procedure, the patient's insurance will receive (and hopefully pay) a bill for a specific CPT code. To be compliant with billing rules, the examination must conform to the description associated with the code.

CPT codes are important for other reasons as well. After the examination, the patient will likely receive an "explanation of benefits" (EOB) from the insurance company showing what payments they have made (or denied) on the patient's behalf. In all probability, this will list the name associated with the CPT code for the examination in question. Though the radiology department can assign whatever name it likes to the procedure, if the name is substantially different from that of the CPT, the department may receive complaints from the patient, who might think he or she is being charged for a procedure he or she did not have.

The descriptions attached to the CPT codes are usually somewhat vague, leaving plenty of room for interpretation. Sometimes, though, they are surprisingly specific. As one example, a radiology department might offer an X-ray examination called "wrist" that consists of three views: "AP," "lateral," and "oblique." This examination would be billed using the CPT code indicating "Wrist, 3 views." However, the radiology department might also offer an exam called "wrist, deviation exam" that consists of radial and ulnar deviation plus AP clenched fist. This examination would be billed using the same CPT code. Conceivably, the same patient could have *both* exams, in which case he or she would receive two bills that look to be the same. In this case, both the insurance company and the patient would be looking for an explanation.

Another example of a vague CPT is the code used to designate CT scans of the extremities (Fig. 5.2).

CPT	Description
73700	Computed tomography, lower extremity; **without** contrast material
73701	Computed tomography, lower extremity; *with* contrast material
73702	Computed tomography, lower extremity; **without** contrast material, **followed by contrast material** and further sections

Fig. 5.2 Typically vague CPT codes for CT scans of the lower extremity. Notice that the same code may refer to a hip, thigh, femur, knee, calf, ankle foot, etc. MRI codes are only slightly more specific, separating the lower extremities into "joint" and "not joint"

Fig. 5.3 In our department, only 388 CPT codes are used to bill for almost 1600 examinations!

Similarly, MRI examinations of the prostate, penis, uterus, sacral plexus, and sacrum would all share the same CPT: 72195.

Sometimes the payment requirements can be quite specific: For example, CPT 76700 (abdominal ultrasound, complete) requires evaluation (and therefore documentation) of the liver, gallbladder, common bile duct, pancreas, kidneys, upper abdominal aorta, and inferior vena cava!

Attempts to fit the somewhat arbitrary CPT coding system into the specificities of real life can have bizarre consequences. For example, if an MRI of the hip were ordered, it would be coded with one of the lower extremity joint codes (depending upon the use of contrast). If both hips are imaged for appropriate clinical indications, then it is considered appropriate to use the same code twice. However, bilateral symptoms might warrant an examination of the pelvis, which would include both hips, and furthermore, evaluation of the pelvis and femur would include the hip that therefore should not be coded.

So you see how things can get complicated quickly: an individual CPT code can be a single examination, or it can be a whole family of related exams. A typical radiology department offers more examinations than there are CPT codes. Our institution offers 1593 different examinations that use just 388 discrete CPT codes for billing (Fig. 5.3). The more examinations offered, the greater the need for specificity in the order, and the greater the need for specificity, the more complex the technologist's task.

5.2   Who Can Create an Examination?

We have already discussed who can order examinations. Now let us look at who can create them.

5.2.1   X-Ray Examinations (Radiography)

In addition to performing the examinations "officially" offered by a department, clinicians might also have idiosyncratic preferences. For example, Dr. X might believe that the ideal wrist examination (let us call it "Dr. X's wrist") consists of AP views in pronation and supination, plus a lateral. The question then becomes: If Dr. X orders a wrist, does he mean a standard wrist or "his" wrist? Also, what happens if other doctors decide they want to order Dr. X's wrist, or perhaps create their own examination?

This individually customized approach will necessarily create an informal set of alternative examinations (including also special examinations for Drs. A-W and Drs. Y and Z). Each of these must be correctly mapped to an appropriate CPT code. The intentions of the order may be clear to the ordering physician but they will be less so for those who are expected to carry them out. Thus the approach complicates the training of technologists and coders and increases the risk of error.

This situation is perhaps most common in plain-film imaging performed for orthopedic surgeons, but it can certainly be found in examinations with other modalities as well. Here, while the radiology department usually defines a "default" that serves as the standard examination, clinicians may be allowed to modify these selections.

Whether or not to allow such additions and modifications to routine radiographic examinations does not seem to be a major concern for departments. Most apparently accept them without much question. A more difficult decision is whether to limit the entire examination to what has been requested or whether there should be minimum standards. For example, if an orthopedic surgeon requests only a scapular "Y" view, should the radiology department require that the "Y" view form part of a minimally acceptable shoulder series? Not doing so could put the radiologist in a very uncomfortable position, having to produce a report on an evaluation that he or she considers incomplete.

But maybe the requested view was intended to supplement an examination that was performed previously, or at another facility, with the result that the images are not available to the radiologist performing the present exam. The likelihood of this happening seems to be decreasing with the ongoing electronic integration of medical records but it might still be some time before it is no longer a concern.

If the department never allows its technologists to perform what it considers to be less than a standard examination, it risks the ire of the referring clinician, and might even be harming patients by exposing them to needless radiation. Of course, there may also be instances in which an insistence upon a standard examination yields important information.

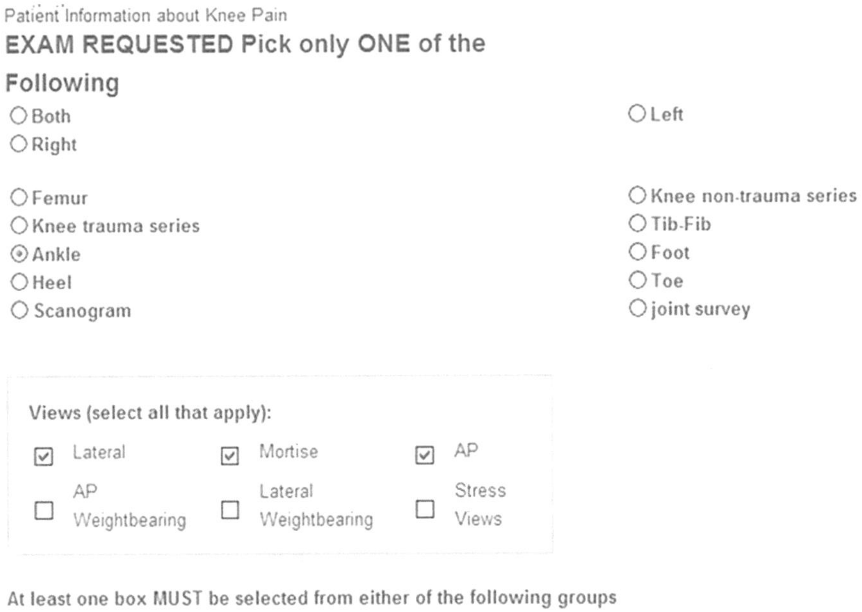

Patient Information about Knee Pain
EXAM REQUESTED Pick only ONE of the

Following
○ Both   ○ Left
○ Right

○ Femur   ○ Knee non-trauma series
○ Knee trauma series   ○ Tib-Fib
◉ Ankle   ○ Foot
○ Heel   ○ Toe
○ Scanogram   ○ joint survey

Views (select all that apply):

☑ Lateral   ☑ Mortise   ☑ AP

☐ AP   ☐ Lateral   ☐ Stress
  Weightbearing   Weightbearing   Views

At least one box MUST be selected from either of the following groups

Fig. 5.4 Plain-film selection in our homemade order entry system was performed as shown. A selection of "ankle" showed all possible views, with the standard series checked by default. Here, the clinician was free to add or remove views. Logic built into the system assigned the correct CPT code in the background. Unfortunately, we lost this capability when our institution implemented a commercial EHR

We believe it is appropriate, in certain circumstances, to honor requests for partial or nonstandard examinations. For plain films on outpatients, we will accept an order for any arbitrary selection of views, as long as they are drawn from a known set of possible views (Fig. 5.4). We would probably not accept seriously incomplete studies (such as a single view) in the emergency department. Fortunately, we rarely if ever receive such requests in our institution.

5.2.2 CT, MRI, Ultrasound

Designing an MRI or a CT study is vastly more complex than designing a radiography study, and fewer clinicians are familiar with how to do so. For such "high-tech" examinations, the limited set of examinations that the department offers is greatly expanded by detailed specifications of the components of the exam known as the "protocol." Just as there are standard examinations, most departments have a predetermined menu of standard protocols intended to address specific clinical issues. Although some institutions also permit certain specialists to design specific examinations, these variations are more often treated as different "protocols." The functional difference between the two is that an examination can be ordered, whereas a protocol is usually selected in a separate step done after the order is placed (although, as we will discuss, specific protocols can sometimes be ordered, making them essentially no different from "examinations").

A protocol can include parameters such as contrast dose and timing and planes of imaging. Although it is essentially the same concept as we have been discussing for radiography, the term "protocol" is usually reserved for the more complex modalities (CT, MRI, ultrasound, PET).

5.2.3   Names Matter!

No matter which examinations you decide to offer, the names you select for them are consequential. For instance, the name of the examination can (and should) be used as the header in the imaging report. If the name is vague as to which CPT applies, the radiologist (or medical coder) might be obliged to provide the missing information, thus leading to internal conflicts. As an example, Fig. 5.5 shows a list of X-ray examinations of the fingers, all of which are billed using CPT 73140 (radiologic examination fingers minimum of two views).

Note that the technologist has 12 (!) options to choose from, not even counting additional examinations for stress views. A similar number of examinations is available for toes. This strikes us as far too many, and as a mistake just waiting to happen. In any event, if a radiologist cannot tell from the images which finger is being examined, perhaps he or she should consider hanging up his or her lead apron!

More importantly, only the first two names on the list indicate that the examination is a "2 or more view" study. If only one view is received, the radiologist would not know that something is amiss, and if the examination name is used as the report

Fig. 5.5 Twelve alternative names used in our institution for a two-view radiographic examination of a finger

1. XR FINGER 2 OR MORE VIEWS (LEFT)

2. XR FINGER 2 OR MORE VIEWS (RIGHT)

3. XR FINGER 2ND DIGIT (LEFT)

4. XR FINGER 2ND DIGIT (RIGHT)

5. XR FINGER 3RD DIGIT (LEFT)

6. XR FINGER 3RD DIGIT (RIGHT)

7. XR FINGER 4TH DIGIT (LEFT)

8. XR FINGER 4TH DIGIT (RIGHT)

9. XR FINGER 5TH DIGIT (LEFT)

10. XR FINGER 5TH DIGIT (RIGHT)

11. XR FINGER THUMB (LEFT)

12. XR FINGER THUMB (RIGHT)

header, the coder will not know that the "2 or more view" code applies. Asking the radiologist to dictate the number of views is inefficient, and potentially dangerous as he or she may contradict the way that the technologist has completed the examination.

Keep It Real!
Protocol standardization and consistency have both obvious and subtle consequences. When imaging is used to follow specific conditions, the follow-up images should be acquired in the same way as the baseline images. This is particularly important for quantitative techniques (such as bone density measurement).

Consistency of examination and series names is important for "hanging protocols" (the way the PACS system displays the examination for the radiologist). Image processing software—from basic display and 3D reconstructions to the most complex AI—often depends on these naming rules. Some post-processing is heavily dependent on fine details of acquisition. For the more intricate post-processing algorithms (such as texture analysis and different flavors of AI post-processing), even the most minute scanner-side noise filtering can affect the quality of the results. Generally, the more ways there are to do an examination, the greater the opportunity to make a mistake.

5.2.4   Protocol Creation

Radiologists are given considerable freedom in designing protocols. Virtually any combination of series and pulse sequences is permitted, and protocol design tends to be highly individualized—at least institution specific, and sometimes individual specific. This variability is currently a major problem in the development of machine learning tools to assist with department operations.

There is one major constraint in protocol design. Protocols must follow certain billing rules. We have emphasized that many different examinations can fit the same CPT code but what about the reverse? What happens if, in designing a protocol, the radiologist or the radiology department creates an examination that requires two or more CPT codes? Is that allowed?

The answer is definitely, probably, possibly, "Yes, but …."

It is a principle of billing compliance that the ordering physician must be informed if an order will result in more than one charge. He or she must be given an opportunity to "opt out" of the additional charge. For example, many radiology departments firmly believe that separating CT of the abdomen from CT of the pelvis is unrealistic. But because there are separate CPT codes for pelvis and abdomen, any examination that includes both must be clearly identified to the ordering clinician, who must also be given an opportunity to order each one separately.

It is quite possible that, in specifying the "protocol," a radiologist may change the applicable CPT. For instance, if an MRI of the brain is ordered for stroke, the radiologist might believe that evaluation of the arteries of the neck is also called for. However, adding an MRA of the neck in the course of specifying a protocol will result in two CPT codes—one for MRI of the brain, and the other for MRA of the neck—and therefore two charges. The same can be true for MR spectroscopy. In both cases, the addition will need to be authorized by the requesting clinician and, when applicable, included in the insurance pre-authorization.

In summary, the "order" is the province of the clinician, the examination to which it applies is defined by the radiology department, and the "protocol" design is the territory of the individual radiologist, with the caveat that "protocols" resulting in additional charges must be authorized by the ordering clinician.

5.3   Protocol Selection

Once a standard set of protocols has been created, the appropriate protocol must be selected for each order. The process of tailoring (or attempting to tailor) each examination to individual patients' specific issues is a laborious and time-consuming one, especially with the imperfect information often provided with the request. Given this, there are several ways to approach it.

5.3.1   By the Radiologist

Generally, the goal of protocol selection is to address the clinical concern as thoroughly as possible. How does the radiologist know what the concern is?

Most orders for imaging studies come with at least a minimal "indication." As discussed in the chapter on ordering, this indication should at least be sufficient to select an appropriate ICD code for billing. Here, though, the information provided is often skimpy, and in some instances so perfunctory as to be misleading. The radiologist might attempt to supplement it by reviewing the medical record, a time-consuming and not necessarily revealing process.

Some institutions try to improve the process of tailoring the examination to patients' specific issues by asking the patients to complete questionnaires. In other cases (when feasible), the radiologist might address the questions to the patient directly. Not surprisingly, studies have shown that direct interviews are more useful than questionnaires, at least to the extent that they help the radiologist decide upon a protocol. Whether the selected protocol is actually "better" than the other options would have been is left unanswered [3].

5.3.2   By the Technologist

In some facilities, especially community hospitals, imaging centers, and smaller academic centers, a senior technologist may select the protocol based on a set of rules established by the facility's radiologists, or through their own prior experience. This approach can work well if the number of options is neither too large nor extremely specialized [4].

Having technologists assume protocoling responsibilities makes sense especially with remote radiology services such as teleradiology, when a radiologist is not available at the imaging site.

5.3.3   By the Clinician

Should clinicians be expected (or even allowed) to specify the protocol? As we mentioned earlier, sometimes the clinician may wish to specify the exact way in which the examination is performed—as in the example of our "Dr. X's wrist exam." This is less often the case for "high-tech" imaging than it is for radiography, but even in "high-tech" imaging there are clinicians who prefer to specify the protocol. These clinicians tend to be specialists who are familiar with the examination they are ordering and what it can show (Fig. 5.6). Primary care doctors are much less likely to want to do so.

On the one hand, allowing the clinician to specify the protocol simplifies operation of the department by eliminating a step and expediting scheduling and preauthorization, based on a clear understanding of the examination to be performed. On the other, it devalues the role of the radiologist (Table 5.1). Determining the key components of an examination is part of radiologists' core competence, and in our experience they are often unwilling to relinquish this role. As a sort of compromise, our department offers certain specific protocols that can be selected as part of our order entry system. Selection of a specific protocol is optional. Generalists who do not wish to specify this level of detail may leave the protocol selection to a radiologist.

Fig. 5.6 A pop-up list of orderable protocols is available to clinicians in our order entry system. Even a cursory evaluation of the protocol names will reveal that only highly specialized clinicians are likely to want to specify the protocol

Table 5.1 Pros and cons of clinicians selecting protocols as part of the order vs. radiologists selecting them

	Specific protocol ordered by clinician	Radiologist determines protocol
Advantages	• Pre-authorization facilitated • Clinician gets exactly what he or she expects • Duration of the examination knowable at the time of the order	• Removes the need for the clinician to understand this level of detail • Permits greater flexibility in keeping up with advances in imaging
Disadvantages	• Some clinicians may not understand the use of more detailed protocols	• May undermine the pre-authorization process • A time-consuming task in which the radiologist attempts to figure out what the clinician needs to know • Duration of examination may be affected, making scheduling more difficult

5.3.4 By Machine ("Auto" Protocols)

Protocol selection would seem to be a good candidate for automation, or at least semi-automation. Tudor et al. [5] reported that, when they used a rule-based system to assign protocols automatically, the protocols selected were seldom changed. In cases where changes were made, the changes tended to fall into predictable patterns. One of the more common reasons for change was consolidation of multiple examination requests into a single performable. In other cases, free text provided with the order led to an organ-specific protocol that was not identified by the automatic selection process.

In our institution, we have been using a semiautomated system for protocol selection. Our system employs both inclusion and exclusion criteria for this process. For example, in order to complete a request for a lumbar spine MRI, the ordering clinician must respond to questions about whether the target of the examination is infection, tumor, or demyelinating disease, and whether the patient has recently had surgery. If the answer to all these questions is "no," then the examination is automatically protocoled as "routine, no contrast." If the answer to any one or more is "yes," then manual selection of the protocol is needed. In addition, if free text provided along with the order includes any of a number of terms (e.g., "MS" or "multiple sclerosis"), the cases are excluded from "auto-protocoling" (Table 5.2).

While not foolproof, this approach offers two benefits. First, a substantial number of cases are removed from the radiologist's protocol list. Second, the process is almost instantaneous, facilitating scheduling of the study for the correct amount of time.

Recent advances in radiology artificial intelligence (AI) make machine auto-protocoling particularly attractive: If properly implemented, machine learning algorithms can process all available patient information (from previously acquired images to full hospital records) and, based on this, recommend the most appropriate scanning sequences.

Table 5.2 Free-text terms that will exclude the case from auto-protocoling if included as part of the order

• Abnormal X-ray bone destruction	• Fluid collection
• Cauda equina syndrome	• Drainage
• CES	• Meningioma
• Primary tumor lumbar spine	• Neurofibroma
• Bladder dysfunction	• NF
• Demyelinating	• NF$_1$
• Gado	• NF$_2$
• Contrast	• Ependymoma
• MS	• Paraganglioma
• Multiple sclerosis	• CIDP
• Schwannoma	• GB
• Staph	• Guillain-Barre
• Septic	• With contrast
• Arachnoiditis	

5.4   Where Does Protocol Selection Belong in the Workflow?

Should protocols be selected before or after the examination is scheduled? You could make a good argument for either answer, depending on the circumstances. If protocol selection and scheduling are independent, they can be done in parallel, rather than in series, and one need not delay the other. However, since the protocol determines the length of the examination, selecting the protocol after the exam has been scheduled can lead to a mismatch between the examination duration and the available time. This would suggest that protocol selection should be done before scheduling.

But there are other issues to be considered. When the insurance company requires pre-authorization, as they commonly do for "high-tech" studies (CT, MRI, PET), the pre-authorization must specify whether contrast is to be used. Clinicians may not know whether or not contrast is needed, preferring to leave that decision to the radiologist. In such cases, the protocol must be selected far enough in advance to ensure that the pre-authorization can be obtained. This, of course, is more easily said than done.

At least one large institution tried to delay scheduling until after protocol selection. Unfortunately, the clinics in that institution habitually batched their order entry at the end of the day, when radiologists were not available to protocol the incoming orders. Although schedulers were available until 8 pm, they were underutilized because of the relative dearth of protocols. To address this, the institution added an afternoon "protocol owner." Although this appeared to have worked for them, such a solution may be inappropriate for more subspecialized departments, since more than one "protocol owner" would be needed [6].

Another study attempted to address schedule mismatches and pre-authorization problems by making the protocol part of the order. When this workflow modification resulted in sky-high rates of subsequent protocol changes (90% in the first week from one department!), the authors of the study created a checklist to help clinicians select the correct examination (the majority of problems appeared to be related to contrast use) [7].

Fortunately, in our area, most (but not all) insurance companies will approve a family of CPT codes (without, with, and both with and without contrast), permitting the radiologist to make the decision about contrast after the order has been scheduled. Clearly, the optimal solution for this dilemma has yet to be found.

5.5   How Should a Protocol Be Designed?

There is a prevailing belief among radiologists that every examination should be "tailored" to the specific needs of the patient. In practice, though, personalizing an exam like this can be exceptionally difficult because the specific needs of a patient may depend upon many details that might be unknown to the radiologist—or to anyone prior to imaging. Consequently, in an effort to avoid "callbacks" (requests for the patient to return for additional imaging), radiologists may decide to include more images and/or use more contrast than is necessary.

Specification of the imaging study thus can be subject to several opposing considerations. Tailoring the examination makes sense as a problem-solving tool, but perhaps not as an initial diagnostic measure—especially as such personalized exams require considerable time and effort and might still fail to address the clinical needs. We believe that initial protocols should be *robust and standardized*, with the recognition that some patients will need to come back for additional imaging. These initial studies can be viewed as a sort of a survey or screening examination. (We acknowledge that, in the strictest sense, a "screening study" is performed on asymptomatic individuals and few advanced imaging studies actually meet this definition.) This situation is analogous to that of screening mammography, in which there is an optimum range for callbacks (usually around 10%, as our hospital records indicate). If the callback number is too high, either the examination was poorly done or the radiologist is insecure. But if the number is too low, patients are being over-imaged. Frequent customization of examinations (as opposed to selection from a menu of standard protocols) should be avoided, as this practice undermines both consistency and the technologist's expertise. Unfortunately, we are not aware of any data that provides guidance as to the appropriate number of "callbacks" for CT or MRI.

A short protocol obviously increases both capacity and revenue [8]. Because of this, many believe that the motivating factors behind reducing the duration of exams pit quality against greed! In fact, abbreviating protocols is an excellent way to make high-tech services less expensive and more generally available. A number of studies have shown that substantially shorter protocols can be devised without compromising quality in any way [9–11]. Shorter protocols are also more patient friendly and, as we have previously discussed, less likely to disrupt the daily workflow, resulting in delayed exams downstream.

Protocols should be as short as possible and, in most cases, general enough to detect a range of different pathologies. Their design should be unambiguous and

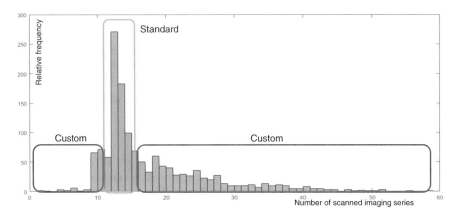

Fig. 5.7 Number of imaging series acquired for the same MR brain examination. While the standard protocol includes a fixed number of required imaging sequences, a much wider range of sequence acquisitions is proscribed for patient- and physician-specific reasons

should rely on techniques with low failure rates. Unless you provide very strong guidelines, you may be surprised to discover how many different ways the same examination can be performed. We alluded to this issue in Chap. 4 (Scheduling) and illustrate this variability with Fig. 5.7, extracted from our PACS data, which shows the frequency distribution for the number of imaging series performed in response to orders for a single examination (MRI brain) over a period of 8 months. Some exams included very few series, likely because they were not completed for one reason or another. Most often, examinations included between 9 and 20 series. These were probably "standard" protocols selected by radiologists for various indications. Still, there is tremendous diversity in the data, and quite a few examinations contained much larger numbers of series. In some cases, this is likely due to technologists performing repeat scans because they were not satisfied with the initial images, though there are simply too many of these exams for that to be the whole explanation (or even the primary explanation). The wide range we see in the number of series surely also includes radiologists' attempts to "customize" the examination to the perceived need.

This type of heterogeneity is unadvisable from an operational perspective, as it makes the duration of the examination unpredictable. In addition, it renders operational improvements impossible: If you have a "gazillion" customized sequences, making any one of them faster or better will have no effect on the overall performance. Finally, as we have emphasized already, the longer the examination, the higher the variability and the greater the chances of an untoward event (such as premature termination due to patient claustrophobia). The use of sequences that have a high probability of failure (those involving breath-holds, for example) should be discouraged. As a teaching institution, we probably have more difficulties with standardization than many community hospitals do. We try to teach the trainees the craft of medicine—the science of selecting protocols according to rational rules—but all too often what gets emphasized is the "art" of medicine. A suggestion by Picasso that one should "Learn the rules like a pro, so you can break them like an artist" also seems to apply in radiology.

Keep It Real!

We briefly referred to the potential of radiology AI for auto-protocoling. We have also seen it applied in the reverse: as a way to clean up protocol messes stemming from custom deviations, manual inputs, and various scanner versions, where even the same protocol sequence may appear under several individualized and confusing names. To group all these acquired sequences into a few protocol groups, as originally intended, one may need all the power of natural language processing and machine learning. In short, the variability we create exceeds our human capacities to manage it.

Protocols map what we observe (patient conditions) onto what we want to examine (patient imaging). If this mapping is not clear-cut, our decisions become irrational—and our work, impossible to manage.

5.6 Safety in Protocoling

Selecting an inappropriate protocol might make an examination less useful than it would have been otherwise. But improper use of contrast can have much worse consequences. The "red flags" warning us about improper contrast use are not very complicated, and electronic health records should contain the information needed to minimize the risk of error. This could fail, though, for one or more of three possible reasons: (1) Information is not always found in the expected places; (2) not everything in the electronic health record is correct; and (3) there are exceptions that must be taken into account.

For example, a chest CT scan may be requested for a patient preparing to undergo radioiodine treatment for thyroid cancer because of possible metastatic disease. Use of iodine-containing contrast media could interfere with the cancer treatment but, unfortunately, the details of the treatment plan might only appear in an office note, or they may not even be present when the scan is ordered. If the radiologist who protocols the scan is not aware of the impending treatment, he or she might improperly select the use of contrast.

Poor renal function is usually a contraindication to the use of iodinated contrast, and can easily be determined by a simple laboratory test. However, iodine-containing contrast use may be appropriate if the patient is scheduled to undergo dialysis shortly after the procedure.

The issue of allergies is even more complex, as physiological responses to contrast injection may be mistakenly recorded as allergic reactions, and mild or moderate hypersensitivity can be managed by pretreatment with steroids.

We rely upon a combination of policy and a custom-made protocoling interface to minimize the chances of something going wrong. Every protocol is categorized according to whether contrast material is included; protocols are selected from a list that always includes this information.

We have developed an in-house system to help prevent errors due to inappropriate use of contrast. If an order specifically states that contrast material is not to be used, we consider this an "absolute" contraindication. Any protocols requiring contrast are hidden from the radiologist. The only way they can be accessed after this is for the clinician to create a new order. If a patient has extremely bad kidney function (eGFR less than 30), the system treats it as another absolute contraindication and makes unavailable any gadolinium-containing protocols for MRI.

However, use of iodine-containing contrast agents in patients with poor renal function is considered a relative contraindication. Protocols for CT that call for contrast will be hidden until the radiologist acknowledges the risk. Similarly, reported allergies are regarded as a relative to contrast and result in a similar warning before the protocol can be accessed.

Figure 5.8 demonstrates how our protocoling software attempts to decrease the risk of error. In this case, the clinician specifically requested that contrast *not* be used (red rectangle). Therefore, protocols that require the use of contrast have been removed from the available menu (yellow rectangle). If the radiologist strongly believes that contrast material is necessary, the individual who placed the order must change it.

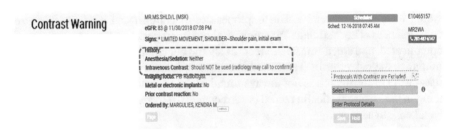

Fig. 5.8 Reducing errors in protocoling application. If an absolute contraindication to contrast use is present in the medical record, protocols that call for the use of contrast are not available. If a relative contraindication is present then the protocoling radiologist must acknowledge the risk before proceeding

---

Keep It Real!

1. Keep protocols as short and error-proof as possible. Standard protocols should be designed to "find" relevant pathology, but not necessarily to evaluate it fully.
2. A limited number of recalls is not necessarily a bad thing.
3. Avoid the pitfall of thinking that longer examinations are somehow "better."
4. Find ways to automate protocol selection, at least partially. This decreases the amount of labor needed and simplifies pre-authorization.
5. Create systems (procedural or software) that protect against errors in protocol selection.

References

1. Carroll L. Through the looking-glass. Illustrated by John Tenniel. 1871 MacMillan Co, London, p. 208.
2. CPT 2017 Professional. 4th ed. Chicago: American Medical Association; 2016.
3. Davis D, Mulligan M, Moszkowicz A, Resnik C. Patient-centered care in diagnostic radiology: lessons learned from patient interviews prior to musculoskeletal magnetic resonance imaging. Qual Manag Health Care. 2015;24(1):38–44.
4. Glazer D, Alper D, Lee L, Wach R, Hooton S, Boland G, Khoraani R. Technologist productivity and accuracy in assigning protocols for abdominal CT and MRI examinations in an academic medical center: implications for physician workload. AJR Am J Roentgenol. 2019;213(5):1003–7.
5. Tudor J, Klochko C, Patel M, Siegal D. Order entry protocols are an amenable target for workflow automation. J Am Coll Radiol. 2018;15(6):854–8.
6. Wessman B, et al. Reducing barriers to timely MR imaging scheduling. Radiographics. 2014;34(7):2064–70.
7. DiRoberto C, et al. Prioritizing the protocol: improving the process of scheduling imaging examinations in a radiology department with partially integrated IT systems. J Am Coll Radiol. 2017;14(3):444–8.
8. O'Brien J, Stormann J, Roche K, Cabral-Goncalves I, Monks A, Hallett D, et al. Optimizing MRI logistics: focused process improvements can increase throughput in an academic radiology department. AJR Am J Roentgenol. 2017;208(2):W38–44.
9. Chhor C, Mercado C. Abbreviated MRI protocols: wave of the future for breast cancer screening. AJR Am J Roentgenol. 2017;208(2):284–9.
10. O'Brien JJS, Roche K, Cabral-Goncalves I, Monks A, Hallett D, Mortele KJ. Optimizing MRI logistics: focused process improvements can increase throughput in an academic radiology department. AJR Am J Roentgenol. 2017;208(2):W38–44.
11. Alaia E, Benedick A, Obuchowski N, Polster J, Beltran L, Schils J, Garwood E, Burke C, Chang I, Gyftopoulos S, Subhas N. Comparison of a fast 5-min knee MRI protocol with a standard knee MRI protocol: a multi-institutional multi-reader study. Skelet Radiol. 2018;47(1):107–16.

Arriving for the Examination

6

Contents

Things That Happen
- Appointment reminders are sent.
- The patient checks in.
- Information is collected.
- A certain amount of waiting ensues.
- The patient is called for the appointment.
- Unplanned arrivals occur.
- "No-shows" are identified and followed up.

Things to Measure

Periodic Reports
- Percentage of reminders delivered
- Effectiveness of reminders
- Causes of "no-show" patients
- Percentage of "no-shows" and effectiveness of successful reschedule
- Patient punctuality
- Patient waiting time:
  - Delays for scheduled procedures
  - Waits for "walk-in" patients

© Springer Nature Switzerland AG 2021
D. Rosenthal, O. Pianykh, *Efficient Radiology*,
https://doi.org/10.1007/978-3-030-53610-7_6

- Reliability of manual data (estimates)
- Equitability of room assignments

Real-Time Reports
- Actual waiting time displayed for arriving patients
- Patients waiting longer than predetermined allowable amount

6.1   When Do We Tell Patients to Arrive?

Despite the fact that there is a historical relationship between surgeons and barbers, a medical appointment is more like an airplane flight than a haircut. If you have a haircut scheduled for 10 o'clock, you arrange your day so that you are available to be seated in the chair at 10 AM; no one tells you that you must arrive 45 min earlier. However, for air travel one is constantly reminded of the need to arrive at least an hour ahead of the domestic flight, and at least two for international. Travelers generally understand the reasons for early arrival and adjust their behavior according to their assessment of how necessary they think it is.

In healthcare, we do similar things for scheduled patients (obviously this does not apply to walk-ins or to inpatients). We tell the patients to arrive in advance of their appointment. But unlike the case of air travel, patients may not understand why this is needed. We often do not explain it, and in fact neither the patients nor we may have a clear understanding of how much time is necessary.

In order to achieve a high level of patient satisfaction, everyone who works in a radiology department must understand expectations. What does the appointment time mean? Air travelers expect that the scheduled flight time means the time that the plane leaves the gate, not when they arrive at the gate or even board the plane. In imaging procedures, the appointment time is usually understood to mean the time that the patient enters the imaging or procedure room, not the time that they arrive, begin answering questionnaires, or start to drink barium.

However, even if the patient enters the room at the scheduled time, the procedure may not begin on time (Fig. 6.1). Just as we would probably not be satisfied to board an airplane and leave the gate on time, only to wait on the tarmac for an hour, so too we would not appreciate entering the procedure room only to wait for a doctor or a technologist. There is another analogy to air travel. Sometime before you take off, the flight attendant will politely inform you that "your safety is our most important priority"—subtly suggesting that your time is not their first priority. In healthcare we encounter similar attitudes. On-time performance is seldom listed high on the hierarchy of "quality" metrics. In fact, in our experience hospital staff may not even know whether they are on time or not!

There is a subtle but important difference from air travel that might be interesting to mention. Airlines know that on-time arrival is at least as important as on-time departure. In fact, many travelers believe that the airlines deliberately "pad" the

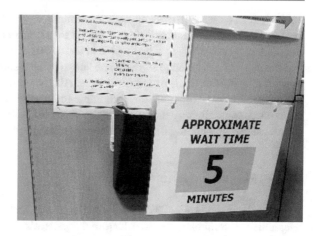

Fig. 6.1 Patient wait time information in a hospital waiting area. This is printed on paper and therefore very unlikely to be current information

schedule, allowing more time than is really required in order to allow for at least some of the more common delays. As far as we know, imaging patients are told when to arrive, but not usually when to expect to be finished.

6.2 Appointment Reminders

Appointments for imaging, especially screening examinations and follow-up studies, may be scheduled weeks, months, or even years in advance. Therefore, it is not surprising that a certain number of appointments are not kept, resulting in "no-shows," as we described in Chap. 4. Clearly, no-shows are undesirable because they limit availability for other patients, and result in idle equipment and technologists. Of course, they are also undesirable because of the potential health consequences to the patient who has missed the appointment. For those reasons alone, no-show reduction is an important goal.

Since this is a universal problem, there have been a number of attempts to deal with it, ranging from simple telephone calls to the most advanced AI models to predict patients at risk for no-show. Studies have shown that a variety of different factors contribute to the problem, many of which can be mined from data that is available in the electronic health record and beyond [1]. Although specifics vary from place to place, socioeconomic and cultural factors play a significant role in the probability of a "no-show." Patients who are economically or educationally disadvantaged, and patients who have difficulty with language, all have a greater likelihood of nonattendance [2–4]. Much of the information that is necessary to suggest the probability of a no-show is available in the health record, and therefore creation of a predictive algorithm that will work with your patient population is feasible and can be very helpful [2].

A variety of appointment reminders have been tried, with varying degrees of success. We think that success depends upon getting the message right and bringing it to the patient's attention. The technology of reminders is well known: They may take the form of a mailing, a telephone call (either by a human or a machine "robocall"), an email, or a text message. The devil is in the details of implementation, as always.

Mailings cannot be done in real time and are increasingly obsolete. This leaves us with telephone, email, or text messages. All three are technically feasible, and there is a wide range of companies providing these services for a fee. This outsourcing reduces the radiology manager's task to selection of the wording and timing of the message—and hoping that the patients will be interested in receiving it.

6.2.1   Phone Call Reminders

To understand the probability that the patients will be "interested" in receiving a telephone call reminder, consider it from the patient's perspective. Automated calls are unpleasant and/or disruptive. To a lesser degree, so are uninvited emails or text messages. There seems to be no particular time of the day when uninvited messages are welcome. For example, many robocalls are made in the early evening because this is a time of day when many people are at home. Although calls that are made at this time do not disrupt the workday, they do interrupt dinner or family time. Many people will not answer or will immediately hang up when they realize that the caller is a machine. One study appeared to show that an automated calling system actually worsened the problem of no-shows and late arrivals, because patients appear to be conditioned to ignore automated calls! [5] Another study reported that when a robocall was replaced by a human being, the percentage of on-time arrivals improved from 56 to 74% [6]. This situation is changing rapidly as our culture adapts to ever-increasing invasions of privacy. Because increasing numbers of individuals will not answer telephone calls if the caller's name or ID is unknown, it may be necessary to leave messages on an answering machine (and hope that someone will listen to them), but this brings up another issue. Since we do not know who will listen to a recorded message, what sort of content is permissible to protect patient confidentiality?

The first requirement for any reminder message is that it must strike the right balance between patient confidentiality (demanded by the Health Information Portability and Privacy Act, HIPPA) and information (to make it useful and specific). For example, an MRI appointment message at our hospital reads as shown in Fig. 6.2.

Notice that the patient is identified by first name only, in an attempt to provide some confidentiality. Also notice that the message states the time of appointment, but then says that the patient must arrive 30 min before the appointment. We will return to this issue slightly later in this chapter. Our telephone message is delivered three business days prior to the appointment, between the hours of 6 and 8 PM (when most annoying robocalls are delivered).

> Hello, this is Mass General Imaging calling to remind you that (*Patient's First Name*) has an appointment on (*Date*) at (*Time*) (*Name and address of imaging location*).
>
> Please arrive 30minutes before your appointment time to prepare for your exam. It will be necessary to complete paperwork, and to change into a hospital gown.
>
> Certain devices may not be safe for MRI. These include: Implantable cardioverters, defibrillators, and other implanted electronic devices. Some stents and aneurysm clips are also not safe. Some one from Mass General Imaging will be contacting you within 48 hours to review these important safety issues. If possible, please be prepared to provide specific information about the manufacturer and model you have any implants.
>
> Please leave your valuables at home. Children are not allowed in the examination room and must be supervised by a responsible party while the scan is underway.
>
> If you need to cancel or reschedule your appointment, please call (*Resource rescheduling telephone number*).
>
> We look forward to seeing you on (*Date*) at (*Time*) (*Name and address of imaging location*).

Fig. 6.2 Mass General Hospital MRI appointment phone call reminder template. The text indicated in parentheses () is drawn from a database table

6.2.2   Texting/Email Reminders

Email and text messages are commonly perceived as more "patient-friendly" options, because they do not require attention at inconvenient times. Also, and quite importantly, emails and text messages "persist" in time—the patient can read and reread them later and can even reply to them if needed. This, along with the increasing adoption of smart phones, makes texting an increasingly popular choice for appointment reminders.

What needs to be considered when thinking about the texting implementation?

First is the best time to deliver the message. Although less disruptive than phone calls, text messages still should arrive at the "most convenient" times. Unlike a telephone call, a text message does not demand an immediate response and receipt does not depend upon being in a particular place. For that reason (recall our daily activity curve) we prefer to use the midday lunch break, one day in advance of the appointment, trying to achieve a balance between "enough time to get ready" and "not enough time to forget." This differs from the time of day of the telephone reminder, partly because we believe that many patients will not keep their cellphones with them at dinner time.

Second, text messages are usually limited to 160 characters, so they must be succinct. You can achieve this in two principal ways:

1. Provide only essential information
2. Use abbreviations: "pls," "appt," etc.

Your MRI appointment is on (*Day of week*) (*Date*)
Arrive at MGH (*Building and floor of specific scanner*) at (*Time*) for safety screening.
Questions call (*Resource rescheduling telephone number*)
Text STOP to stop messages

Fig. 6.3 Mass General Hospital MRI appointment text message template—the text in () is automatically filled with specific examination information

Your MRI appointment is on (*Day of week*) (*Date*)
To prepare for contrast injection, arrive at MGH (*Building and floor of specific scanner*) at (*Time*).
Questions call (*Resource rescheduling telephone number*)
Text STOP to stop messages

Fig. 6.4 Mass General Hospital MRI appointment text message template, intravenous contrast version. The text within parentheses () is supplied from data tables drawn from the specific appointment

We are not fans of the second option, which seems cryptic and amateurish: With some effort, it should be possible to keep the message short and readable. After many experiments with our radiology messaging, we have arrived at the baseline template shown in Fig. 6.3.

The items shown in parentheses () are autofilled by our texting software from a database.

Notice that instead of the examination *scheduled* time, this system tells the patient when and where to *arrive*, with arrival time being earlier than the scheduled imaging appointment. This is done to accommodate necessary pre-procedure activities (see our Chap. 4), so that the procedure can indeed start on time. The message tells the patient why it is necessary to arrive prior to the appointment (safety screening) in an attempt to improve compliance.

The content of our message is modified depending upon other available information at the time of texting. For example, if a protocol requiring intravenous contrast has already been selected, we change our message to the one shown in Fig. 6.4.

We have evaluated the success of adding the text message to the traditional telephone call. Almost 7000 patients were randomly assigned to receive either telephone calls only or both telephone calls and text messages reminding them of their upcoming MRI appointments. Sending texting appointment reminders in addition to phone calls helped us significantly reduce patient no-show rates. When patients received a text message reminder in addition to a telephone call the no-show rate was 3.8%, but when no reminder was sent, the no-show rate was 5.4%, a very significant difference.

However (and surprisingly), patients receiving a text reminder were no more likely to arrive the requested 30 min ahead of their appointment than those that did not receive the reminder [7].

Figure 6.5 illustrates what we observed.

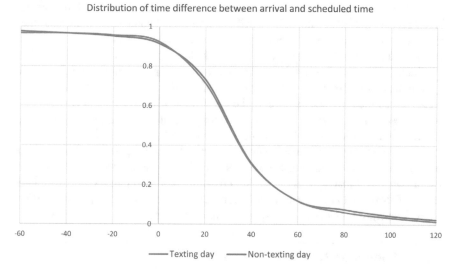

Fig. 6.5 The fraction of patients who have arrived is shown on the vertical axis. The horizontal axis shows the time of arrival with respect to the scheduled appointment time (shown as "0"). Patients who arrived in advance of their appointment are shown to the right, and those who arrived after the scheduled start are shown to the left. Notice that although the great majority (75%) of patients arrived at least 20 min before their appointment, there is a significant fraction (20%) who arrived only 10 min or less in advance. Although the text message decreased the no-show rate, it made no difference whatsoever in the "on-time" arrival (reproduced from Liu et al. [7])

Keep It Real!

Asking your patients to arrive prior to their scheduled time may lead to unexpected conflicts with your own staff. When we implemented our texting reminder program, asking our patients to arrive 30 min before their scheduled examinations, we started receiving patient complaints from one of our facilities. The patients were arriving as prompted only to find themselves in front of the locked facility door, where no one was waiting for them!

You can probably guess why this was happening. With the first examination scheduled for 8:30, our staff had developed a habit of coming to work just a few minutes before this time. But the patients started to arrive at 8:00 as requested by our messaging—with no one expecting them. This is what we meant at the beginning of the chapter when we said "it is necessary for everyone who works in a radiology department to understand expectations." Make sure that your staff schedule is put in complete sync with what you expect from your patients.

Another unpleasant discovery came from a revision of all our departmental web pages, calling scripts, and patient communication resources. Developed by different people at different times, they turned out to be completely uncoordinated, all suggesting different arrival thresholds. "Why does your text message ask me to arrive 30 min earlier, and your web page, 60?" was among the most typical complaints. Same recommendation: Make sure that all arrival instructions come from a single current source.

From this we conclude that reminders are not sufficient to ensure "on-time" arrival, either because patients do not believe in the importance of compliance or because they are caught off-guard by the amount of time needed to comply. Achieving "on-time" arrival, and therefore "on-time" performance, is clearly a work in progress!

Finally, some texting services offer patients the opportunity to confirm their appointment with a text response. While a confirmation is undoubtedly a reassuring piece of information to have, it raises the question of what to do about patients who do not respond. If done sufficiently far in advance, it might be possible to make further attempts to contact the patient by telephone, text, or email, but ultimately there will be some patients who do not respond and cannot be contacted. It does not seem right to give the time to another patient without waiting to see if the patient will arrive, but if management is sufficiently nimble, it might be possible to substitute another patient (such as an inpatient, or an outpatient who has arrived early) at the first indication that the non-responding individual is late.

6.3   Following Up on "No-Shows"

Despite reminders, some patients will not keep the scheduled appointment and will not reschedule. When a patient fails to show up for an appointment there may be a variety of explanations:

– The patient may have forgotten the appointment or been confused.
– The patient may be frightened of a potentially unpleasant visit or of getting bad news.
– The patient may not believe that keeping the appointment is important.

These issues are particularly relevant to screening examinations such as mammography. Screening mammograms are often scheduled long in advance, making it possible for patients to forget about them. There is some anxiety about each screening appointment, since the patient knows that there is a small risk she will be told that she has cancer. Finally, since she feels fine, it might be difficult to believe that keeping the appointment is important.

These examples represent true missed appointments. However, there may be other reasons that a patient fails to show up. For instance, the scheduled appointment may be a duplicate. This can happen if an appointment is rescheduled without cancelling the original. Sometimes a patient may have decided to go to a competing facility because an appointment was available at an earlier date, and neglected to cancel the appointment with us. These occurrences are an undesirable waste of appointment time, but do not result in a lapse of care.

The problem of no-shows is not limited to our institution, or even to our part of the world, and may actually be greater in third-world countries. A recent study from the Near East reported that 49% of outpatients failed to show up for their MRI appointments—an enormous number by our standards. In that part of the world female patients were less likely to show up for their appointments than males [3]. This is the reverse pattern to that which is seen in the United States and Canada, and suggests that there is a cultural component to this behavior.

An enormous recently published retrospective study of the problem of no-shows [8] demonstrated that the most important indicators that a patient might not show up for a scheduled examination were median income, distance, daily temperature, and snowfall. Temperature and snowfall affected all income groups. Travel distance was also predictive, but less so among higher socioeconomic groups. This interesting study was drawn from HIS data and relied upon the user having entered no-show manually as the reason for nonattendance. As we have repeatedly emphasized, manual entry is a weak link in the information chain.

There is another way to identify "no-shows" without depending upon manual data entry. We do this by defining a missed appointment as one in which a patient has failed to show up for a scheduled examination, and has not had the same examination within the past week, or had one scheduled within the next 2 weeks at either our facility or any affiliated facilities for which we can access appointment data. Of course, we have no way of knowing if the patient has scheduled the appointment at an unrelated facility.

Using this definition, our no-show rate is about 6.5% overall [2], although it is 4.2% for MRI, suggesting that patients value their MRI appointments more highly than some other types of imaging appointments. Other institutions have reported similar percentages for MRI [9]. For mammography our no-show rate is over 10%. Overall rates reported by others seem to range mostly from 6 to 12% with much higher numbers among vulnerable populations [4].

Our data indicates that failure to show up for an examination is the single most important factor predicting the likelihood of future no-shows. Other important predictors include the time interval since the examination was scheduled and younger patient age [2]. The dependence upon the time interval is illustrated in Fig. 6.6,

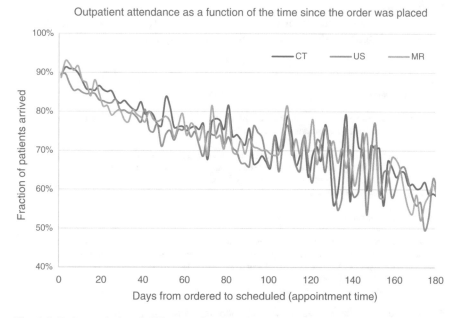

Fig. 6.6 Patient arrival probability as a function of order age—number of days since the date when order was placed to the date when the exam was scheduled to take place. Note the same declining pattern for all three major outpatient exam types

where we see how the probability of patient attendance declines as the time between placing the order and the examination date increases. This is another good example of a pattern which becomes completely intuitive once you see it. The more days pass from the date of the order, the more unforeseen circumstances may intervene in the original plans, resulting in less guaranteed attendance. Also note how noisy this metric becomes with time—essentially meaning that patient attendance not only decreases, but becomes less and less predictable.

Know Your Tools
Other working definitions of no-shows are possible. For instance, one can use two principal timestamps from HIS data—exam cancellation and scheduled time—and define an exam as a no-show if the examination was cancelled after it was due to have been performed. A more pragmatic approach would be to consider a no-show to be any cancellation that occurs after it is too late to fill the time with another patient. This is somewhat analogous to the policy of certain hotels that permit cancellation up to 24 h before check-in. This definition stretches the definition of no-show to a certain extent, but might be adopted if you are considering applying charges to unused appointments.

For those patients who have been identified as no-shows using these criteria, we follow up with a telephone call offering the opportunity to reschedule. Our follow-up script is shown in Fig. 6.7.

Responses to this message permit us to reschedule almost half (43%) of the no-show exams.

Perhaps most difficult to manage are appointments that are missed because of cultural or linguistic differences. A recent investigation from own department

No-show Script Live Version:

Hello, this is Mass General Imaging calling as a courtesy regarding your recent imaging appointment. If you would like to heart his message in English please press1; for Spanish, please press2.

Our records indicate that you have recently missed an appointment for an imaging study. If you have questions or wish to reschedule this appointment, please press1 now and you will be transferred to our scheduling department. You may also contact us at your convenience by calling (*Phone number*).
Thank you and have a good evening.

No-show Script Answering Machine Version:

Hello, this is Mass General Imaging calling as a courtesy regarding your recent imaging appointment. Our records indicate that you have recently missed an appointment for an imaging study. If you have questions or wish to reschedule this appointment, please contact us at your convenience by calling (*Phonen umber*).
Thank you and have a good evening.

Fig. 6.7 No-show communication scripts for following up with the patients

showed that race, household income, and language were all significant factors in predicting the likelihood of a missed appointment, with minorities, immigrants, and less affluent individuals all more likely to miss appointments for imaging [10].

6.4 Arrival

6.4.1 Checking In

Good manners matter. When a patient arrives, he or she must be greeted as soon as possible. This is common courtesy, but also ensures that the arrival time is accurately recorded. If the receptionist is on the telephone when the patient arrives, and the call is necessary, the receptionist should apologize to the patient before completing the call. Personal calls should never occur in front of patients. The receptionist should look at the patient (not at the computer screen or countertop), and should be dressed professionally. What this means is constantly evolving but in our institutions jeans and tee shirts are not acceptable. Managers should have metrics for each of these requirements.

The patient's arrival time must be consistently and accurately recorded: See our little investigation in Fig. 6.8. You might recall that in Chap. 2 we cited a facility in which the percentage of time that the front desk captured this information was one of the dashboard metrics. Manual processes such as these are easy to forget, and therefore require constant monitoring. Whether you take the same approach or not, capturing accurate arrival time is important for two reasons:

1. You need it to track patient punctuality in scheduled facilities—that is, comparing patient arrival times to their scheduled examination times. Patterns of late arrival should lead to an examination of your scheduling and reminder systems.
2. You need it to calculate patient waiting times (as the time from arrival to the beginning of the examination).

Good practice requires unambiguous identification of both the patient and the examination that is to be performed. Our current safety procedures require two forms of identification.[1] Having confirmed this information, an identification bracelet is placed on the patient's wrist so that the technologists need not repeat the identification procedure. Patient identification should be done with respect for the confidentiality and anonymity of the patients, preferably not within earshot of other waiting patients.

Occasionally there is a discrepancy between the examination that the patient believes is to be performed and the one which is indicated on the schedule. In most cases this is a "simple" matter of laterality—for example, an orthopedic surgeon

---

[1] We *never* use social security numbers for identification. The risk of a data breach makes this an unattractive practice.

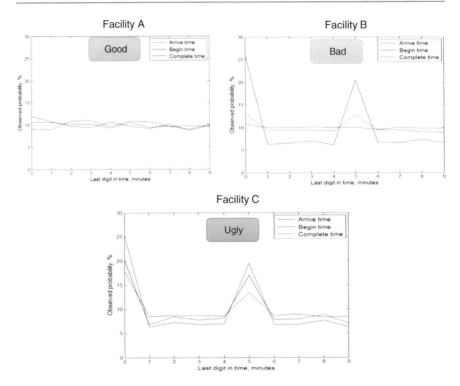

Fig. 6.8 How do you know that your manual entry timestamps, such as patient arrival time, are entered correctly? A couple of years ago, we did this simple check in three of our imaging facilities: A, B, and C. When we, fallible humans, have to enter the time after the fact, we tend to round the minutes to a multiple of 5 or 10: Recalling a past event, instead of "12:21," we would most likely say "12:30" or "12:15." As a result, when a timestamp is entered after the fact, there will be a higher probability that it will have the digits 5 and 0 in its minutes (higher than 10% one would expect for a randomly chosen number between 0 and 9). As you can see, facility A does not show this "after the fact" human bias, meaning that the times were most likely recorded correctly. Facility B shows significant guessing of the examination complete time, and some for the begin time. In facility C we see the full-blown pattern of "human guestimated" times, patient arrival time included

writes "left ankle" and the patient asserts that it is actually the right side. Discrepancies are corrected after a call to the requesting clinicians' office.

As we alluded to in Chap. 4, the time required for pre-procedure activities may vary considerably with the type of the examination, the quality of the information available ahead of time, and the patient condition. Some of the newer electronic information systems offer patients the opportunity to complete the check-in questionnaires from home. A link to the questionnaire may be provided along with the appointment reminder. There is no doubt that such electronic check-in (another airline parallel!!) can save time. However, at the present time a high level of compliance cannot be expected because the practice is recent, and because the healthcare population tends to be older than the general population and perhaps not as e-savvy. A recent study found that only 26% of the eligible patients had completed the form prior to arrival [11].

6.4.2 Dealing with Late Arrivals

Why do patients arrive late? It is possible that patients fully expect to comply with our arrival expectations but are surprised by the difficulties of traveling to our hospital and finding parking. It is also possible that they do not understand or do not believe that it is necessary to arrive early (if so, perhaps the explanation may help). Yet another possibility is that the patients are more likely to arrive on time for appointments that they perceive as being of greater importance. Support for that possibility comes from a recent study of our interventional units, which showed that late arrival was very seldom a cause of delay when the patient is undergoing an interventional procedure (Fig. 6.9).

If, despite your best efforts to schedule and remind patients, they still arrive late, what should you do? The answer partly depends upon how you define "late." As already mentioned, most procedures require a certain amount of preparatory work before they can begin: changing into hospital attire, safety screening for MRI, etc. The time necessary for these activities should be measured, and a patient who arrives when there is insufficient time to perform these preliminaries is "late." For example, if a patient is scheduled to have a contrast-enhanced MRI at 8 AM, we know that this cannot occur on time unless the patient is on-site by 7:40. Therefore, at 7:40 if the patient has not yet arrived, but a later patient is present, we will "swap" the order—beginning the later patient first. This permits the rest of the day to remain on schedule. Of course, some patients object to being delayed, but all patients are

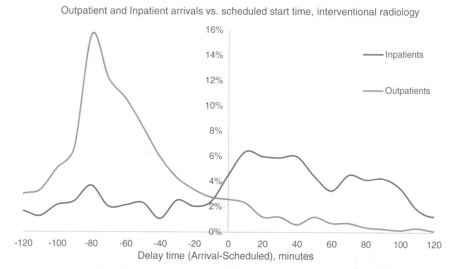

Fig. 6.9 Relationship between arrival and scheduled start times, interventional radiology. Note that outpatients mostly arrive well in advance of the scheduled time, possibly reflecting the high importance that patients attach to this type of examination. Inpatients are far less predictable, being dependent upon other hospital activities and transport

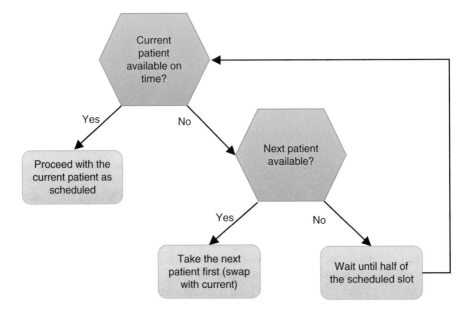

Fig. 6.10 Flowchart for add-on arrival management

told to arrive a half hour ahead and if they do not do so, it seems to us unfair to delay the others to accommodate the late arrivals.

If no later patient is available to substitute, we still face a scheduling challenge, but in this case we must work with the current patient only. As a result, if the late patient is delayed by less than half the expected duration of the examination, we will proceed. If half of the anticipated duration has expired and if the next scheduled patient has already arrived, we will begin the second patient. The first patient will have to either wait or reschedule the examination (Fig. 6.10).

6.4.3   Waiting

As we pointed out in Chap. 4, there is an inherent conflict between the patient's interests and the interests of the radiology department. If the patients wait for their imaging, the department's time is optimized. On the other hand, if the department waits for the patient, the patient's time is prioritized.

Waiting is unpleasant. A substantial number of the complaints that a radiology department receives are related to waiting [12]. Even if a patient must remain in the hospital or clinic after the appointment for other reasons, they will still perceive waiting for the imaging examination to be a cause of dissatisfaction. In our experience—and probably in yours as well—a waiting time of up to 15 min for a walk-in examination is acceptable, but longer times are perceived as onerous. Figure 6.11 shows the results of a national survey of patient satisfaction with a visit to a primary

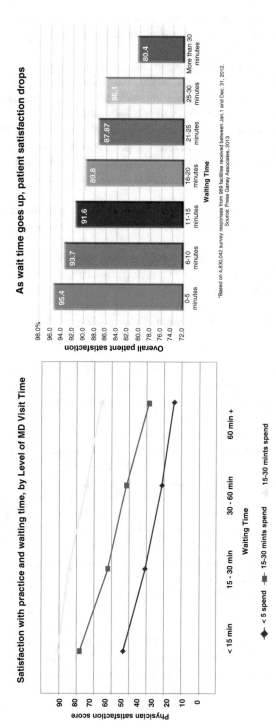

Fig. 6.11 Left: The chart on the left shows the decline in patient satisfaction as a function of the time spent waiting to see the doctor. Notice that for those appointments in which the doctor spent more time with the patients, the patients were willing to wait longer. However, even for the longest appointments (yellow line) satisfaction declined with time. This study was done with primary care practices, but the findings are undoubtedly applicable to radiology [13]. Right: A similar study of patients waiting in a hospital shows a sharp decline in satisfaction when patients wait more than 30 min [14]

care doctor. Notice that the more time that the physician spent with the patient, the longer the patient was willing to wait, but in all cases satisfaction declined once the wait exceeded 15–30 min.

The problem is obvious: Radiology departments must develop methods for managing patient waits. Such methods might include staffing to demand, hardware purchases and upgrades, and changes in operating hours. Larger departments may have the option of moving patients from busier to less busy areas.

It is useful to devote some effort to managing patients' perceptions of the wait in addition to managing the wait itself. In general, perceived waits are inversely correlated with satisfaction. If the patient waiting experience is made comfortable and friendly, patients will tend to underestimate their actual wait, and report higher satisfaction levels [15].

Managing expectations can be difficult. Sometimes, what seems like a good idea is actually not. For example, adding a television to patient waiting areas does not seem to improve satisfaction [16].

Patients who are sitting together in a waiting room may notice that some who have arrived later might be called sooner. Of course, some might have appointments for scheduled examinations and others might be walk-in patients. Even among the latter group, some patients may be waiting for a particular piece of equipment to become available. In such an environment, it is impossible to work on a "first come, first served" basis, giving the impression that some patients are receiving preferential treatment.

Although it may sometimes be distressing to them, we have found that patients appreciate knowing how long their wait is likely to be. Waiting times can vary a great deal depending upon the time of day, day of week, and location. This is especially true of walk-in facilities where patient arrival is uncontrolled (Fig. 6.12).

Fortunately, a rough calculation of wait time for walk-in plain-film appointments is fairly straightforward, being based upon the known capacity of the available examination rooms, the duration of the examinations for which patients are waiting, and the number of patients currently waiting. This makes it possible to develop real-time displays of current waits. In our version of this, the number of minutes that they should expect to wait is displayed to the patients at the time that they check in to the department for their appointment (Fig. 6.13). We do not try to personalize this for each patient. For example, if a patient sees that at the time of arrival the predicted wait is 7 min, it is quite possible that when the next patient walks in the wait might be 9 min for the newly arrived patient, but only 4 min for the patient who had previously arrived. In order to display patient-specific information it would be necessary to identify each waiting patient in some way, running the risk of violating patient confidentiality.

Our simple approach to waiting time will not suffice when there is a mixture of scheduled and unscheduled modalities. The concept of "wait time" does not translate directly to a scheduled modality. A patient who arrives early for a scheduled appointment may wait a considerable amount of time and yet still begin his or her

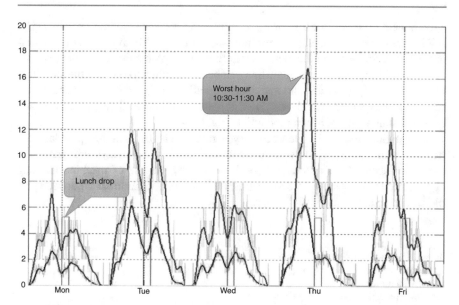

Fig. 6.12 Number of patients waiting for imaging in one of our walk-in X-ray facilities. The average number of patients waiting for the given day and time is shown in black, whereas the largest number is shown in blue. Note that there are significant differences depending on the time and day of week. Tuesdays and Thursdays are clearly worse than Mondays, Wednesdays, and Fridays. The red bar indicates the lunch hour (noon). The dip that occurs at lunchtime probably reflects the lull in activity of the referring offices (another manifestation of the "Asian camel" HAP curve)

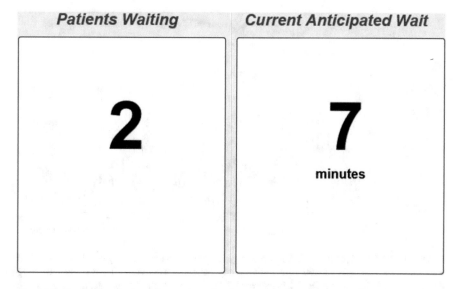

Fig. 6.13 A monitor displays the number of patients currently waiting as well as the anticipated wait at the time of patient arrival to one of our walk-in facilities

appointment on time. Because of these considerations, for scheduled patients (CT, MRI, ultrasound) we display *delays*, not waiting times. "Delay" means the anticipated difference between the appointment time and the time that the patient will be called in for imaging. We calculate this number by taking into account the start time of the previous patient and the anticipated duration of the case. This display uses real-time data (patient arrival, scheduled appointments, and available resources) and clearly distinguishes between modalities (Fig. 6.14).

This digital display is updated every 5 min. It has been highly popular with patients who prefer to know what to expect, even when delays are predicted. Predictive accuracy has recently been improved by the use of machine learning approaches [17]. Figure 6.15 demonstrates the excellent concordance between predicted and actual delay times for X-ray.

Fig. 6.14 A monitor that displays both waiting times for walk-in patients and delays (if any) for scheduled patients. Note the disclaimer at the bottom

Walk-In Patients

Modality	Location	Patients Waiting	Anticipated Wait
X-ray	Yawkey 6	0	3 min

Scheduled Appointments

Modality	Location		Anticipated Delay
CT	Yawkey 6		On Time
MRI	Yawkey 6		23 min
Ultrasound	Yawkey 6		16 min
Procedures	Yawkey 6		18 min

Your actual wait time may vary based on the complexity of the previous exam and resource availability.

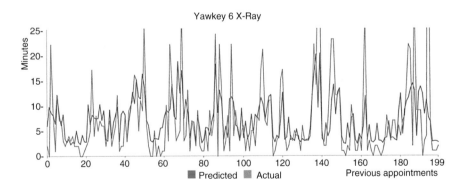

Yawkey 6 X-Ray

■ Predicted ■ Actual

Fig. 6.15 Predicting patient wait time for a large outpatient imaging facility (predicted vs. actual wait times for a sample of 200 consecutive X-ray patients). This view of the delay-predicting model was provided for the facility managers: Clicking on different data points, they can see the patient and examination data behind them, to better understand their delay patterns

Keep It Real!

Note that wait time displays, popular with the patients, could be less popular with the front-desk staff: When the facility runs late, they make these delays very visible to the patients. One example is particularly interesting: Soon after we developed and implemented the displays, we started receiving calls from the front desk about "patients complaining about long wait time." One instance of complaints was particularly frequent: when the first patient comes in the morning, and the display shows some 45 min of estimated wait time. Why would the first patient have to wait, if there is no one else in front of him or her?

The answer was simple, and came from a brief investigation of the historical data: The physicians and staff were arriving and starting the examinations late. As a result, the first patient was indeed delayed by 45 min not because of the other patients in front of him or her, but because of the delayed facility "warmup"! Thus, the display (and the underlying machine learning model, predicting the delay times) was correct, but exposing the lack of facility punctuality to the patients was resulting in many unpleasant questions from the patients to the front desk.

6.4.4   Managing Delays

Real-time knowledge of how long patients are waiting and which devices are behind schedule is an important tool for managers. The waiting time/delay time displays that what we have created can be viewed from anywhere in the department, including the relevant manager's office. The information can also be used to page a manager when delays exceed predetermined thresholds. Finally, additional in-depth views can be provided for the facility administrators to see and examine their delay instances.

In our practice, once waiting time for plain radiographs exceeds 20 min the manager is alerted, and consideration is given to moving patients to another location (unless the other location is also delayed). For modalities with no alternative location, patients might be offered the option to reschedule. This is not often practical, since many patients come for X-ray examinations on the day that they are scheduled to see a clinician.

6.5   First Come, First Served?

The waiting time display is built on the expectation that walk-in patients will be seen in the order they arrived. How does the technologist know what this is? It could be determined by a monitor that displays arrival times, but many places still manage patient queues by pieces of paper stacked in the order of patient arrival. This is obviously subject to human error and errant breezes. Moreover, there may be a temptation for technologists to take patients out of order intentionally. For example, if technologist performance is evaluated by the number of examinations they perform, there may be a perverse incentive to "cherry-pick" easier or shorter examinations. If the facility is not working at full capacity there may be a tendency for the more energetic technologists to absorb the lion's share of work, resulting in "high-productivity" and "low-productivity" rooms. We have all played the game of trying to guess which checkout line (or bank teller, or airline check-in, etc.) is moving faster, but this is clearly not equitable. Apart from inherent differences among technologists in the rate at which they work, just before a change of shift, or preceding a lunch break, a technologist may be disinclined to begin a case that might be long or difficult. A more innocent cause of inequality can be facility design, especially in a large department. If some rooms are more remote from the waiting area than others, creation of "sub-waiting" areas dedicated to specific rooms can operationally turn one large department into several small ones, resulting in uneven waiting times.

Keep It Real!
A couple of years ago, while trying to implement an electronic patient queue in one of our facilities, we discovered another interesting pattern of human behavior—the lunch block.

The facility had four examination rooms and four technologists. During normal operations, each technologist would take the next patient from the queue. But as the lunch hour approached, the smooth pattern abruptly changed. Each technologist wanted to leave for lunch, and a sort of game ensued to see who would take the last patient of the morning. As a result, there might be one patient in the waiting room, while all four technologists, completely idle, were waiting in their exam rooms to see who would take the last patient, setting the rest of them free!

You would never think that an excessive capacity could lead to a bottleneck, but this is a perfect illustration!

An objective, automated patient distribution system can solve these problems. We implemented such a system with an online app, as illustrated in Fig. 6.16. Patients are automatically placed in an electronic queue upon arrival. All radiographic rooms that are in operation (by which we mean staffed and capable of accepting a patient) are shown in a display that can be viewed using a handheld device. "Open" rooms are shown in green, along with the time that it has been in "green" status. A facilitator guides the waiting patient to the room that has been open for the longest period of time. On arrival, the technologist has a desktop function that is used to "toggle" the room status to "red" (in use). After completion of the case, the room is again toggled to "green" status. The time that the room remains in the "red" status is tracked, to ensure that technologists do not forget to reopen their room at the conclusion of the examination.

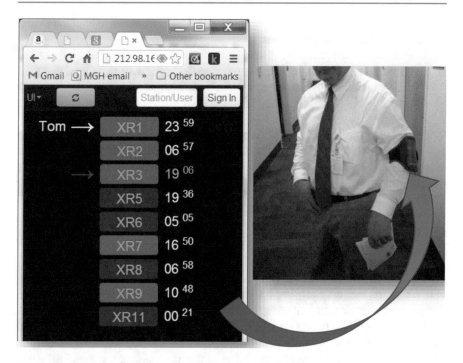

Fig. 6.16 Our patient distribution app, running as a web page on a mobile handheld device. Busy X-ray rooms are shown in red, with their busy time indicated. Similarly, idle rooms are shown in green with their idle time indicated. When the next patient has to be seen, the app picks the green room that has been idle for the longest time (see red arrow next to XR3). As the facilitator leads a patient to the open room, he or she clicks on that room button, and it turns orange (see XR1). This informs the technologist in this room, equipped with the same app, that the patient is coming

We have found that this system improves patient throughput by making sure that all rooms are kept occupied, and results in a more equitable distribution of work among technologists. However, implementing this system of patient distribution met an unforeseen amount of resistance due to the way in which it forced the technologists to keep moving while patients were waiting. It also led to a few sad discoveries. We were surprised to discover that some technologists did not know how to do certain examinations—because they used to cherry-pick only the ones they liked! We received a barrage of complaints that the "electronic queueing makes our work slower"—a claim that was supported by neither logic nor data. Therefore, a word of caution. If you intend to implement a similar system, prepare yourself for some surprises! Your organization's culture, as we know, may well eat your technology for breakfast.

Eventually the green/red system was very successful, and took on an organic life of its own. What accounts for the ultimate success?

- The patients were dispatched to the technologists by a pair of "facilitators." This put an end to the practice of cherry-picking.

- Room and equipment use was optimized, helping to lessen complaints from patients and referring physicians.
- It became clear to all that the distribution of examinations was fair.
- The facilitators, who did most of the work on the "patient front," found that their work became easier because the hassle of locating the next available room was eliminated.

Finally, we experienced another important aspect of introducing technology into any environment. Where there is resistance, it is necessary to find allies. Whereas some technologists might wish to "take it easier," the facilitators were motivated by the goal of satisfying the patients that were assigned to them and thus became natural allies of the technology.

6.5.1 Unplanned Additions to the Schedule

As we have seen many times in this book, healthcare workflow is full of unpredictable events, including unplanned additions to the schedule. The best known, and in some ways the easiest to deal with, is the STAT examination—something that is so medically urgent that it takes precedence over all others. STAT cases might even displace examinations that are about to begin or are already underway. Different institutions may have different approaches to this type of issue, but all will agree that a medically urgent examination will displace an elective procedure, even if it means making subsequent examinations late.

However, often it is not so simple. Many procedures are urgent, yet not STAT in the strict sense. For example, a patient is being seen in a doctor's office and a decision must be made whether a hospital admission is required. This is a decision that can wait a few hours, but not a few days. What is the best procedure for handling such a patient? And what is the least disruptive and most equitable way to fit this patient into a schedule that might already be full?

If by some good fortune there is an open appointment, the problem may appear solved, but appearances are deceiving. For example, in some departments "open" appointments are routinely used to catch up on a schedule that is overloaded or unrealistically planned. Filling one of these imaginary appointments with real patients might guarantee that the remainder of the day will be chaotic.

Keep It Real!
We have focused attention upon eliminating no-shows in this book, and for good reasons. But in some facilities no-shows are often met with joy, as the only way to catch up with an overloaded schedule. Therefore, when you plan your no-show reduction project, be sure to take this into account.

An opportunity may arise if a case finishes early—but most likely this will be only a fractional time, insufficient for an add-on examination, and once again your stressed staff will be hoping for the next patient to be a no-show.

Thus, it is desirable to develop some rules for "add-ons" to minimize their impact on workflow. If possible, it is best to add on patients at the end of the day since double booking early in the day causes delays in all subsequent patients [18]. That approach may or may not be feasible depending upon clinical considerations. Our approach to this situation is that if a scheduled outpatient has already arrived for an appointment, we will begin their examination early, rather than inserting the unscheduled patient. If not and the available time is at least half of the expected examination duration, we use it to accommodate the "urgent" addition. If the available time is less than half of that necessary for the examination, then we refer the scheduling dilemma to a manager to see if another device might be better able to accommodate the addition.

6.5.2 What Is Your Strategy?

This discussion brings us to a rather interesting point: We can—and should—be developing our patient arrival management rules as a consistent strategy, optimized to achieve the maximum gain. In essence, this is a game theory approach, where we are trying to attain the best possible result—staying on schedule—despite all the possible moves our "opponents" can make. The opponents can be the patients themselves (who have their own goals, sometimes opposed to ours), the "moving parts" of our own workflow, or even the heavy rain outside, which slows everything down. We cannot predict most of them, but can model some of them based on the probabilities captured in our HIS data.

Let us suppose that we are attempting to use game theory to calculate how much time we should wait for a scheduled patient to arrive before moving on to the next patient (Fig. 6.17). We compare two models. In the first model (MS, "model for scheduled"), we take the patients only in the order that they are scheduled: If a patient is late, we wait for him or her for D minutes before moving on to the next scheduled patient. In the other model (MA, "model for arrived"), we take them in the order of their arrival (still taking into account that a fraction of them will be at least D minutes late). Obviously, the longer we wait, the better it is for the scheduled patient, but the worse for everyone else who is waiting. As a result, we are interested in finding the optimal D value—how long we should wait for the scheduled patient to take the next available. Figure 6.17 provides an example of such modeling, built with the real data from one of our facilities. Even without exact numbers it highlights a few interesting insights. First, it demonstrates that the stricter MS strategy—taking the patients only as they are scheduled, whatever it takes for them to arrive—is a lose/lose game: MS wait/idle times are consistently higher compared to their MA equivalents. This makes intuitive sense—sticking to the schedule at any cost is a very rigid approach, which does not adapt well to reality.

Second, and more interestingly, each strategy has its optimal point, depending on the parameters we use. In Fig. 6.17, we have chosen to wait D minutes after the scheduled time for the patient to arrive (similar to Fig. 6.10 logic). As Fig. 6.17 demonstrates, depending on the facility parameters and the chosen strategy, there may be optimal D values, in which the parameter under study (either idle time or patient wait) is minimized.

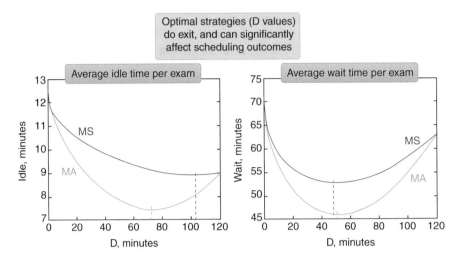

Fig. 6.17 Comparing two strategy models for patient arrivals. Model MS—take everyone strictly as scheduled; model MA—take as arrived. D on the horizontal axis shows the average delay in patient arrivals (D minutes after the scheduled time). The chart on the left shows the effect of the two models upon "idle time" and is thus a "department-optimizing" model. The chart on the right shows the effect on patient waiting time, thus a "patient-optimizing" model. D is the amount of time that we are willing to wait for a scheduled patient to arrive before we consider replacing him or her with any other patient available to us; both models used the probability of a patient to arrive at least D minutes late

These tools provide quantitative data, but they do not address fundamental value judgements. If a strategy eliminates 5 min of idle time, but at the expense of 10 min of increased wait, is that better or worse? From the left chart, you can see that the decrease in room idle time due to the optimized schedule is only a few minutes, which might or might not be impactful for department operations. However, the reduction of the wait time shown on the right chart is very substantial. Someone must still decide whether this trade-off is "worth it," a decision that will probably depend upon factors that are beyond our abilities to calculate.

6.5.3   When All Else Fails: Service Recovery

Even the most carefully planned and managed operation will have regrettable days—days on which data science cannot help. Some of the many things that can go wrong include the following:

1. A scheduled appointment must be cancelled or rescheduled. This might occur if a time is preempted by an emergency, or if a necessary individual or piece of equipment is not available for any reason. (Even doctors become sick!)
2. Patients must wait for excessive periods of time because:
   (a) Many arrived simultaneously, exceeding the capacity of the facility.

   (b) Previous procedures or imaging studies have taken much longer than expected.

   (c) A piece of equipment has broken.

3. There is confusion about the examination to be performed due to communication difficulty.

4. An interpersonal issue occurs with a staff member.

When our subway system performs poorly, the public message is "we are experiencing delays" as though delays are a sort of natural phenomenon, like rain or snow. Do not hide behind this shield of impersonality. Take responsibility! Follow the size recommended steps to service recovery [19]:

- Apologize and acknowledge the problem
- Listen and empathize
- Fix the problem quickly and fairly, if possible
- Offer atonement
- Follow up
- Remember your promises

Patients who are facing excessive waits and who are able to do so might be encouraged to leave and return at a later date or to another location. Remember, however, that patients also have the option of going to a competing facility. To minimize this risk our managers will provide a phone number so the patient can call in advance and be guided to the location that is most convenient for them where they will not experience the same delays when they return.

Patients who have any of these unpleasant experiences in the department may be offered a small gift in recognition of the fact that we have not lived up to our own standards. A certificate to our coffee shop or a free parking pass is a token of goodwill. For those patients who had to return due to our delays we offer a parking pass for the return visit. For patients who are dependent upon public transportation, we also offer taxi vouchers. In extreme (and fortunately rare) instances the manager has bought trays of cookies and fruit for patients in the waiting room, along with apologies. Patients were delighted by this gesture!

Recognize that outpatients have a choice of where to have their imaging done and you appreciate the fact that they chose your department.

References

1. Glover M, et al. Accuracy of self-reported specialty and practice location among radiologists. J Am Coll Radiol. 2017;14(11):1403–11.
2. Harvey H, Liu C, Jaworsky C, Guerrier C, Flores E, Pianykh O. Predicting no-shows in radiology using regression modeling of data available in the electronic medical record. J Am Coll Radiol. 2017;14(10):1303–9.
3. AlRowaili A, Ahmed E, Areabi HA. Factors associated with no-shows and rescheduling MRI appointments. BMC Health Serv Res. 2016;16(1):679.

4. Mander GTW, Reynolds L, Cook A, Kwan MM. Factors associated with appointment non-attendance at a medical imaging department in regional Australia: a retrospective cohort analysis. J Med Radiat Sci. 2018;65:192–9.
5. DiRoberto C, Henderson S, Lehto C, Baccei SJ. Prioritizing the protocol: improving the process of scheduling imaging examinations in a radiology department with partially integrated IT systems. J Am Coll Radiol. 2017;14(3):444–8.
6. Recht M, Macari M, Lawson K, Mulholland T, Chen D, Kim D, Babb J. Impacting key performance indicators in an academic MR imaging department through process improvement. J Am Coll Radiol. 2013;10:206–8.
7. Liu C, Harvey HB, Jaworsky C, Shore M, Guerrier CE, Pianykh O. Text message reminders reduce outpatient radiology no-shows but do not improve arrival punctuality. J Am Coll Radiol. 2017;14(8):1049–54.
8. Mieloszyk RJ, Rosenbaum JI, Hall CS, Hippe DS, Gunn ML, Bhargava P. Environmental factors predictive of no-show visit in radiology: observations of three million outpatient visits over 16 years. J Am Coll Radiol. 2019;16(4):554–9.
9. Nickel S, Schmidt UA. Process improvement in hospitals: a case study in a radiology department. Qual Manag Health Care. 2009;18(4):326–38.
10. Glover M, Daye D, Khalilzadeh O, Pianykh O, Rosenthal D, Brink J, Flores E. Socioeconomic and demographic predictors of missed opportunities to provide advanced imaging services. J Am Coll Radiol. 2017;14(11):1403–11.
11. Pirasteh A, VanDyke M, Bolton-Ronacher J, Xi Y, Eastland R, Young D, Escobar J, Hernandez C, Toomay S, Browning T, Pedrosa I. Implementation of an online screening and check-in process to optimize patient workflow before outpatient MRI studies. J Am Coll Radiol. 2016;13(8):956–9.
12. Loving VA, Ellis RL, Rippee R, Steele JR, Schomer DF, Shoemaker S. Time is not on our side: how radiology practices should manage customer queues. J Am Coll Radiol. 2017;14(11):1481–8.
13. Anderson RT, Camacho FT, Balkrishnan R. Willing to wait? The influence of patient wait time on satisfaction with primary care. BMC Health Serv Res. 2007;7(1):31.
14. Stempniak M. American Hospital Association. The Push is on to Eliminate Hospital Wait Times, Marty Stempniak, November 1, 2013. https://www.hhnmag.com/articles/6417-the-push-is-on-to-eliminate-hospital-wait-times.
15. Holbrook A, Glenn HJ, Mahmood R, Cai Q, Kang J, Duszak RJ. Shorter perceived outpatient MRI wait times associated with higher patient satisfaction. J Am Coll Radiol. 2016;13(5):505–9.
16. Pruyn A, Smidts A. Effects of waiting on the satisfaction with the service: beyond objective time measures. Int J Res Mark. 1998;15(4):321–34.
17. Curtis C, Liu C, Bollerman TJ, Pianykh OS. Machine learning for predicting patient wait times and appointment delays. J Am Coll Radiol. 2018;15(9):1310–6.
18. Santibanez P, Chow VS, French J, Puterman ML, Tyldesley S. Reducing patient wait times and improving resource utilization at British Columbia Cancer Agency's ambulatory care unit through simulation. Health Care Manag Sci. 2009;12(4):392–407.
19. AHRQ. CAHPS ambulatory care improvement guide. December 2017. [Online]. https://www.ahrq.gov/cahps/quality-improvement/improvement-guide/improvement-guide.html. Accessed 2019.

Creating the Images

7

Ma'am, this vacuum cleaner will cut your work in half!
Then I would like to buy two!

Mathematical joke

Contents

Things That Happen
- Patients arriving for examinations are matched to available resources—both equipment and technologists.
- Pre-procedure work:
    - The room and the equipment are prepared for the examination.
    - The technologist talks to the patient and verifies patient information and condition.
- The technologist begins the examination (in RIS).
- One or more series of images is created.
- The technologist ends (completes) the examination (in RIS).
- Post-procedure work:
    - Patient exits the exam room.
    - The technologist performs image QA and post-processing.
    - The room is readied for the next patient.

© Springer Nature Switzerland AG 2021
D. Rosenthal, O. Pianykh, *Efficient Radiology*,
https://doi.org/10.1007/978-3-030-53610-7_7

Things to Measure

Periodic Reports
- Demand:
- Hourly demand for walk-in services
- "Acceptable" turnaround time (no complaints)
- Capacity:
  – Potential productivity (capacity) of the equipment and workforce
  – Required room turnaround time
  – Appropriate scheduling interval (based on distribution of examination lengths)
  – Room and equipment idle time
  – Utilization charts
- Performance:
  – Time required to perform examination (by examination type, technologist, and radiologist, where appropriate)
  – "Hidden" repeat examinations (deleted images)
  – On-time starts
  – "Priority creep"
  – Adherence to standard protocols

Real-Time Reports
- Examinations that appear to exceed expected durations
- Examinations with missing data points:
  – Begin time
  – End time
  – Process owners

This chapter is about what happens once all the preliminaries (ordering, scheduling, protocoling, checking in, safety checking, and waiting) have been completed. Since we are concerned with operations, and not with clinical issues, we do not address the actual methods of creating images. Instead, we focus on the workflow activities that surround this process.

To produce an imaging examination, the technologist is expected to follow the prescribed protocol and generate a number of images or image series. For an intervention, a plan of action should be in place (to obtain a tissue sample, for example, or to place a device or catheter in the patient). Procedures, equipment, and manpower should be in place to ensure that these activities are done correctly, safely, and reasonably promptly.

How long should this take, and how many people will it require? To answer these questions, let us first look at the capabilities of individual imaging rooms, setting aside for the moment the issue of human productivity.

7.1   Productivity, Capacity, Utilization, and Downstream Effects

The term *productivity* is typically used in describing the actions of people—in our case, the people would be either radiologists (as we will discuss in Chap. 9) or technologists. There is relatively little information about the productivity of technologists in the literature. The few analyses that are available focus on how much of the technologist's employed hours is actually spent creating images. Such studies begin with an observational period in which the amount of time taken to perform certain examinations is manually recorded. The measured durations are then applied to counts of the number of cases performed. An early study of this nature found that technologists were engaged in image creation 79% of the time at the beginning of the study period, but this rose to 113% by the end! [1] The fact that the productivity appeared to exceed 100% of capacity indicates that the technologist's ability to complete studies was actually greater than it appeared from the initial observation period.[1] A more recent attempt to determine the same information came from the Mayo Clinic. As in the previous study, manual time logs were kept over a 2-week period for a variety of examinations (all radiography). The amount of time required for each study was multiplied by the number of examinations shown on the weekly logs. This number was compared to the number of employed hours to determine what percentage was actually spent on imaging. The researchers found that this was a mean of only 50%! [2]. Simply as the result of bringing this number to light, the authors report that "productivity" improved to 61%.

Of course, the amount of time spent working is not equivalent to productivity. Still, such a measure can be useful because, if a technologist worked very slowly, he or she might be credited with only a few hours of "work equivalent" because of low output, even if the work in question took an entire day to complete. This type of study offers no insight into what an appropriate degree of productivity should be, but clearly it cannot be 100%. Even if the amount of time allotted for the procedure included all necessary pre- and post-procedure activities, it could not account for 100% of the day because of lunch (or dinner) breaks, the need to allow adequate capacity to respond to urgent demands, and so on.

There will be instances in which the productivity of the technologist is less important than the combined technologist/device productivity. For this reason, because the hourly capital and operating costs of the equipment might outweigh the technologist's salary, a combined metric that takes all three into account could be measured against the value of the output (RVUs).

Most managers will want to have metrics related to equipment as well as to workforce productivity. *Utilization* refers to a device. It can only be understood in connection with the related-but-different concept of *capacity*.

Capacity refers to the ability of a resource (in this case, the combination of a room, an imaging device, and the available staffing) to produce images,

---

[1] The tendency for workers to perform differently when they know that they are being observed is known as the Hawthorne effect.

examinations, and/or revenue. Capacity can be increased to some extent either by adding staff or by optimizing facility design; both of these will be discussed later in this chapter. Capacity can be theoretical, considering optimal staffing and design and 24/7 operation, or it can be more pragmatic, taking into account the existing realities of staffing and hours of operation.

Utilization, on the other hand, refers to the percentage of capacity that is being used. The most easily understood aspect of capacity is *time*. Since there are 24 h in a day, each device has, in theory, 24 h of use capacity. If the device is used for 6 h a day, its theoretical utilization is $6/24 = 25\%$. However, if the facility is available for only 12 h a day due to staffing or access issues, a more realistic capacity is 12 h. Thus, the same 6 h of use represents $6/12 = 50\%$ of capacity utilization. It can sometimes be quite arbitrary which numbers to use. For example, in the United States, Medicare payment policy arbitrarily considers that a freestanding imaging facility will operate 5 days a week for 10 h a day. So those 10 h would represent 100% capacity, from the point of view of Medicare [3].

Another consideration: What exactly do we mean by "use"? If 12 1-h appointments are available for a particular device, and every one of them is filled, is utilization 100%? This is actually an example of *schedule utilization (SU)*: the percentage of scheduled appointments for which the resource was used (busy). While schedule utilization makes some sense as a measure of outpatient capacity, it is subject to manipulation. For example, time blocked for "catch-up" or for other purposes will not appear as available, and therefore will not show as unused capacity. No-show patients contribute to schedule utilization but actually result in unused capacity. More importantly, this metric can be seriously misleading if your institution uses "appointments of convenience" as placeholders for patients who will not necessarily be seen at the scheduled time (as is frequently done, for example, for inpatients and for walk-in outpatients). In such cases, available appointments may not reflect the actual ability to perform examinations.

Time utilization (TU) is different from appointment utilization inasmuch as it represents the percentage of the available time when the resource was actually busy. For example: During the same 12-h day filled with 1-h appointments, how many hours was the scanner, or scan room, actually in use? The measure of time utilization will always be less than that of schedule utilization because some amount of time is always required for room turnover. Also, if you prefer to start procedures on time, and of course you should, the schedule must be managed to ensure that the room is not in use immediately prior to the start of the next scheduled case.

The TU metric can be determined by summing the begin to end times and dividing by the available time.

However, because these timestamps are manually generated and thus subject to human error, you may want to consider an alternate approach in which the imaging device is deemed busy only while it is acquiring images. This metric is identical to TU except first image time and last image time during the image acquisition are used instead of begin and complete time [4].

The time utilization metric is particularly important because, in the United States, it is used by the government to determine the payment component based upon equipment amortization. As of 2011, the average self-reported utilization rate for facilities nationwide was 25 h per week, or 48–54% of the mandated 50 h per week, with rural facilities falling into the lower end of the range. Despite this, the Affordable Care Act of 2010 established a 75% utilization rate as the basis for payment, ensuring that in many places technical component reimbursement would be inadequate to cover equipment amortization [3].

This can be a very informative metric, showing how efficiently we use the device itself. It may happen that only a small fraction of the time spent on some imaging examinations is spent actually creating images, with the remainder spent on non-scanning activities (patient communications, device configurations, etc.). On the other hand, the time utilization (TU) metric has a couple of principal limitations:

- For some of our imaging devices (mostly MRIs), the scanners do not provide reliable imaging timestamps. For instance, some imaging series will assign the exact same time to all of their images, making this computation impossible.
- Imaging requires an available room, not just a device, and this is what begin and complete times capture. That is, it is not enough to have an idle device—its room needs to be available as well.

These three metrics (schedule, time, device) give us some idea of capacity utilization, but they are still overly simplistic. Just because a device is being used does not mean that it is being used *productively*. What we really need are measures of useful productivity.

7.1.1   Images/Hour

The images/hour metric makes some sense for modalities in which the amount of time it takes to generate images is largely the same across different types of examination. Plain-film radiography and CT generally fall into this category. However, even for modalities in which the production of images/hour is relatively constant, examinations differ in the number of images that are required, and therefore it is possible that two facilities producing the same number of images per hour would result in very different numbers of examinations per hour.

Other modalities can be much more variable, though. With ultrasound and MRI, for example, the number of images produced per hour depends on the pulse sequences used, real-time sweeps vs. static images, number of image captures, etc. Similarly, nuclear studies show considerable variation in images/hour with photon flux among other factors. Also, generally speaking, newer versions of a technology can generate more images per hour than older versions. Still, this metric is useful when appropriately used: For example, in cases where a device yields a large number of images per hour but a small number of examinations, it can reveal an inefficient case mix or excessively long examinations (protocols).

7.1.2   Examinations per Hour

This important metric is highly dependent on case mix, device capabilities, and examination design (protocol). If the device is able to produce images at a more or less fixed rate, examinations that require more images will take more time, resulting in a lower capacity of examinations/hour.

7.1.3   Revenue per Hour

This metric is closely tied to the number of examinations per hour, since payment is typically derived from the RVUs which are assigned to each examination. It is important to consider it separately, though, because RVUs differ greatly among modalities. It is quite possible, even likely, that two different devices with the same schedule utilization, the same time utilization, and the same number of examinations per hour will have very different RVU generation. In fact, as counterintuitive as it may sound, one could be profitable while the other is losing money. Therefore, this metric can have a profound impact upon where your institution is willing to devote resources: for example, in staffing, hours of operation or facility design.

7.1.4   Determining Capacity

Here we address the question of how to determine capacity. With time and schedule capacity, the answers are relatively straightforward, as one represents the hours of operation and the other the number of available appointments (with all the caveats that we have mentioned). But how do you determine capacity when you are dealing with examinations (and by extension, revenue)?

One method is to add the number of minutes needed to complete a representative set of examinations and the sum of the required room turnaround time and divide the number of available minutes in the day by the sum of the two. This will work if the examinations selected are truly representative and if neither the imaging time nor the turnaround time has been artificially shortened or lengthened.

Another way to accomplish this is empirical. With a sufficiently large data sample, it should be possible to retrospectively determine the greatest number of examinations that were completed within a given time frame on a particular device. In theory, if your staff members have achieved this level of productivity once, they can achieve it again. It may not be sustainable, but it would at least be useful to know what is possible.

Optimizing capacity to consistently approach this level of performance requires staffing levels that match demand. This is not easy when demand is uneven or unpredictable, or when high demand occurs during times that are difficult to staff. Using modern, data-driven methods, you could design a shift optimization approach to more effectively align workload with personnel. Once you have done this, though, you will have to convince the employees to rearrange their work lives, and often their work culture as well. In one study, sharing data with staff became a powerful driver for buy-in and willingness to implement change. According to the authors, morale improved once the staff recognized the benefit of improved staffing levels during peak volume periods [5]. As anyone with experience with management will tell you, though, getting your staff to agree to such things is not always easy. And even if you do, the results may not be as impressive (read: publishable) as these studies suggest.

Know Your Tools

Many mathematical tools have been used to build "optimal" schedules. The most versatile of them is known as *linear programming* [6]. This can be used to assign different workloads to different staff or different shifts while taking into account various constraints (such as lunch break, or total staff counts). Although initially designed for minimizing cost functions (such as total idle time, or average expense), with creativity linear programming can be extended to virtually any scheduling problem [7, 8]. It encounters limits, however, when more realistic scenarios need to be accommodated. It is less satisfactory when it is necessary to account for randomness and variability. Stochastic modeling and machine learning are much better adapted for such applications [9].

It is important to remember that a schedule that appears to be mathematically optimal is of little value unless it is reasonably robust. If it is easily destroyed by unforeseen disruptions and schedule alternations, it cannot be considered optimal.

For modalities that require advance scheduling, the workload can be kept relatively level (although possibly at the cost of a schedule backlog) and staffing can be adjusted accordingly. But in cases where demand is driven entirely by forces outside radiology and service expectations are immediate (walk-in outpatients, emergency departments, operating rooms), you will need to use an empirical approach. And the situation can change substantially from day to day. Let us look at the latter scenario first.

Before proceeding with this discussion, it is important to point out that optimization, in the sense of best use of equipment and personnel, can be completely outweighed by significant downstream effects. For example, we would probably all agree that it is better to have periods of time when technologists and equipment are idle than to delay an operating room. Similar arguments could be made with respect to an emergency ward, or even to the length of hospital stay.

"But surely," you might say, "this doesn't apply with outpatient imaging." Actually, it does. In some cases, for example, access to prompt imaging can help avoid an emergency room visit. Finally, there are strategic issues that might render a simple cost/benefit calculation irrelevant. Can the institution (or department) afford to delay a major "customer" by operating its resources close to capacity?

All of these considerations make it extremely difficult to create rational metrics that will allow you to determine the appropriate use of people and equipment. That said, as you might guess, we have a few thoughts on the matter.

7.2   Right-Sizing a "Walk-In" Facility

Most radiology departments experience peaks and valleys in demand driven by activities largely outside their control. Because of referring offices' schedules, for example, outpatient arrivals might peak in the late morning and the midafternoon, with a break at lunchtime (recall our examples of human activity curves in the beginning of this book). Operating rooms typically ramp up relatively early in the morning and begin to slow in the late afternoon. Emergency department volume usually increases later in the day and into the evening (when patients' medical problems continue but physicians' offices are closed). Radiology staffing and equipment needs must be calculated based on the following:

1. Hourly patterns of demand
2. The productivity of each staff/equipment combination
3. Acceptable amounts of delay (waits)

Here is an example: Imagine a single isolated radiographic facility serving a sports medicine clinic. It is generally accepted that an all-purpose radiographic room (not a dedicated chest facility) can accommodate four or five examinations per hour if it is fully staffed. This room is open from 7:30 AM until 6 PM, giving it a theoretical capacity of approximately 47 examinations per day. The facility sees a total of 40 patients each day, suggesting a daily excess capacity of seven examinations. However, because they depend on the schedules of various doctors' offices, patient arrival times are not uniform. Table 7.1 shows a typical patient arrival

Table 7.1 Nonuniform patient arrival patterns affect patient wait times

Time of day	Patients arriving per hour	Capacity	Average wait in minutes
7:30–8:30	4	4.5	0
8:31–9:30	7	4.5	33
9:31–10:30	6	4.5	53
10:31–11:30	4	4.5	47
11:31–12:30	1	4.5	0
12:31–1:30	2	4.5	0
1:31–2:30	7	4.5	33
2:31–3:30	6	4.5	53
3:31–4:30	2	4.5	20
4:31–5:30	1	4.5	0
5:31–6:00	0	2.25	0
Totals	40	47.25	

For simplicity, the table assumes that the patients who arrive each hour arrive uniformly across the hour. This, of course, is rarely if ever the case. For example, it is likely that the four patients who arrive between 7:30 and 8:30 arrive closer to 8:30 than 7:30, meaning part of the hour's productive capacity will be lost waiting for the patients. Conversely, if all four patients arrive at the beginning of the hour, one of them will inevitably wait 45 minutes. This unpredictability will cause "real-life" delays even greater than we have estimated in this model

pattern, with peaks in the midmorning and the midafternoon, and its influence on wait times. Even though the room is only working at approximately 80% of its capacity (40 of 47 possible examinations), it still runs late much of the time!

This system appears to "work" only if the number of arrivals in a given time frame is roughly equal to the room capacity. In reality, though, the numbers align only in the first hour of the day. For the rest of the morning, the excess arrivals are "smoothed out" by making them wait until the lunchtime. Similarly, excess arrivals in the peak afternoon hours have to wait for the late-afternoon slowdown. Thus, though "capacity" appears to be adequate, wait times of more than half an hour for almost half of the day are guaranteed to result in dissatisfied customers: both patients and referring doctors. Note also that, in this example, we show four patients arriving for the first hour of operation—almost equal to the room capacity. However, if the first patient was not available when the facility opened at precisely 7:30, the capacity lost could never be recovered. This type of issue can lead to the seemingly paradoxical situation of a facility that is working at less than "capacity" having to use overtime!

This is another example where averages can fail us: As Table 7.1 shows, facilities can experience delays even with "excess" capacity. Worse, if they tried to accommodate an additional eight patients a day to reach the theoretical capacity, they would create bottlenecks with wait times of up to 1.5 h! (Table 7.2) We know from our own, regrettable experience that delays of this magnitude (or even much shorter ones) are unacceptable to both patients and referring physicians.

Table 7.2 Hypothetical example of what would happen if a facility tried to increase the number of patients to 100% of the room's theoretical capacity (47 patients)

Time interval	Patients arriving per hour	Wait in minutes
7:30–8:30	4.8	0
8:31–9:30	8.4	33
9:31–10:30	7.2	88
10:31–11:30	4.8	92
11:31–12:30	1.2	48
12:31–1:30	2.4	0
1:31–2:30	8.4	52
2:31–3:30	7.2	88
3:31–4:30	2.4	60
4:31–5:30	1.2	16
5:31–6:00	0	0

Note that the wait time peaks at 92 min! For this example, the patients' hourly arrival rate was assumed to be the same as that in Table 7.1

Keep It Real!
Why are these types of bottlenecks so common? Unfortunately, facility planners tend to think in terms of average capacity. If projections show that 48 patients are expected in a given day at a particular facility, the naïve planner will conclude that one radiographic room is adequate. We now know, however, what average capacity really means: It assumes a perfectly uniform workload, in which the facility receives the same "average" number of patients every hour. Clearly, this seldom happens in real life, meaning that the likelihood of having perfectly balanced workload is next to nil. Ultimately, with respect to walk-in imaging suites, "capacity" is little more than a theoretical concept. Facilities should never plan to work at, or even close to, 100% capacity.

The lesson is clear: Nonuniform demand can cause massive disruptions for an operation.

Of course, if you work in a busy imaging facility, you (re-)learn this lesson on a daily basis.

This phenomenon has interesting consequences. For example, let us examine the relationship between patient wait time and percentage utilization of rooms and technologists. Many years ago, a member of our department performed an analysis of four radiographic rooms in our emergency department radiology suite [10]. The study showed that, as the percentage of utilization climbs, the effect on wait time is much greater than linear. His conclusions remain valid.

In this analysis, the equation that described the *mean* waiting time was

$$\text{Waiting time} = 43.7 \times \text{Utilization}^{1.82},$$

while, for *maximum* waits, the equation was

$$\text{Waiting time} = 135 \times \text{Utilization}^{1.69}$$

Though this work was done in the era of analog imaging, when productivity of the equipment was not quite as high as with digital equipment today, the principle has not changed. Figure 7.1 shows some of our recent experience, extracted from the HIS data for one of our facilities.

Both examples lead to the same conclusion: When the arrival of patients cannot be controlled, attempts to optimize the utilization of the equipment and manpower will come at the expense of soaring patient wait times and dramatic drops in satisfaction.

A general approach to this type of issue can be found in queuing theory, in what is known as the Pollaczek–Khinchine formula. In simple terms, this formula states that the size "L" of the waiting line (such as the line of patients waiting to be scanned) depends on the utilization ratio U as follows:

$$L = \frac{C}{1 - U}$$

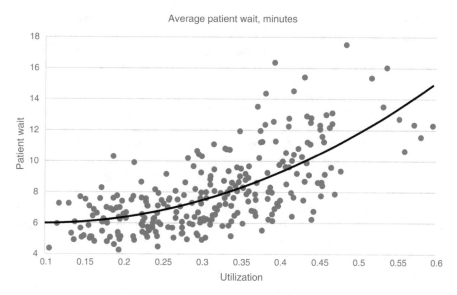

Fig. 7.1 Average patient wait as a function of facility utilization. A busy outpatient facility with nine X-ray devices was considered; facility utilization (per X-ray unit) and wait (per patient) were averaged for each day. As can be seen, as utilization increases, wait time grows at a rate that is greater than linear (simple math suggests a quadratic trend). This phenomenon occurs well before theoretical capacity is reached

where C is a constant coefficient. That is, when utilization approaches 100% (utilization ratio U approaches 1), L goes to infinity. Hence, the facility's operation breaks down and chaos rules.

Keep It Real!

This might all sound like no more than a fascinating theory. Rest assured, though, it is as real as it gets. In fact, we run into this formula all the time in our daily lives. Consider the following scenario: You are in a grocery store and want to check out. If the store is not busy, you can probably find a register with no line and check out quickly. If it is, though, you are going to encounter lines. And as the store gets busier, not only will the lines get longer, they will grow much more fragile as well. You probably picked the cash register with the shortest line but what if the man in front of you gets to the cashier and only then starts looking for his wallet, slowly going through all of his pockets and bags. After a few minutes of this randomly prolonged service time, not only has your line doubled in size, because your line is no longer accepting its share of the customers, the other registers have jammed up as well. There is no flexibility to absorb the unanticipated delay.

The capacity of a facility therefore should not be regarded as the theoretical capacity of each device multiplied by the hours of operation. Rather, it should be determined by the patient flow and the acceptable wait time, which is driven by four factors: medical urgency, patient satisfaction, referring doctor satisfaction, and cost.

If all examinations were medically urgent (STAT), the ideal wait time would be close to zero. To achieve this, you would need to keep the average utilization rate low. Think about how other types of emergency responders keep themselves available. Everyone knows that there is considerable downtime in fire stations, for example. There has to be. If our firefighters were always busy they would not be able to respond promptly to calls. Delivery of true emergency services is expensive!

Medical urgency is only one issue that demands available (excess) capacity. Another is *economic* urgency. If operations at another, expensive facility (for example, an operating room, or an emergency ward) are held up because of limited imaging availability, costs would quickly begin to snowball. Therefore, wait times must also be kept low to prevent delays in these facilities.

The important issues of medical and economic urgency will be taken up again in Chap. 9. For now, let us turn our attention to the two other major drivers: patient satisfaction and doctor satisfaction. As we have shown, for outpatient visits, patient satisfaction starts to drop off when wait times exceed about 15 min. Even when the *mean* wait time is less than 15 min by a comfortable margin, some patients will inevitably have to wait considerably longer. We have found in our emergency department that we will not receive complaints from either patients or doctors if we have a mean wait of 8 min or less. But to maintain such levels when patient arrival is unpredictable, the facility must be sized and staffed so utilization is only approximately 50% of capacity! Higher rates of utilization might save money in radiology equipment, manpower, and space, but they will leave you with unhappy patients and doctors; may compromise patient safety; and, due to increased transit time through the ED, could wind up costing more money than the required investment in imaging capacity.

Finally, consider the wait time issue from the clinicians' point of view. We noted earlier that, in our emergency department, we need to maintain mean wait times of 8 min or less to avoid receiving complaints. An 8-min wait may not sound especially long, but remember that the clinicians' *perceived* delay is more than just those 8 min. It is the sum of the wait time and the time it takes to perform the examination, plus any time needed for communication, transport, and check-in and return. Consider, for example, the following rather optimized scenario: An emergency physician places an order at 8 AM and it is communicated to radiology at 8:05 AM. The radiology department receives the patient at 8:10 AM and the patient waits 8 min for the examination, which takes 15 min to perform. The examination is completed at 8:33 AM and the patient is returned to the emergency ward at 8:38 AM. Thus, the perceived wait for imaging *from the perspective of the clinician* is almost 40 min, despite what seems to be a very high level of performance!

7.3 Right-Sizing a Scheduled Facility

This topic introduces several new issues.

– Is the capacity of the system adequate to meet the demand for appointments?
– Is the performance of the facility adequate to perform the examinations as scheduled?

We have already discussed the first question in Chap. 2 when we talked about the metrics for appointment availability (3rd Next, Outpatient Availability Score, OAS).

Unlike walk-in or emergency facilities, scheduled imaging should be performed as scheduled, implying a commitment to "on-time" performance, something that can be extremely difficult to achieve.

7.3.1 Starting on Time

Some years ago, we observed that our interventional procedures did not start at the scheduled time, even for the first case of the day! Why was this happening?

The first hypothesis we considered was that perhaps the patients were arriving late. To test this hypothesis, we extracted patient arrival times from our database and compared them to procedure start times. Figure 7.2 shows the results.

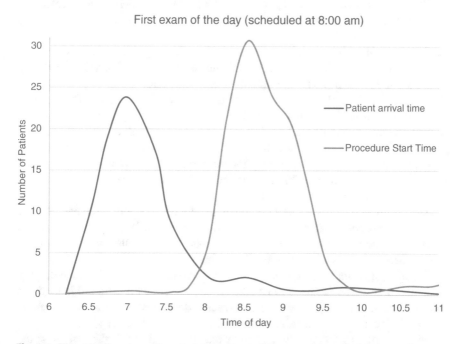

Fig. 7.2 The solid line shows the actual time of arrival for outpatients scheduled to undergo an 8 AM interventional procedure. Note that, though a few patients arrived late, most arrived well in advance of their scheduled start time. Even so, the start times were considerably delayed. In fact, while the average patient arrived at 7 AM, the average start time was 8:45 AM!!

Table 7.3 Breakdown of staff responsibilities

	Mean duration, min	Std dev, min	Median duration, min	Number of observations
Chart review	8	4	8	15
Nursing workup	18	8	17	30
MD/patient interaction	12	8	10	10

This analysis showed us that, for a scheduled 8 AM start, 42% of the patients arrived before 7:00 AM and 78% arrived before 7:30. So clearly, the late starts were not the result of late patient arrival.

So what was the cause? Following a patient's arrival, two nursing steps occurred in sequence: chart review and patient evaluation. These steps were followed by a patient/physician interaction (explanation of the procedure, obtaining of informed consent). Each of these processes takes time, added to which is the time lost in the "handoff" from one group to another (receptionist to nurse, nurse to doctor). Table 7.3 outlines the amount of time all of this required.

In total, the pre-procedure interaction took an average of 38 min! Now, what was our capacity to perform all of these functions?

A review of our staffing pattern revealed the following:

1. Patient care assistants (receptionists) arrived at 6:00 AM. They greeted the patients and had them change their clothes but had no ability to do any of the other steps.
2. At 6:30 AM, either one or two nurses arrived. During the 90 min prior to the scheduled start of the procedures, these nurses might have been able to handle three patients each (26 min of nursing time per patient).
3. At 7:00 AM, both the charge nurse and the resource nurse arrived. These nurses were not expected to evaluate patients.
4. The rest of the nursing staff arrived at 7:30 AM. Even if all of the nurses immediately started helping with patient preparation, a half hour was not enough to complete the pre-procedure evaluation because, when the physician component was added, an average of 38 min was needed for the workup.

The upshot is the nursing staff could completely process only three patients (for 11 procedure rooms!). No wonder the first case started late 88% of the time! This is a classic example of a bottleneck due to a mismatch between the procedure rooms' requirements and the capacity of the nursing staff.

It is also an example (though a less obvious one) of a common fallacy in facility planning. If several steps need to be taken in sequence, and if different individuals perform the various steps, the total time required can never be less than—and is frequently greater than—the sum of the time taken for each activity.

Handoffs often prevent a facility from reaching its theoretical capacity. If the same person were to check in patients, have them drink contrast material, have them change their clothes, perform the safety checks, obtain the scans, check the images for quality, perform the necessary post-processing, forward the images to PACS, and discharge the patients, each step would likely flow into the next more or less seamlessly. But when multiple individuals are involved, delays are almost inevitable. This principle applies to every aspect of operations. For example, having a radiologist check the images prior to a patient's departure (a common practice in breast imaging and MRI) almost invariably results in delay. Of course, this does not mean you should or even could eliminate these practices, only that, to whatever extent possible, the amount of time devoted to them should be minimized.

Our experience in the interventional suites reinforces what others have also reported: The single most important cause of bottlenecks is delays between the time the patient arrives and when the radiologist actually begins the procedure [11].

This sorry situation is brought about by a number of factors: unrealistic understandings of how much time is required before a procedure can begin, unrealistic or injudicious staffing plans, and inefficient operations (handoffs). There may also be a not-very-well-hidden 800 lb gorilla to reckon with. The care assistants, the nurses, the technologists, and/or the radiologists may not actually want to arrive early and begin promptly. This is an important issue, but one that falls outside the domain of data science.

7.3.2   Staying on Time

The healthcare industry as a whole is not good at keeping on schedule. Why is this? One reason: Unanticipated events can interfere with the predictability of the workflow. One study found, for example, that nearly 17% of MRI cases were interrupted by an unplanned event. Such occurrences were reported much more frequently in university hospitals than in community hospitals [12].

Some observers argue that every examination is unique and that it is therefore impossible to predict duration. As we will show later, this argument is completely specious. Similarly, the argument that some sort of emergency could disrupt the schedule at any moment is often nothing more than an attempt to throw sand in the eyes of a disgruntled patient. In reality, our inability to predict when the examination will be completed is often due to sloppy or unrealistic scheduling, and sometimes due to a lack of sensitivity to patients' needs.

7.3.3   Tracking Exam Duration

It is only possible to stay on time if one has a good idea of actual examination duration. Therefore it is important to develop consistent and useful operational definitions of this term. Clearly, duration is the difference between the time the examination began (Tb) and the time it was completed (Tc). However, definitions of "begin" and "complete" can vary wildly. For this reason, each department should establish clear, useful, unambiguous, and easily communicated definitions for the terms. We consider the procedure to have begun when the patient enters the room, and to be completed when the patient leaves the room, because that is the interval during which the room is not available for any other use. Thus, activities such as image post-processing can be performed after the examination is completed. Consistency in this definition is particularly important for interventional procedures that may have elaborate pre- and post-procedure requirements.

As we discussed in the first part of this book, begin time and completion time are usually entered into the system manually and therefore are subject to human error. We noted that when the times are not entered contemporaneously but later, after the examination itself, they tend to be suspiciously round numbers. A technologist is much more likely to think that a case started at about 9:15 than to remember it starting at exactly 9:12!

There is another consequence of human error that may be more easily corrected using intelligently designed information systems. If the technologist has not completed the examination by the time the images have been received in PACS, it is reasonable to assume that he or she has forgotten. This is a problem because, in our implementation (and probably in most), dictation of the report cannot begin until the examination has been fully transferred to PACS. Requiring transfer of the examination within a certain time window following acquisition is a safeguard against losing images and reporting upon incomplete image sets. Therefore, in our department, when images are manually completed but cannot be found in PACS within the expected time window, an automatic page is sent to alert the manager of the problem. We will discuss this implementation in more detail in the next chapter, when we talk about image delivery.

Practical Advice
Once you know the actual start time of the examination it is possible to estimate the expected time of completion. If a time stamp has been generated to mark the start of an examination (exam begin time, Tb), you should have some approximate understanding of when the exam will be completed (complete or end time, Tc). If no begin timestamp has been generated (that is, if the technologist begins the examination while it is still in "scheduled" status), the time (Tp) of arrival of the first images in the PACS can be used to estimate the expected time of completion.

This is important because the completion event must be entered into the information system before dictation of a report can proceed. Although some dictation systems permit dictation of reports for examinations that remain in "scheduled" status, this is generally not a good idea because it relieves the pressure to complete the examination in a timely fashion, and because there is no guarantee that all of the images have been reviewed by the radiologist. Estimates of expected completion time can be used if the technologist fails to record the completion time.

Similarly, if the interval between the begin and the complete times exceeds a chosen threshold (this will be examination dependent but, for CT and plain radiography, it could be half an hour, whereas for MRI it might be 1 h), a manager should be notified that a case has exceeded the expected duration, regardless of whether the images have been received in PACS. Our electronic patient distribution system, described in the previous chapter, does just this. Managers are automatically alerted if radiographic rooms are flagged as being "in use" (begun but not completed) for more than 30 min.

Keep It Real!
X-ray acquisitions rarely require more than 20 min. This is why one of us was surprised to see a technologist—let us call her Mary—still busy with her patient after more than 40 min. When I asked another tech why Mary was taking so long, the reply was strikingly simple: "No surprise, her vacation starts tomorrow." Self-interest can have an enormous impact on operations.

7.3.4 Mindfulness

As we mentioned in Chap. 6, healthcare professionals do not, as a rule, place on-time performance at the top of their priority lists. Try this experiment: Walk over to a working technologist at a scheduled facility and ask, "are you on schedule?" In our experience, you might get a clear answer if you do this at a small facility with only one or two imaging devices. However, if you ask a technologist at a university center, you are more likely to hear something along the lines of "I don't know, let's see," or maybe a smokescreen like "the next patient is here but he is drinking his contrast," or a defensive, "our patient didn't speak any English so we needed to get an interpreter," none of which actually answers the question.

After we experienced this time and again, it became clear to us that most technologists simply do not know the answer to what seems a rather simple question.

To help technologists to be aware of timelines, we built special displays for their work areas (Fig. 7.3). These not only show whether a particular case began on time, but also tell the technologists when other patients have arrived for similar procedures, in the event it is necessary to substitute a patient who has arrived for one who is late.

These efforts, while not completely successful, have produced a slow but sustained improvement in "on-time" performance (Fig. 7.4).

Daily Schedule

Name	MRN	Exam	Arrive	Scheduled	Begun	Start	Completed	Duration	Status
		MR.BI.BRST@/B	6:51 AM	7:15 AM	7:14 AM	1 Minutes Early	7:49 AM	35	Exam Ended
		MR.XS.SPECT	7:18 AM	8:00 AM	8:02 AM	2 Minutes Late	8:35 AM	33	Exam Ended
		MR.AB.ABD@	8:09 AM	8:45 AM	8:47 AM	2 Minutes Late	9:33 AM	46	Prelim
		MR.AB.ABD@	10:30 AM	11:00 AM	10:55 AM	5 Minutes Early	11:38 AM	43	Exam Ended
		MR.AB.ABD		12:30 PM					Scheduled
		MRP.BI.BXBR/R	12:37 PM	1:15 PM	12:59 PM	16 Minutes Early			Exam Begun
		MR.XS.LSPINE		2:15 PM					Scheduled
		MR.BI.BRST/B		2:45 PM					Scheduled
		MR.MS.PELVIS		3:15 PM					Scheduled
		MR.MS.FOOT/R		4:00 PM					Scheduled
		MR.BI.BRST/B		4:45 PM					Scheduled
		MR.BI.BRST/B		5:30 PM					Scheduled
		MR.BI.BRST/B		6:00 PM					Scheduled
		MR.BI.BRST/B		7:15 PM					Scheduled
		MR.AB.PELVIS		8:00 PM					Scheduled
		MR.NE.BRAIN		8:45 PM					Scheduled
		MR.AB.ABD		9:30 PM					Scheduled

Arrived Outpatients (all scanners)

Name	MRN	Exam	Arrive	Scheduled	Resource
		MR.XS.CSPINE	11:01 AM	2:00 PM	MR1L6
		MR.XS.TSPINE	11:03 AM	2:30 PM	MR1L6
		MR.MS.ELB/R	12:34 PM	12:45 PM	MR3Y6
		MR.AB.ABD	12:41 PM	3:00 PM	MR2Y6
		MR.NE.BRAIN	12:48 PM	1:30 PM	MR2Y6
		MR.MS.SHLDAR/L	12:52 PM	1:30 PM	MR1Y6
		MR.CA.HEART	1:15 PM	3:45 PM	MR1Y6

Fig. 7.3 Screenshot of the "on-time" dashboard that hangs in the technologists' control room. The display is intended to increase the technologists' awareness of the timeliness of their work. The top portion is the daily schedule (in this case, for an MRI scanner). Cases that start after the scheduled time are highlighted in red. A daily on-time performance score (the percentage of cases that begin on time) is calculated and tracked. The lower half of the display lists patients who have arrived for MRI scans at other locations. This information is useful as it allows technologists to call for one of those patients if there is a very late arrival or a no-show

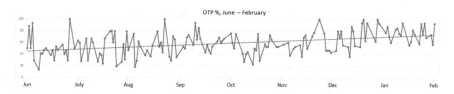

Fig. 7.4   Slow but sustained improvement in on-time performance, chiefly due to management's sustained attention to the issue

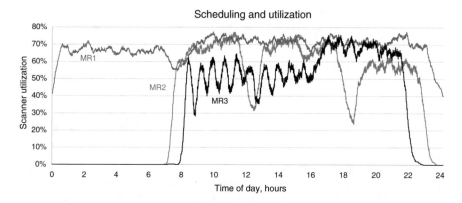

Fig. 7.5   Scheduling patterns seen in MRI scanner utilization. Note that there are three different patterns. Scanner 1 operates at a plateau of 65–75% utilization pretty much all the time. Scanner 2 operates at a similar plateau except between the hours of 11:30 and 12:30 (lunch) and 5:30 and 6:30 (dinner). Scanner 3 has a jagged waveform most of the day but switches to a plateau in the late afternoon

7.4   One Size Does *Not* Fit All

A pragmatic approach to the issues of utilization and productivity would be to build a utilization chart specific to each device. To do so, take a few months of data—say, the most recent 60 days—and calculate how often the machine was busy at each hour of the day. For example, if you pick 10 AM, count all the days from your data sample in which there was an examination that started before 10 AM and ended after 10 AM, indicating that the resource was busy at 10 AM. If you find this to be the case for 30 of the 60 days, the probability that the device is busy at 10 AM is 30/60 = 50%. Repeating this simple data science exercise for every minute from 0:00 to 23:59 will give you an interesting chart, like the one shown in Fig. 7.5. Here, you can see that some equipment is equally likely to be busy at all times, such as MR1 shown in red in our example, which is from our emergency ward. The chart

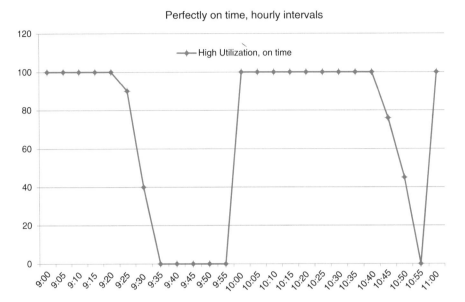

Fig. 7.6 In this (imaginary) situation, cases are booked on the hour. Since every appointment is taken, and the cases are on time, utilization is 100% at the beginning of each hour. In order for the subsequent case to begin on time, utilization must drop to "0" at some point prior to the next hour. Note that, at the 9 o'clock hour, the case is short, ending at 9:35, leaving the machine idle until 10. The 10 o'clock case is longer, ending at 10:50

shows that this device is approximately 65–75% likely to be in use at all times of the day. The blue line shows a scanner that is closed overnight but then exhibits comparable levels of use for two shifts except for two obvious dips—one at noon, and the other at 6 PM (20:00)—that clearly represent breaks for lunch and dinner.

Scanner 3 (**black line**) exhibits yet another pattern, with a wavy component in the morning and a more plateau-like one in the late afternoon. How can we explain this? To understand better what this figure is telling us, consider the theoretical utilization chart in Fig. 7.6. For the purposes of this illustration, the chart assumes a perfect operation in which cases are scheduled at hourly intervals, every hour is fully booked, and the cases are always on time. In this highly stylized situation, the imaging room will always be busy at the start of the hour, since the cases start on time and the room is fully booked. The room becomes available as each case ends. The timing of this will be variable due to differing examination durations but the room will always be open prior to the start of the next hour, since, in our perfect scenario, cases always start on time. This results in the very jagged, or "wavy," shape we see in the utilization curve, similar to MR3 in Fig. 7.5.

A slightly more realistic situation, although still hypothetical, is depicted in Fig. 7.7. This figure depicts utilization of four different procedure rooms, which are also booked at hourly intervals. Since utilization is never 100%, the highest rates of utilization are in the range of 80%, suggesting that, for each hour of the day, there is

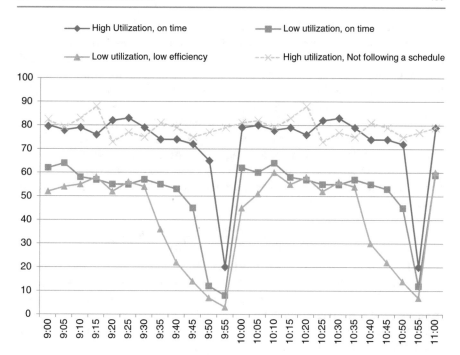

Fig. 7.7 Hypothetical utilization charts. Note that, when attempting to follow a schedule of 1-h intervals, utilization drops prior to the start of the next hour. If cases are substantially shorter than the scheduling interval, room use is inefficient. Note that utilization falls well before the hour is over. Late starts are represented by a slow climb in the utilization curve following the scheduled start time. Utilization is random when no schedule is being followed. Therefore, all times are equally likely to be used (yellow curve). This type of pattern can be seen with either high or low utilization rates

a 20% chance the room will not be in use. The blue line represents a room similar to the room shown in Fig. 7.7, a scheduled facility in which utilization drops prior to the scheduled start of the next case, allowing the facility to run on time. The orange line shows the same phenomenon but with a lower overall utilization rate. The grey line is different. Here, the cases are substantially shorter than the scheduled interval, resulting in longer idle time, and the technologists clearly realize this, because, even though the first case ends early, they often begin the second case late.

Having walked through the hypothetical utilization charts above, we can better understand the actual utilization chart shown in Fig. 7.5. There, the wavy pattern in MR3 during the first part of the day indicates that the room is being utilized in short spurts separated by intervals of relatively idle time, telling us that the room is following a predetermined schedule.

The pattern changes in the late afternoon. Here, the absence of waviness in the pattern suggests that MR3 is no longer following a schedule—either because of longer (and less predictable) exams or because its schedule is more packed (with add-on patients, for instance).

We have found this graphical approach to be extremely flexible, especially as it allows us to modify our expectations based on the room. It is essential to be able to do this when dealing with different generations of equipment. Also, the approach helps illustrate another fundamental point for us. We have shown how high utilization rates cause the waiting time to explode for walk-in procedures. Similarly, high utilization rates are inimical to keeping on schedule. Suppose we want to guarantee (to ourselves as well as to our patients) that a high percentage (P) of our examinations will begin on time. We can designate P as 90 or 95% or whatever rate we promise. To achieve this, we must allocate enough time between examinations that, when procedure duration is added to necessary pre- and post-procedure activities, P% of all exams will fit into the scheduled interval between cases. Our time utilization for any choice of P can be expressed as

$$\mathrm{TU}(P) = \frac{\text{Average examination length}}{P - \text{th quantile of exam lenth distribution}}$$

(if TU exceeds 1.0, we truncate it to 1.0).

As P increases, the denominator will grow and the numerator will stay the same, so TU(P) will decrease. Exactly how it can be seen in Fig. 7.8, which is derived from our MRI examination durations.

As the curve demonstrates, there is an inverse relationship between resource utilization and on-time guarantee:

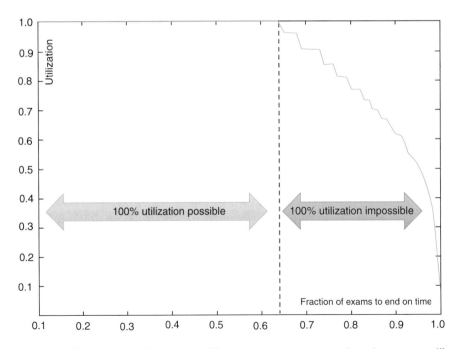

Fig. 7.8 Utilization vs. service guarantee. The more we want to stay on time, the more we will have to reduce our utilization rate

- It is possible to achieve 100% utilization if our on-time guarantee rate is low— under 65%, in this particular instance. If we do not care about keeping on schedule, we can pack our resource until it is fully or nearly fully used.
- After a certain threshold, increasing P results in a rapid drop in utilization. For instance, 90% of on-time service will achieve only 62% utilization, and 95%, only 51% utilization.

Another way to look at this curve is to mentally swap its axis. Thus, the increase in resource time utilization translates into a decrease in on-time performance (P).

7.5 Can Productivity (Throughput) Be Increased?

There are only four ways to achieve higher throughput:

1. Accelerate one or more steps of the process.
2. Perform steps in parallel with one another, rather than in a series.
3. Eliminate re-work.
4. Minimize interruptions.

Let us take a look at each of these.

7.5.1 Accelerate the Steps

Throughput can be increased if either:

- The actual time spent imaging the patient can be shortened
- The pre- or post-procedure steps can be shortened

Consider the MRI safety screening process. This, of course, plays an important part in keeping the MRI patients safe, but it can also take up a substantial amount of time. In our facilities, patient care assistants were handing arriving patients a two-page "screening" form with 49 questions for them to answer. The form had clearly been designed by committee. It contained an assortment of general "screening" questions ("are you allergic to any medications/drugs? If so, please list ….") alongside highly specific questions using technical language ("do you have a Swan-Ganz or thermodilution catheter?"). When patients conscientiously wished to complete the form, the patient care assistants often were not able to explain the technical language. As a result of this collective nonsense, many patients simply gave up.

When we started looking into this, we observed that a positive answer or an unanswered question almost always required a medically trained individual to interview the patient. Because we were doing this so often, we realized that the questions did not need to have so much detail to begin with. By creating general questions in lay language, with the expectation that all positive responses would be followed up by a conversation, we were able to reduce the number of questions from 49 to between 6 and 10, depending on whether the patient was male or female and whether contrast was going to be used. This greatly shortened one of the key pre-procedure steps.

Technology has helped by enabling shorter imaging times. CT scanning offers the most striking example of this. With modern CT scanners, the imaging time is typically on the order of 1–5 min—a huge improvement over scanners from 20 years ago, when scanning might have taken 20–30 min or even longer. Today, the actual imaging of the patient takes only a fraction of the entire imaging appointment. So, while further tech-nological improvements may shorten the patient imaging time, they probably cannot do much to shorten the total visit. MRI has also made substantial, though less impres-sive, gains in speed. However, these gains have been offset by an increased ability to create specialized sequences, which add to the total duration of an examination.

Other activities can also contribute to the overall length of an imaging session. For example, a recent study of the time savings due to a shortened MRI protocol for breast cancer screening showed that increased technologist activities (that otherwise might not have occurred at all) consumed some of these gains [13]. This finding should not be surprising, if only because of the well-known principle "work expands to fill the time available."

Also, improvements expected from technological advances may not materialize because the improvement does not address some rate-limiting step. For example, the transformation from analog (film) to digital imaging resulted in a marked decrease in the time needed before images were available for viewing. Nonetheless, its impact on radiographic facilities' throughput was only modest, indicating that the processing step was a relatively small contributor to the total appointment dura-tion (see below).

7.5.2   Perform Steps in Parallel if Possible

Technical advances yielding faster throughput are not within the radiology depart-ment's control, except to the extent that it has the resources to keep its equipment current.

A proactive adjustment that departments *can* make is performing actions in par-allel. In the old days, a technologist might obtain four or five conventional expo-sures and submit them for chemical processing. If the patient waited in the radiographic room for completion of the processing (steps performed in series), the next patient would be delayed. But if the technologist handed off the films to a dark-room technician and moved on to the next patient (steps performed in parallel), the technologist's productivity would be increased, perhaps explaining why the intro-duction of digital technology did not have a large impact on total productivity.

In a modern radiology department, one technologist can prepare the second patient while the another is producing images for the first. Or one technologist can help a patient from the room while another is preparing for the next patient.

Table 3. Model B: Weekly and annual potential computed tomography patient throughput, at 100% and 85% capacity, using a 15-hour weekday operation and a 12 hour per day weekend operation with a 1-, 2-, or 3-technologist model

Technologist No.	Weekly No. of Patients		Annual No. of Patients	
	100% Capacity	85% Capacity	100% Capacity	85% Capacity
1	207	174	10,764	9,048
2	514	436	26,728	22,672
3	745	634	38,740	32,968

Fig. 7.9   The effect of adding technologists on the productivity of a CT scanner [14]

A few years ago, our department performed a study of the effect on productivity of "overstaffing" a CT facility [14]. The study looked at the impact of staffing with one, two, or three technologists per CT room on potential patient throughput. When the facility was assumed to be working at 100% of capacity the addition of a second technologist more than doubled the theoretical number of patients who could be scanned, and the addition of a third technologist almost doubled it again! (See Fig. 7.9.) Even using a somewhat more realistic value of 85% capacity, there was a doubling of capacity with two technologists and a somewhat smaller increment with the addition of a third. This striking gain in productivity was possible because, when you have multiple technologists, many of the steps in their workflow can be performed in parallel rather than in series. (See discussion above concerning pre-procedure tasks.)

A single technologist can perform all of the activities necessary to operating a CT scanner. The addition of a second or third technologist will result in a certain amount of time when one or two of them may not be engaged in productive work, and thus might be regarded as overstaffing. Was this "overstaffing" worth it? In purely economic terms, the cost of adding a technologist to the staff is equal to salary plus benefits. Given this, how many more studies would the department need to do for the financial benefit to equal the additional staffing costs? When we did this math, it became clear that performing only three additional CT scans per shift would cover the costs. Since we nearly doubled the number of scans, we gained financially.

Clearly, the use of multiple technologists per CT scanner can result in substantial increases in throughput. The exact gain will vary, though, depending on the workflow, the technology, and the staffing model. Other institutions have reported results similar to ours. One of these studies placed the optimum number of technologists per MRI scanner at 1.5 [15].

This approach has proved so successful for CT scanning because technological progress has made the actual scanning time a much smaller percentage of the overall imaging interaction, with the rest of the time taken up by pre- and post-procedure activities that can be done in parallel with the imaging. For MRI, where imaging time is a much larger percentage of the total encounter, smaller gains can be expected (Figs. 7.10 and 7.11). However, the dollar value of a small increase in throughput can be substantial, because of the higher cost of the equipment and higher rates of reimbursement.

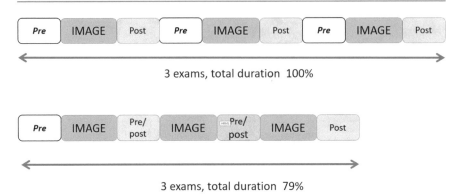

Fig. 7.10 Time is saved by performing steps in parallel. In this example, the imaging time is a relatively small percentage of the total examination time, which includes a significant amount of time devoted to pre- and post-imaging work. Using two technologists to perform pre- and post-procedure work in parallel can reduce the overall time by approximately 21%

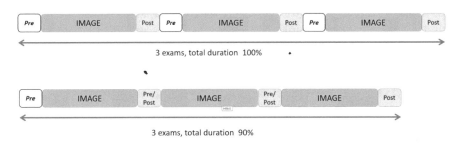

Fig. 7.11 The percentage savings that can be achieved with parallel workflow is lower when imaging occupies a larger percentage of the total time (in this example, about 10%)

Obviously, "overstaffing" in this way means technologists will be less busy at certain times than they otherwise might have been. Hospital administrators need to recognize that having all employees busy at all times is not necessarily a good strategy! Another interesting way to take advantage of working in parallel is illustrated by the experience of a major medical center in New York. This center divided the patient encounter in radiology into three components:

- A value-added component, which produces information of direct importance to the patient
- A "business value-added" component, which does not directly help the patient but is important to the ongoing operation of the equipment (cleaning, setting up, coil placement, etc.)
- Entirely non-value-added component (essentially, "wasted" time)

Turnaround time for an imaging room falls into the category of "business value-added." The authors of the study found that this could be minimized by proper room design. By laying out a new facility with two dock-able tables per scanner, adjoining patient prep rooms, and two doors per scanner, and angling the doors and gantry in such a way that minimal angulation of the table was required, their center was able to perform many of the setup steps while the scanner was in use with the previous patient. Optimizing the physical layout shortens the time needed for these activities and having two tables per scanner makes it possible to perform the steps in parallel rather than in sequence, resulting in a more-than-50% reduction in turnaround times. On average, this corresponded to a savings of 5 min per examination—a savings that, if it could be captured as increased throughput, would easily justify the increased costs of the facility (Fig. 7.12, [16]). This type of modification benefits from BOTH working in parallel and reducing the number of steps for room turnover.

Two prep rooms, two tables, two doors, and two technologists, all serving a single MRI scanner, appears to be the way to go!

Fig. 7.12 Architectural drawing of relationship between the preparation room and the MRI scanning room, and the angulation of the scanner within the scanning room. *EQUIP* equipment, *RM* room, *PREP* preparation (Recht 2019; used with permission from NYU School of Medicine)

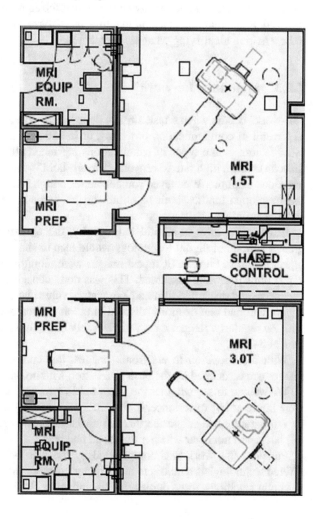

Can we further improve efficiency by co-locating scanners? The short answer is: Yes. As we have noted, efficiency will increase if two "queues" can be handled as one, because if one examination finishes early there is a greater probability another can begin early. This works well if both examinations take roughly the same amount of time. But what if the two scanners are scheduled for slots with different lengths of time—for instance, one every half hour and one every 45 min? If a 30-min scan finishes early, taking a patient with a 45-min examination can cause delays that propagate throughout the day—a perfect example of good intentions gone wrong. Exactly this situation was described in the operational study [15].

This discussion highlights the dangers of using benchmark data to determine appropriate levels of staffing and equipment. It is naïve to assume that if facility A uses a certain number of technologists to produce a certain number of examinations and facility B has 50% more technologists for the same number of scans, then facility B is overstaffed. Similarly, if facility A is producing fewer scans per device than facility B, one cannot necessarily conclude that the equipment in facility A is underutilized. Benchmarking is useful in telling us we have a problem. It is far less likely to be a help in identifying what the problem is.

7.5.3   Minimize "Re-work"

"Re-work" occurs when a task already done needs to be repeated. This can happen as a result of communication problems, or insufficient training, or any number of other factors. Some types of examinations are inherently fraught with difficulties that can create a high rate of re-work. "Breath-hold" sequences in MRI are just one, notorious example. Whenever you encounter a high rate of repetition, you should look for opportunities both to eliminate the particular type of problem and to improve training.

In the early days of digital radiography, the manufacturers claimed that the greater latitude of digital technology would lead to sharp decreases in the need for repeat imaging. Previously, repeat images were monitored by the number of (hard copy) films that were discarded. This was done conscientiously because film was expensive and discarded film had a monetary value due to silver reclamation. Each department had one or more "discard bins," and discarded films were weighed or counted regularly. Repeat rates varied widely but were mostly reported to be in the area of 5–10%.

With the transition to electronic images, this control method was lost. Now, images can be deleted by the push of a button with no one the wiser!

We wanted to see whether the promised low repeat rates of digital radiography were borne out by experience. Initial reports following the implementation of digital radiography had suggested that the retake rates had dropped precipitously [17, 18] but it was not clear whether this trend had held.

Pursuing this work was complicated by the fact that the manufacturers have offered technologists a means to make images disappear without a trace. According to Hindu teachings, three deities rule the universe: Brahma, who is responsible for creation; Vishnu, who preserves and maintains; and Shiva, the destroyer. Surely Shiva is responsible for the "delete" key. Only by disabling this function were we able to show that the retake rate had climbed to over 13%! We had to implement a training and education program to bring it back under control [19].

Retakes add to a patient's radiation dose and make the examination longer. These are truly costs without benefits—a problem for which there is no "solution," only perpetual management (not unlike mowing the lawn). Periodic review of this aspect of performance—and retraining, if necessary—is needed, perpetually, with no end in sight.

7.5.4 Minimize Interruptions

One of the common disruptions in an imaging facility is the unanticipated arrival of a patient in need of an urgent or "STAT" examination. During the day, this will cause delays or cancellations of scheduled examinations. At night or on weekends, it might require the services of an on-call team. In either case, it is expensive.

We cannot think of any ways to eliminate such events. However, it is possible to mitigate their disruptive effects, as long as they are handled thoughtfully. We have already discussed the need to maintain excess capacity to minimize waits in facilities that see patients with high levels of acuity and unpredictable patient arrivals (such as emergency departments).

Elsewhere, managers should take measures to limit inappropriate demands for emergency services, since emergencies will displace and disrupt routine services. For example, the time spent clearing a scanner and holding it open for the arrival of an emergency is lost, never to be regained. Some departments have reported that STAT requests can comprise as much as 74% of certain examinations. We refer to the practice of requesting a higher priority than seems medically appropriate as "priority creep." Not only does this practice impair efficiency, it can also cause a dangerous situation, one where a truly urgent medical issue might be overlooked or delayed. We have had some success in controlling this problem that we will discuss in Chap. 9.

References

1. Williams B, Chacko R. Increasing radiographer productivity by an incentive point system. Radiol Technol. 1982;53(5):409–17.
2. Witt M, Miranda R, Johnson C, Love P. Measuring and improving productivity in general radiology. J Am Coll Radiol. 2010;7:774–7.
3. Sura A, Ho A. Enforcing quality metrics over equipment utilization rates as means to reduce Centers for Medicare and Medicaid Services imaging costs and improve quality of care. J Clin Imaging Sci. 2011;1:31.
4. Hu M, Pavlicek W, Liu P, Zhang M, Langer S, Wang S, Place V, Miranda R, Wu T. Informatics in radiology: efficiency metrics for imaging device productivity. Radiographics. 2011;31:603–16.
5. Aloisio J, Winterfeldt C. Rethinking traditional staffing models. Radiol Manage. 2010;32(6):32–6.

6. Wikipedia. Linear programming. Wikipedia. [Online]. https://en.wikipedia.org/wiki/Linear_programming.
7. Van Huele C, Vanhoucke M. Analysis of the integration of the physician rostering problem and the surgery scheduling problem. J Med Syst. 2014;38(6):43.
8. van der Veen E, Hans E, Veltman B, Berrevoets L, Berden H. A case study of cost-efficient staffing under annualized hours. Health Care Manag Sci. 2015;18(3):279–88.
9. Leeftink A, Vliegen I, Hans E. Stochastic integer programming for multi-disciplinary outpatient clinic planning. Health Care Manag Sci. 2019;22(1):53–67.
10. Rhea J, StGermain R. The relationship of patient waiting time to capacity and utilization in emergency room radiology. Radiology. 1979;130(3):637–41.
11. Zhang L, Runzheimer K, Bonifer E, Keulers A, Piechowiak E, Mahnken A. Improving efficiency of interventional service by lean six sigma. J Am Coll Radiol. 2015;12(11):1200–3.
12. Sadigh G, Applegate K, Saindane A. Prevalence of unanticipated events associated with MRI examinations: a benchmark for MRI quality, safety, and patient experience. J Am Coll Radiol. 2017;14(6):765–72.
13. Borthakur A, Weinstein S, Schnall M. Comparison of study activity times for "Full" versus "Fast MRI" for breast cancer screening. J Am Coll Radiol. 2019;16(8):1046–51.
14. Boland G, Houghton M, Marchione D, McCormick W. Maximizing outpatient computed tomography productivity using multiple technologists. J Am Coll Radiol. 2008;5(2):119–25.
15. Recht M, Macari M, Lawson K, Mulholland T, Chen D, Kim D, Babb J. Impacting key performance indicators in an academic MR imaging department through process improvement. J Am Coll Radiol. 2013;10:202–6.
16. Recht M, Block K, Chandarana H, Friedlane J, Mulholland T, Teahan D, Wiggins R. Optimization of MRI turnaround times through the use of dockable tables and innovative architectural design strategies. Am J Roentgenol. 2019;212(4):855–8.
17. Weatherburn GC, Bryan S, West M. A comparison of image reject rates when using film, hard copy computed radiography and soft copy images on picture archiving and communication systems (PACS) workstations. Br J Radiol. 1999;72:653–60.
18. Peer S, Peer R, Giacomuzzi S, Jaschke W. Comparative reject analysis in conventional film-screen and digital storage phosphor radiography. Radiat Prot Dosim. 2001;94(1–2):69–71.
19. Fintelmann F, Pulli B, Abedi-Tari F, Trombley M, Shore M, Shepard J, Rosenthal D. Repeat rates in digital chest radiography and strategies for improvement. J Thorac Imaging. 2012;27:148–51.

Image Delivery

8

Contents

Things That Happen

- The technologist performs image quality checks.
- Any necessary post-processing and measurements are performed.
- If needed, images are divided into different examinations.
- The technologist "completes" the study in the RIS.
- The images are forwarded to the PACS, either manually or automatically.
- The images appear in the PACS ready for interpretation.

Things to Measure

- Periodic reports
  - Wrong completion
  - Image counts that differ between imaging devices and PACS
  - Network speed, compared to peak requirements
  - Expected time to PACS
- Real time
  - Delayed times to PACS
  - Delayed completion
  - Late image arrival

© Springer Nature Switzerland AG 2021
D. Rosenthal, O. Pianykh, *Efficient Radiology*,
https://doi.org/10.1007/978-3-030-53610-7_8

8.1   Finishing Up

Once all the images have been acquired, there are still several tasks that need to be performed before the radiologists can view the examinations.

8.1.1   Quality Assurance

Many technologists prefer to review their own work prior to sending it to the radiologists. This allows them to delete any unsatisfactory images, thus sparing the radiologists from having to examine sub-par or duplicate images. From a more self-interested perspective, this step also gives weak technologists a chance to conceal poor-quality work. As we discussed in Chap. 7, electronic image deletion may conceal the true repeat rate, and with it the technologist's competence, to say nothing of causing an increase in the patient's radiation exposure!

8.1.2   Post-processing

Images acquired in one plane often must be reformatted into others. This is particularly true of CT images, which are nearly always acquired in the axial plane and often reformatted into coronal and sagittal images. With most modern scanners, this is easily done using the scanner hardware and software. Sometimes, though, special reformats or other processing (3D, image segmentation, disarticulation, etc.) might entail the use of freestanding workstations, to which the images need to be sent before they are forwarded to the PACS.

8.1.3   Labeling and Other Annotations

In some departments and for some examination types, the technologist might be asked to label and measure particular structures. This is especially common in ultrasound examinations, where clinicians might request measurements of aortic diameter, infant head size, or other structures.

8.1.4   Image "Splitting"

A set of continuously acquired images might include body parts that should be evaluated by different radiologists. This is particularly true of CT. For example, a continuous acquisition might include images of both the chest and the abdomen, which will be evaluated by a chest specialist and an abdominal or body imager, respectively. To accomplish this, the images might be forwarded to an intermediate workstation in which the single acquisition is divided into two or more examinations, each with its own accession number, before they are forwarded to PACS.

8.1.5 Examination "Completion"

The study must be designated as complete ("completed") within the information system. This requirement has always seemed strange to us. In this high-tech day and age, why should we have to tell such things to a computer? Well, there are at least three reasons:

1. In completing the examination, the technologist specifies which examination was done—was it one view of the hand or several? Was contrast material used? What type of ultrasound probe was used? Details such as these determine which CPT code applies and are essential for correct billing. In some cases, they may also determine which radiologist will review the images and which dictation "macro" applies.
2. Having the technologist specify which examination was performed at the time of completion allows the order to be more general, and therefore relieves the ordering clinician from the need to know the department's performable "menu."
3. The information system (RIS) may be unable to recognize that the examination is complete because, as noted in Chap. 5, the number of images, series, etc. is unpredictable.

Failure to complete the examination is one of the more frequent errors of omission that we see. We have pointed out that manual steps such as "beginning" and "completing" the examination are weak links in the chain of information. In Part I, Chap. 2, of this book we noted that technologists frequently forget to perform the "begin" step, and that estimating examination start times after the fact results in spikes of apparent "beginnings" at 5-min intervals. To encourage compliance, some facilities track how often technologists enter specific start times on their operational dashboard (recall the "good-bad-ugly" figure in Chap. 6).

Surely there must be a better way! Perhaps someone reading this book will invent one.

Another concern related to "completion" times: The language itself is misleading. Yes, the examination is "completed" from the technologist's point of view, but it is not actually over until the images have been examined, the report has been finalized, and results have been communicated to the responsible clinicians.

Failure to complete the examination has definite operational consequences. In many departments, the radiologist cannot issue a report until the examination has been marked as "completed" by the technologist. Failure to perform this step in a timely manner can therefore cause the report to be delayed.

Can we address this issue by allowing the radiologist to issue a report before the technologist has completed the examination? Well, yes and no. While technically feasible, this solution could have unintentional negative outcomes. For example, suppose a radiologist creates a report while the case is still in "scheduled" or "begun" status. If the radiologist realizes that there are images missing, this report could be held until the examination has been completed and then sent.

However, because of the variability of examinations, radiologists might not know if and when the complete set of images has been received. They certainly would not want to create a report if images are missing. Also, creating a report before the technologist has completed the examination could result in an unhappy circumstance in which the report contradicts the billed examination.

For these reasons, we do not allow radiologists in our institution to dictate reports before the examination is completed. If a radiologist tries to issue a report for a case that has not been completed, the dictation system will stop him or her. At this point, there are three options:

(a) Put the case aside until the technologist has completed it.
(b) Complete it himself or herself.
(c) Contact the technologist to explain that the examination must be completed.

Putting the case aside may not be a good option. Someone is waiting for it, and likely needs it promptly. Or maybe the technologist has forgotten the case and will not complete it in an acceptable time frame, if at all. If the radiologist competes the examination himself or herself, how will he or she know whether the images in front of him or her constitute a complete set?

In a small practice with a limited number of imaging rooms, contacting the technologist may be relatively easy. However, in the modern world of digital electronic images, radiologists are increasingly seeing cases from many different locations. For this reason, our image QA system sends real-time alerts notifying the technology manager when a case needs to be completed. Chapter 9 includes a fuller description of the functions of this system.

In our institution, we encounter incomplete examinations or incorrect completions fairly often. We see these errors most often with cross-sectional studies (CT, MRI) in which the use of contrast is not correctly specified. It is unfortunately relatively easy for radiologists to overlook these errors, creating the potential for an embarrassing and even fraudulent claim. For example, consider a situation in which contrast was not given but the technologist has incorrectly completed the examination as "with and without" contrast. The radiologist, seeing no contrast, might state in the report that contrast was not used. However, the bill, being based upon the examination as completed, is rendered for an examination with and without contrast.

To address this issue, the default report templates for our dictation system include a technique line that indicates the examination as completed by the technologist. In the example given above, the report template would say that an examination was performed with and without contrast, because that is how the technologist completed it. This should make the radiologist aware of the completion error. He should correct it—not by dictating the correct technique (which might not affect billing)—but by contacting the technologist, either directly or through the QA system, and asking him or her to recomplete the examination correctly.

We will discuss this matter in greater detail when we talk about the radiologist's role in quality assurance (Chap. 9).

Keep It Real!

Unfortunately, we cannot count on imaging standards or devices to provide the completion time automatically. For instance, the DICOM protocol used to transmit images to PACS has no concept of the "last image." The technologist (or the physician supervising the acquisition process) may decide to add more images—at least in theory, they can decide to do so whenever they deem it important, regardless of how much time has passed since the previously acquired image. This can cause a rare but important problem, as we will discuss below.

8.2   Delivering Studies to PACS

Once all post-imaging activities are complete, the images must be forwarded to PACS, either from the imaging device itself or from an intermediate workstation such as a 3D processing workstation.

Sending images to PACS would seem to be a simple process. Like any process, though, it can be plagued by any number of problems. We have already described why the "autosend" feature is not used consistently. While it is true that reformatted images and labeled images can be sent independently of the original images, and thus are compatible with the "autosend" mode of transmission, quality assurance and image splitting are not compatible. For this reason, we prefer manual means of initiating transmission to PACS.

Whether transmission is done manually or automatically, technicians generally assume that there is no room for error once it has been initiated. It is reassuring and convenient to think this way. The fact is, though, they can still be caught off guard by unanticipated turns of events.

We tend to trust automated processes. Maybe this is simply wishful thinking, born of a desire to expend as little effort as possible. When you send an email, you do not call the intended recipient to verify it has arrived, do you? You certainly do not check to see whether the message he or she received had the same number of words as the one you sent. Similarly, once images have been transmitted to PACS, no human verifies that the images are actually received. As a result, if images happen to get lost, their absence might escape notice for a considerable length of time. This probably would not be a major issue for plain radiography as the components of a full set of images are generally predictable so there is a good chance someone would notice if any views were missing. However, for CT, MRI, or ultrasound, a full examination can include an extremely large and variable number of images. As a result, lost images or even entire missing series could easily be overlooked.

A few years ago, we were shocked to discover such "image leakage" in our department. Following this discovery, we decided to take a deeper dive into what we had believed to be a foolproof system [1].

You may ask: What could possibly disrupt an automated, standardized image transfer? In fact, a number of things can go wrong during the process. Some of these are regular and reproducible—for example, vendor DICOM incompatibilities and database failures. Radiology data exchange standards such as DICOM or HL7 are not carved in stone. Different versions and different vendor-specific interpretations of the standard make it virtually impossible to guarantee 100% compatibility. Such mismatches expose a fundamental problem of automated processes. *Unlike* humans, machines usually have no "self-recovery" mode, and no sense of importance or priority. Trivial data mismatches will likely be handled in the same way as critical issues.

Keep It Real!
The more you work with automated tools and software, the more you realize one principal difference between these and "organic thinkers"—that is, those built by Mother Nature. The latter can evolve, adapt, and recover: A worm cut in half will grow again; a swarm of ants running into a wall will find a way to go around.

The story is completely different in software and hardware: Changing a single byte of code, or misconnecting a single wire, will most likely send even the most advanced machine into a downward spiral. Engineers and software developers seldom take this into account; most will let the systems crash. When they do crash, some systems will write an error message into a hidden log file while others will simply go "missing in action," losing whatever transaction was in progress when the failure occurred. This can be a dangerous feature, especially when combined with natural human laziness and the effort required to monitor automated processes. Remember this when you implement any kind of automation: You need to have additional processes to control the quality of the automation, and alternative means to recover from its failures.

As an example of what can go wrong, Fig. 8.1 illustrates a simple DICOM incompatibility. The DICOM standard allows vendors to add their own data elements to the standard data dictionary. This generally works well—if the elements the different vendors add do not collide with one another, as in this case. Here, two vendors used essentially the same data element names to store completely different data. As a result, an attempted image transfer from one system to the other failed because the data was not in the expected form. The images were ignored because of the "invalid" data, even though the data mismatch was clinically irrelevant. They were simply dropped, and no one received any kind of notification that they were gone!

(0028,1054) Rescale Type	LO	1	BQML
(0028,1055) Window Center & Width Explanation	LO	2	WINDOW1\WINDOW2
(0029,0010) Private Creator	LO	1	SIEMENS MEDCOM HEADER
(0029,0011) Private Creator	LO	1	SIEMENS MEDCOM HEADER2
(0029,0012) Private Creator	LO	1	SIEMENS MEDCOM OOG
(0029,0013) Private Creator	LO	1	MITRA PRESENTATION 1.0
(0029,1031) PMTF Information 1	LO / OB	1	202.0.8317148 <Binary Data>
(0029,1032) PMTF Information 2	UL / OB	1	131072
(0029,1033) PMTF Information 3	UL / OB	1	0
(0029,1034) PMTF Information 4	CS / OB	1	DB TO DICOM
(0029,1160) Not in Dictionary	LO / OB	1	com
(0029,1208) Platform OOG Type	CS / OB	1	MEDCOM OOG 2
(0029,1209) Platform OOG Version	LO / OB	1	VD30C
(0029,1210) Platform OOG Info	OB	1	<Binary Data> <Binary Data>
(0029,1301) Not in Dictionary	LO	1	1197
(0029,1302) Not in Dictionary	LO	1	-463

Fig. 8.1 Example of a data encoding collision between two medical imaging vendors. This medical data was encoded using the DICOM standard, which all radiology devices are supposed to support. In this instance, though, the two devices were trying to read the same data using different DICOM VRs (data formatting conventions, circled in the middle column). As a result, image transfer failed, and no one was alerted to this fact

8.3   Time-to-PACS (TTP) Performance Metric

How long should it take for images to reach the PACS once they have been completed? We refer to our metric for this step as time to PACS, or TTP.

Measuring TTP is fairly simple if you have both PACS and RIS running at your department. RIS will provide you with the exam completion time, Tc. PACS will usually have a timestamp for a study arriving to PACS (often called "study create time" in PACS database lingo), Tp. Thus, you can calculate TTP as Tp − Tc. In many cases, Tc will be a manual entry by techs. Tp is automatically stamped by the PACS server, making it much more reliable.

Once you know how to derive your TTP values, you can (and should) take a close look at them. How consistent (or variable) are they? If some are higher than others, there may be a simple explanation. Some delays can be caused by your devices or network. These might appear to occur at random, or they might tend to coincide with times of high network traffic. However, many TTP delays will be the result of manual image transmission and common workflow disruptions: techs getting distracted by their patients, shift changes, lunch breaks, etc. There are any number of reasons the technologist might fail to send the images promptly.

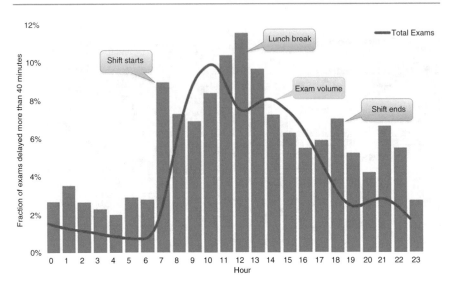

Fig. 8.2 Hourly TTP delay patterns. The blue bars represent the percentage of cases in which it took more than 40 min for the images to reach PACS and are therefore classified as "delayed." The smooth black curve represents the volume of exams acquired during the same hours of the day. It is clear that high overall volume contributes to the TTP delays: Perhaps the techs get busy, and more forgetful, or perhaps high network traffic is to blame. Other patterns are also evident, including effects of shift changes and lunch breaks [2]

Figure 8.2 shows the results of an analysis we performed a few years ago, when it became obvious that some cases were taking too long to get to PACS [2]. After reviewing the spectrum of our TTP times, we determined that the overwhelming majority (90%) of cases reach the PACS within 40 min. It is important to recognize that this surprisingly long stretch of time does not represent the pure "transmission time" between pushing the "send" button and arrival of the images. It is the apparent time interval between manual "completion" of the case in RIS and the first image arriving in PACS. It is therefore subject to various activities, both necessary and unnecessary, between completion and "send," in addition to the actual transmission time (and sometimes to errors in entering the completion time).

For example, as noted above, in some cases it is necessary to separate a continuous image acquisition into two or more distinct examinations so they can be viewed and reported by different radiologists. We refer to this as "image splitting," a process that requires the entire image set be sent to a separate workstation as an intermediate step before transmission to PACS. Clearly, a certain amount of time is needed for this. Figure 8.3 demonstrates the magnitude of this effect. This figure compares the time to PACS for two different examinations: CT of the head and CT of the chest, abdomen, and pelvis. When performed by itself CT of the head never requires splitting. However, in our institution CT of the chest, abdomen, and pelvis is split into separate chest and abdomen components. The activities associated with the process of "splitting" introduce a delay of about 15 min, although in some cases it can be much longer.

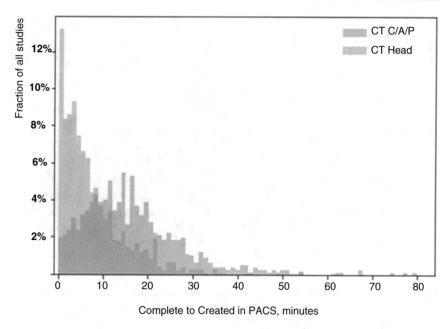

Fig. 8.3 Time to PACS. Comparison of examinations that do not require "splitting" (head CT) with those that do (chest/abdomen/pelvis CT). The need to separate images introduces a delay in arrival to PACS of approximately 10–15 min, but in some cases it can be much longer

Although image splitting and other necessary operations might prolong the TTP, they do not adequately explain what seemed like an excessively long interval. We tried a number of different approaches to decreasing the TTP, including displaying the times on a website, but finally settled on the most direct and proactive solution: automatically paging technologists and managers when the TTP exceeds 40 min. The local manager is contacted first. If the problem has not been resolved within 40 min, a page is sent to both the local and the modality supervisor informing them of the issue. Further pages are sent every 40 min until the problem is addressed.

We re-evaluated performance after 3 months of paging alerts and were pleased to note a spectacular improvement, with a nearly two-thirds reduction in the number of delayed cases. These results are illustrated in Fig. 8.4. Interestingly, the results also show a much smaller relationship between delays and overall volume, indicating that network traffic played a minimal role and human error was largely to blame.

Our system alerts technologists when entire examinations are missing from PACS. The system works well if the examination is completed (a manual process) but not sent (also a manual process), but it does not work if the examination is neither completed nor sent. If the examination is sent (either manually or automatically) but not completed, the radiologist will see the problem when he or she attempts to interpret the examination. We have created another system to address the latter possibility. We will discuss this system as well as the typical problems that it records in Chap. 9, where we cover the radiologists' role in operations. Finally, our

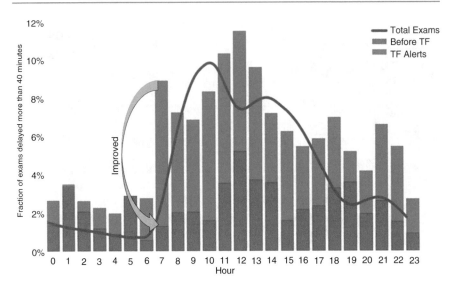

Fig. 8.4 Automatic paging of technologists when TTP exceeded 40 min drastically reduced the overall number of delayed exams. The blue bars show delays prior to implementation; the red bars show the improvement. The black line shows overall examination volume. Note that there is still a delay during the lunch hour. Overall, though, we no longer see a correlation between volume and delay [2]

TTP alerting system does nothing to reconcile the number of images generated at the acquisition device with the number received by the PACS. As noted above, we strongly recommend implementation of a reconciliation process wherever possible.

Keep It Real!
We chose a 40-min threshold for an important reason: alert fatigue. Using our data, we found that TTP above 40 min accounts for some 5% of our overall image transfers. Practically, this translates into an alert for only 1 in 20 imaging studies, or 1–2 alerts per day for most imaging modalities.

A lower threshold would have resulted in much more frequent alerts. We all know what would happen in this case: Modality managers would stop responding, turning their pagers off. In developing any computer-to-human interface, you absolutely need to consider the limits of human "bandwidth."

8.3.1   Network Issues

Other failures can be erratic and unpredictable. For example, a variety of networking "glitches" can disrupt image transmission and even cause permanent loss. Sometimes the glitches are obvious, such as network downtime (when everything gets stuck and needs to be resent). In a well-run system, such events should be rare.

Much more common are bandwidth fluctuations, which usually do not create substantial problems but occasionally will if the fluctuations exceed the equipment functionality thresholds. For instance, while all DICOM devices are configured to tolerate brief communication timeouts, the connection will be dropped if the timeout exceeds a certain, preset threshold (usually a few seconds) and the data will not be transmitted. Network and equipment overloads can sometimes cause these longer timeouts, resulting in a loss of data.

A dedicated and well-managed network is a must-have for any radiology department. Your IT support team needs to be in charge and must know exactly what is going on. This is particularly true when you fetch images from remote sites (e.g., teleradiology). In such cases, you might be dependent on several intermediate networks, and as a result your control over performance may be minimal, opening the door to unpredictable fluctuations in the bandwidth of your connection. Ask your IT team to do the simple math: Take the volume of studies (images per hour), multiply it by the image size, and divide the product by the speed of the weakest link in your network. This will give you a minimal bandwidth requirement. If the result does not fit your expectations, you need a network upgrade.

Practical Advice
Did you know there are two types of IP addresses? Most devices use dynamic IP addresses, which the network assigns to a device when it connects. Dynamic IP addresses may change over time. However, the DICOM standard, used for all medical imaging, requires a fixed ("static") computer address. This is why the majority of radiology networking disasters always look something like this: A new engineer makes an update on your CT or MRI scanner (or worse, your PACS archive) and accidentally changes its network name or address. Then—kaboom!—one machine no longer talks to another. Even once you have identified and fixed the problem, it can still take hours for the system to recover.

8.4   Ecce Homo

As we have seen many times in this book, human behavior patterns can have a significant impact on workflow. A plain lack of interest or motivation can certainly play a part, but habitual patterns of behavior can be so deeply ingrained that we accept them almost entirely unconsciously. Shift breaks and mealtimes, as shown in Chap. 7, can have a profound impact upon efficiency. Personal preferences and cherry-picking, described in Chap. 6 in connection with our work distribution system, can also play an important role.

This idea is expressed in the maxim "Culture eats strategy for breakfast." If gains are to be sustainable, you need to change the workplace culture surrounding the issue. This can be difficult to do.

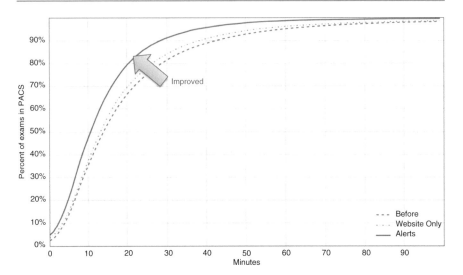

Fig. 8.5 The percentage of cases received in PACS as a function of the time since "completion." Note that, prior to any intervention (dashed line), slightly less than 90% of the cases had arrived at 40 min. An intermediate step, in which times were displayed on a website, produced a small improvement but the biggest change came after we implemented a paging system in which technologists were alerted when a case was delayed by 40 min. This change improved the performance across the board, even for cases that did not generate alerts!

We believe that our time-to-PACS optimization project, described above, was one that succeeded in changing our work culture. After we implemented the TTP alerts, we observed the expected improvements for cases that exceeded the threshold and resulted in an alert. However, we also observed improvements in functions we had not directly targeted (Fig. 8.5).

We hypothesized that alerting technologists when cases were 40 min late would reduce or even eliminate the "tail" of delayed cases. In fact, the entire curve shifted to the left. So, by the time the 40-min paging threshold was reached, 96% of cases had already arrived in PACS!

The only explanation we can think of is a change in culture: The technologists grew accustomed to the idea that sending images to PACS in a timely manner is critical (not to mention, the only way to avoid alerts, which are viewed as evidence of fault). Note that while active alerting (paging) made a sizeable difference, passive alerting (displaying a list of delayed cases on a web page) had a rather small effect on delays.

8.5   Delayed Image Arrival

What happens if an image that did not make it to PACS is identified and resent or, as sometimes happens, a supplementary image is created to add to an existing examination? In both cases, there will be a delay in adding the images to the case. If the delay is substantial, it might occur after the study has been reviewed, or even worse, after a report has been created, signed, and distributed.

This would put us on treacherous ground, since the report would be generated without full knowledge of what all the images together show. As far as we know, there is no PACS system that alerts the radiologist to the fact that an image has been added to a previously reviewed or reported examination.

A few good housekeeping rules should help mitigate the risk. When possible, the radiologist should have an idea of how many images to expect. This is generally not feasible with CT or MRI examinations, but it is often possible with radiography, where the technologist can indicate the number of images to be expected using the examination name and/or the dictation macro. We will return to this idea when we discuss dictation macros.

As a matter of policy, technologists should be trained never to add images to an examination without direct communication with the radiologist responsible for dictating the report.

Now that the study has been properly completed by the technologist, has been sent to PACS—either manually or automatically—and has transited the network and safely arrived in PACS, it is ready to be evaluated and reported. We will discuss the latter two processes in the next chapter.

References

1. Oglevee C, Pianykh O. Losing images in digital radiology: more than you think. J Digit Imaging. 2015;28(3):264–71.
2. Pianykh O, Jaworsky C, Shore M, Rosenthal D. Improving radiology workflow with automated examination tracking and alerts. J Am Coll Radiol. 2017;14(7):937–43.

From Images to Reports

9

"All meanings, we know, depend on the key of interpretation."

George Eliot

Contents

Things That Happen
- Studies are selected from the PACS using individual or group worklists.
- The cases are sorted by priority, or by other features such as examination type.
- The images are presented to the radiologist, along with prior comparisons.
- The radiologist checks the images for quality and completeness.
- Information regarding the examinations that require reports is forwarded to a dictation system.
- A report is created and, after one or more steps, a final, signed document is generated.
- The finalized report information is forwarded to both the information system and the PACS.

The original version of this chapter was revised. The year "1985" in the first line of Section 9.1 is corrected as "1895". The correction to this chapter can be found at https://doi.org/10.1007/978-3-030-53610-7_11

© Springer Nature Switzerland AG 2021
D. Rosenthal, O. Pianykh, *Efficient Radiology*,
https://doi.org/10.1007/978-3-030-53610-7_9

Things to Measure

Periodically
- QA issues: Look for patterns in type of issue and individuals involved
- Time intervals
  - From arrival in PACS to preliminary interpretation
  - From preliminary to final report
  - Overall time from completion to final report
- Productivity: RVUs/FTE

Real Time
- Total number of examinations awaiting interpretation
- Cases in which quality issues require timely intervention
- "Overdue" cases falling outside expected windows
  - Not assigned, not dictated (possibly not on any worklist)
  - Assigned, not dictated (especially procedures)
  - Dictated, not signed

9.1   "Ich habe meinen Tod gesehen!": The First X-Ray Report

December 22, 1895, was a truly remarkable day in Dr. Röntgen's life. Typically, a university physicist spends time pursuing routine and often fruitless experiments, but not today. Today saw the culmination of a month of secret experiments following a striking observation of a "faint flickering greenish illumination" from a new kind of light, experiments that finally yielded a true masterpiece of biomedical research.

He has just completed a strange kind of portrait of his wife—an odd, provocative image that would produce immediate insights into how we perceive the body, and almost as quickly change the world. Proudly, carefully, he lifted the image from his desk and handed it to Anna.

Frau R.'s face, lit with the same excitement she read in her husband's eyes, suddenly turned pale. She clearly "saw the bones of her living hand" (Fig. 9.1).

Fig. 9.1 Radiograph of Anna Bertha Röntgen's hand from late 1895. Used with permission: German Röntgen-Museum, Remscheid

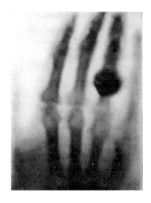

"I have seen my death!" she cried. "I have seen my death!" [1].

Just like that, the first radiology image, and the first radiology interpretation, were born.

Many years have passed since that historic day in December 1895, and untold amounts of hard work, experimentation, and technological advances have gone into perfecting the production of medical images and interpreting what the images reveal. But the strange mix of science and art needed for the conversion of images into words continues in the present day. From the fuzzy hand X-rays of 1895 to the most modern (yet equally fuzzy) diffusion-weighted images of stroke, from the emotional words of Frau Roentgen to the nearly incomprehensible interpretive algorithms of machine learning, we continue to be challenged to extract as much information from our diagnostic imagery as we can. Proceeding from images to reports remains an essential piece of diagnostic radiology.

> **Keep It Real! (?)**
> Many of us have our own history of expressive radiology reports. Some time ago, one of us underwent a chest X-ray after experiencing chest pain. His radiologist friend looked at the image and summarized it in two brief sentences:
> "You will definitely die"—was the first.
> Several long seconds passed before he added, with a smile:
> "But not from this."

9.2 Viewing the Images: Quality Assurance

The days when a radiologist would greet a patient at the office door, shake hands, and sit with him while producing the image are long gone. Now, only after the examination has been completed (by a technologist), reconstructed from digital data (by image algorithms), manipulated and modified (by post-processing algorithms, and possibly by specialized 3D technologists), delivered into the PACS archive (by a sophisticated computer network), and even partially reviewed (by a state-of-the-art black-box AI cloud) does the radiologist have the opportunity to examine it on a workstation. Even then, in a modern department, order and selection of the images to be presented to radiologists are usually done by one or more worklists. We will have more to say about organization of these worklists later in this chapter.

The first step after the radiologist receives the images is quality assurance. Are all of the expected images present? Has the proper anatomy been included? Are there artifacts that can interfere with interpretation? Is the study otherwise ready for interpretation?

As we mentioned in our chapter on image acquisition, technologists will likely already have performed their own quality checks, and any images they deemed unsatisfactory will have been deleted and/or redone. Still, radiologists should also perform quality assurance, as they are better able to determine whether the images are suitable to answer the clinical question at hand.

Given all this, what happens if something is amiss?

Once upon a time, the radiologist knew all of the technologists and could quickly reach them either in person or by telephone. Thus, it was relatively easy to correct any problems they encountered. Unfortunately, such close communication has become increasingly difficult. Especially because of the steadily growing demand for timely reporting, radiologists are finding that they have less time to devote to technologist education. Exacerbating this trend is the greater physical separation between the radiologists and technologists. Oftentimes, technologists are not in the same building, city, or even country as the radiologist who will be interpreting their images.

This problem can be very difficult to manage. Specialized tools can help, though. There are essentially three types of scenarios that may need to be addressed:

1. Something is either missing or simply amiss, making it impossible to produce a report—for example, the examination has not been properly "completed," or critical images or series are missing. This type of issue must be treated as urgent.
2. Something is suboptimal but it is still possible to produce a report, though it likely needs to be qualified in some way. This type of issue should be communicated to the technologists to help with their training and education.
3. Something has been done particularly well and the radiologist wishes to compliment the technologist or document the result for teaching purposes.

To bridge the widening chasm of time and space between the radiologist and the technologists, we have created an electronic QA system [2]. This system allows radiologists to generate two sorts of notifications. Issues that are educational and not time sensitive (for example, technical recommendations for future cases) are stored in the system for later review by the technologists and managers. Other issues are critical and must be addressed before the report can be created (for example, examination completion errors or missing images). In these cases, the manager is notified of the need for immediate action by pager.

Figure 9.2 shows an example of the data entry form that our quality assurance system uses. This form can be accessed from any workstation at any time. Note that once the urgency of the issue is identified (highlighted in blue here), the radiologist can either select from a list of the most common issues or enter a description of the issue as free text.

Not all quality assurance reports require a response. Some may reflect a radiologist's personal idiosyncrasies, others, an incorrectly reported issue. Still others may suggest deficits in training or individual performance. The manager is given the option of categorizing the report so he or she can identify trends and patterns over time. Figure 9.3 shows an example of the manager's screen.

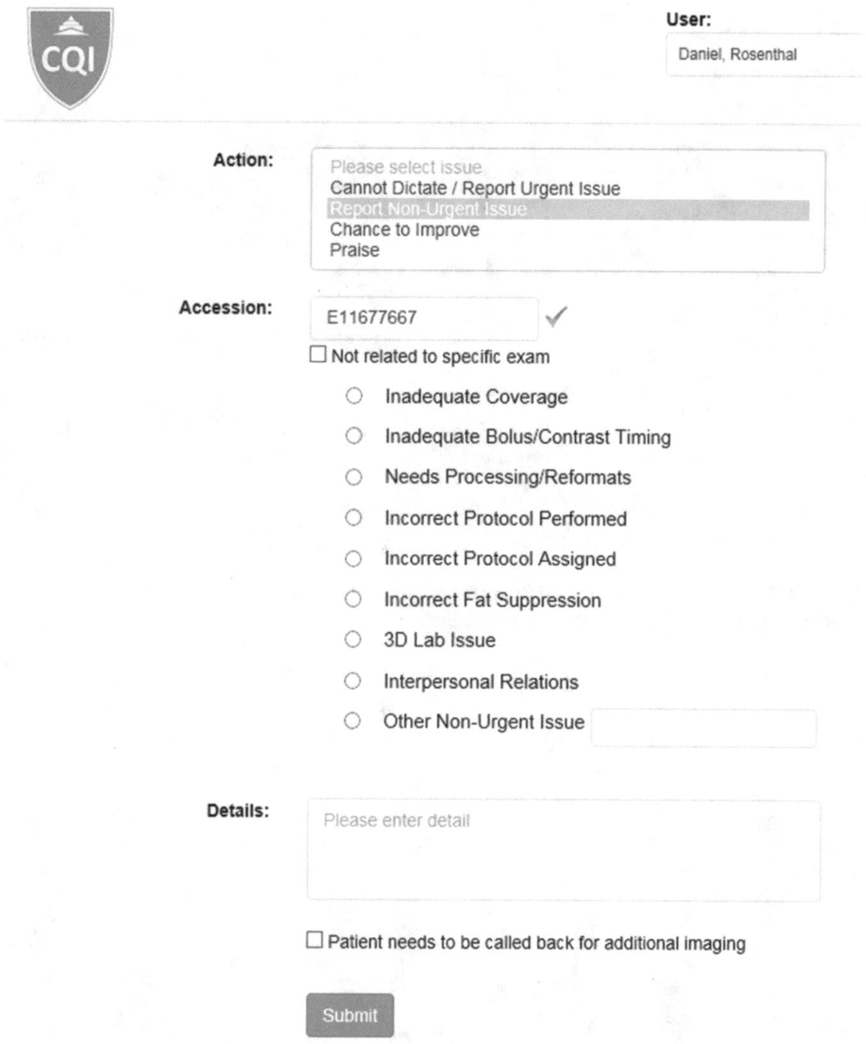

User:

Daniel, Rosenthal

Action:

Please select issue
Cannot Dictate / Report Urgent Issue
Report Non-Urgent Issue
Chance to Improve
Praise

Accession:

E11677667   ✓

☐ Not related to specific exam

○   Inadequate Coverage

○   Inadequate Bolus/Contrast Timing

○   Needs Processing/Reformats

○   Incorrect Protocol Performed

○   Incorrect Protocol Assigned

○   Incorrect Fat Suppression

○   3D Lab Issue

○   Interpersonal Relations

○   Other Non-Urgent Issue

Details:

Please enter detail

☐ Patient needs to be called back for additional imaging

Submit

Fig. 9.2 Data entry screen that radiologists use to report quality issues. Urgent issues lead to a page being sent to the appropriate manager. Less time-sensitive issues are stored for periodic review

This easy-to-use system has proved highly effective in remedying problems. Following its introduction, technologist errors dropped by 66% overall [2]. Figure 9.4 summarizes some of the typical quality issues reported with the system. We designed the system with the intent to use it to report image quality problems, an idea we derived from older quality assurance projects in which radiologists would comment on issues such as positioning and exposure. In retrospect, though, that idea seems rather quaint and old-fashioned. In fact, the greatest number of issues reported involved work the technologists did after creation of the images but

Manager Issue

Fig. 9.3 The data entry screen used by managers to classify and categorize quality issues. Every case must be "closed" even if no action is taken

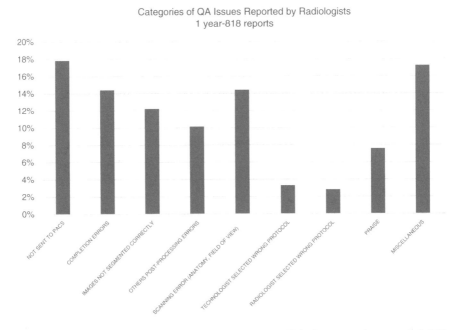

Fig. 9.4 Categories of quality-related issues reported by radiologists over a 1-year period (818 examples). Note that a total of 55% of the errors involved activities that took place between when the images were created and when the radiologist saw them. While failure to send the images to PACS was the single most common error, failure to complete the study was not far behind. It is also interesting to note that protocol selection errors were equally likely whether the protocol was selected by the radiologist or by the technologist

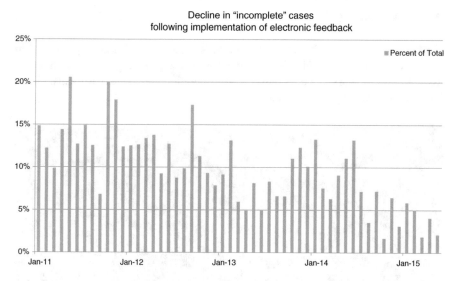

Fig. 9.5   Improvements in the percentage of "incomplete" cases observed after implemented electronic feedback system at Massachusetts General Hospital

before the radiologist saw them. A full 55% of the errors were completion errors, post-processing errors, segmentation errors, and failure to send to PACS!

A particularly troublesome error was the failure to manually complete the examination before the radiologist reviewed the case. Figure 9.5 shows the percentage of examinations that were still in "incomplete" status when the radiologist initially viewed them, before and after implementation. There was a marked decrease in such cases after implementation, from 10–15% to less than 2%.

The reporting system produces a permanent record of the issue, which allows tracking of the problems encountered as well as identification of patterns over time. This transparency is probably one of the major reasons technologists responded so well to its introduction. At the same time, though, it had an unanticipated consequence.

Initially, everything went well. Radiologists reported quality-related issues and technologists improved. But then a curious thing happened. The technologists' managers began using the data generated by the quality assurance system as part of their performance reviews. Consequently, the technologists began surreptitiously asking the radiologists not to file reports "against" them, and use of the system dropped precipitously. A successful, proven system was undermined by an informal compact to conceal problems!

This should probably not have come as a surprise, since one of the features of a successful incident reporting system is freedom from blame. As a result of this experience, we decided to follow the lead of the aviation safety reporting systems in which safety reports are protected from operational consequences by taking the operation of the reporting system out of the hands of the line managers [3].

9.3   Worklists

Worklists determine which cases will be presented to which radiologists, and in what order (Fig. 9.6). Typically implemented as computer algorithms with work-assigning logic, worklists are central to the operation of most departments. Given this, how should they be designed?

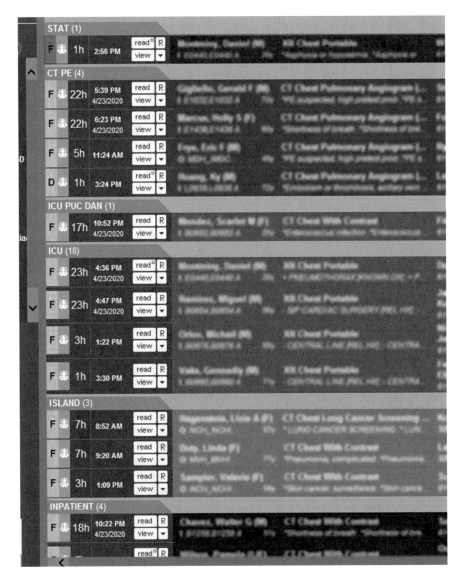

Fig. 9.6 Radiology worklist example, Primordial, Nuance (patient information blurred). Different priorities are indicated by color

The PACS and RIS vendors have not been particularly helpful to department managers in designing their products. In an effort to satisfy all possible customers, they have created systems that allow individual radiologists to design their own worklists. While this might be desirable in certain circumstances (for example, in research studies in which a specific individual is doing the interpreting), it is disadvantageous for departments that want to be able to conform to standards of practice with predictable turnaround times.

Users who want to have individualized worklists present another example of the tension between standardization and customization. If all radiologists and examinations were equivalent, there would be only one worklist and no confusion as to who is responsible for the report. This is not the case, though, and as long as individual radiologists have the option to customize their worklists, it will be extremely difficult for departments to uphold service guarantees. Radiologists who are so inclined may decide what is and what isn't "their" work, or cherry-pick cases for ease of reporting, for their RVU value, or for any number of other reasons. Generally, the more worklists there are, the more places a case can "hide."

For example, when our department decided to offer interpretations of "outside" studies done on patients admitted to our facility (when specifically requested by clinicians), we found it difficult to convince our radiologists that the studies were just as important as those done at our institution, because they involved patients our institution was currently seeing. In an interesting naturally occurring experiment, one group of radiologists decided to isolate the outside studies by capturing them in a separate worklist while another decided they would intermix them with all of their other cases. In all other respects, the overall performance of the two groups was comparable, but interpretation of the outside studies from a separate worklist consistently underperformed.

We have encountered this principle before: *The more subdivided the work, the worse the overall efficiency.* Imagine if, when you went to a grocery store, you had to stand in different checkout lines to buy produce, meat, dairy, dry goods, etc. It would be virtually impossible for the store to match the capacity of each individual line to the demand, and overall wait times would increase. At the same time, many customers would find themselves waiting in more than one line. Does this sound familiar? Of course it does! In radiology, a patient having both a knee MRI and a chest X-ray in a single visit may receive reports from two different radiologists, possibly at different times. There are certainly valid reasons for why this might happen—that is, for dividing the interpretation work into different lists. For instance, the radiologist who interpreted the chest X-ray may not be qualified to interpret the MRI of the knee. However, to the extent that the number of worklists can be reduced, efficiency will improve.

Regardless of how the worklists are designed, all examinations must be included on one worklist or another. We believe a case should not appear on more than one (with the exception below) because, if it does, responsibility for the case becomes ambiguous. If the same examination appears on more than one worklist, it is human nature to assume that someone else will deal with it.

However, the worklist designation might have to change with the time of day or the day of the week. For example, "after-hours" cases may need to be interpreted by emergency radiologists or "nighthawks." Therefore, an ideal system would be able to account for the possibility that after a certain hour, cases meeting appropriate criteria would appear on a "night cover" or "emergency" worklist.

9.3.1   Interpretation Priorities

In what order should the worklist present cases to the radiologist? In an ideal world, the speed with which an examination is interpreted would be based on the clinical urgency of the condition. In reality, this is extremely difficult to accomplish, partly because the urgency of the examination is often unknown until after it has been interpreted. As a matter of practicality, most radiology departments allow the requesting clinician to specify the priority in some way. Here, "priority" could refer either to obtaining the images or to producing a report. These priorities are sometimes the same, but not always. For instance, obtaining the images might be a high priority if an examination is requested to document a patient's condition at the time of discharge from the hospital, but the report itself may be less pressing. With our order entry system, clinicians cannot make the distinction between "perform" priority and "read" priority, although some systems might have this capability.

One interesting publication reported on a trial in which technologists were asked to assign an interpretation priority at the completion of each case, selecting one of nine tightly defined "read priorities." The authors believed that the radiologists were able to respond to these priorities because the turnaround time for the report was more or less in the order of priority. However, there was no statistical difference between several of the categories, suggesting that the radiologists had only a limited repertoire of responses, whatever the designated priority was (we will discuss priorities and radiologists' work habits later in this chapter) [4]. If there is only a limited repertoire of possible responses, there may be a practical ceiling for the number of distinctly different examination priorities a department can support.

How many different priorities do we think we need? Examinations that might be assigned priorities other than "routine" include:

- Patients with acute and potentially severe problems
- Inpatients
- Patients in the emergency department or in other urgent care facilities
- Patients in ICUs
- Patients undergoing procedures (such as surgery) that cannot be completed without imaging
- Patients whose next step (doctor visit, discharge) is dependent upon imaging
- VIP patients
- Patients from facilities for which there are specific contractual obligations. This is an increasingly important category as competition for medical business has

increased. To gain referrals from a new source, marketing or contracting arms of a department or institution might make assurances that service will be provided within certain time frames.

Although it might be morally objectionable to some, it is also conceivable that a special priority status might be considered for more lucrative lines of work—for example, MRI vs. plain radiography. By way of justification, we point out that there are many societal precedents for this type of prioritization, including expedited passport issuance and expedited citizenship processing, to say nothing of expedited aircraft boarding.

In addition, there may be some types of examinations for which slower than usual handling might be tolerated. Examples include:

- Research cases
- Screening examinations in which no pathology is expected
- Cases that are highly specialized and require the attention of a particular individual

The longer the list of priorities becomes, the harder it is to make the distinctions meaningful. Psychological studies have shown that humans can effectively consider (at best) only about three or four variables in their decision-making [5, 6]—meaning that juggling a longer list of priorities can be practically impossible.

In addition, the number of possible priorities can easily exceed the number of available workflows to respond in a meaningful way, by which we mean a predictable time. Most clinical needs are defined in terms of time, not priority. We doubt very much that an ICU doctor would be satisfied to learn that his or her cases are priority 3 out of a possible 9 without knowing how long they will actually take. Contracts for interpretation services are usually written with a guaranteed turn-around time. Priority is irrelevant unless it is supported by an on-time service guarantee.

Finally, the meaning of a priority can be ambiguous. For instance, if "same day" is an option, is it a request or a guarantee? In the old days of paper requests, a handwritten "today please" was clearly a request. However, when your order entry system offers a selectable priority of "today" it sounds like a service offered by the department. Is it possible that the radiology department understands it as a request while the referring clinical believes it to be a service guarantee? Is the department even able to perform and interpret the examination the same day it is requested? If so, how late in the day will it accept an order for same-day service? Does "same day" suggest that the final report will be available that day, or only that the imaging will be done? How you define your priorities gives you an opportunity to look especially effective or especially ineffective based on your ability to meet your definitions.

Keep It Real!

Prioritizing comes with responsibilities, and responsibilities come with liabilities. The public (and the courts) might reasonably expect that cases designated "urgent" will be handled promptly. This is difficult enough when the designation is made by the clinician at the time of ordering. The emergence of artificial intelligence has added another convolution. Many AI vendors claim that their products can prioritize radiology examinations based on the features their algorithms detect in the images. An imaging study, even before it is presented to the radiologists' eyes, can be sent to a wonderfully smart neural network, which can find certain abnormalities requiring immediate attention (stroke, aneurism, pleural fluid), bumping the study to the top of the radiologist worklist.

This sounds great, but what does it mean in practice? Does the AI priority supersede other top priorities? What happens if the algorithm fails? It is unlikely that the AI vendor will be held liable for a clinical error, even if the error is based on the incorrect results from the AI. This creates a rather difficult situation in which a radiologist may be responsible for something before even looking at the images.

We do not yet know the solution to this dilemma. For now, we recommend each department establish a small, clearly defined set of priorities with equally clearly defined performance expectations.

With all of these issues in mind, we recommend the following:

– Assume that the clinician will regard all priorities in the order entry system as a service commitment.
– Keep the number of available priorities to a minimum.
– Offer only those you can manage, and those for which you can support service expectations.

9.4   Service Expectations

Our discussion of priorities inevitably leads to consideration of service guarantees. These generally take the form of a turnaround assurance (e.g.: "95% of cases will have final reports available within 6 h of completion") or a similar service guarantee (e.g.: if the images are completed by noon, a final report will be available by 5 PM in 95% of cases). Consultants are fond of quoting national benchmarks for turnaround times. These are often expressed as median performance at various percentiles and can be derived from nothing more reliable than survey data. However, the seemingly simple benchmarks conceal a world of complexity. Unfortunately, you need to delve into this complexity if you hope to be able to manage it.

Like priority types, service guarantees can grow unwieldy fairly quickly. For example, do the guarantees apply 24 h a day, 7 days a week? Or do they apply only to working hours (e.g., Monday to Friday, 8 to 5)? Does each weekday require two reporting standards or three (that is, for cases done from 8 to 5, 5 to 11, 11 to 8 AM)? What about weekends? Holidays? Are all modalities and patients covered or are some exempted? If the latter, what reporting standards should apply to the "exempt" examinations?

In the extreme case, one can imagine a nightmarish table of priorities with three shifts on workdays, three shifts on weekends, and three shifts on holidays. Applying this to each of the ten clinical contexts listed above would result in 90 different service expectations! The authors are not aware of any radiology department in the world that can manage such complexities!

9.4.1   STAT Examinations: A Special Case

"STAT" is an anomaly among priorities. All other categories of service can be created at the discretion of the individual radiology departments—or, in many cases, their parent institutions. However, the Joint Commission (an independent nonprofit organization that accredits healthcare organizations and programs in the United States) specifies that there must be a category called STAT, although it does not specify what the performance expectations for STAT should be.

In our view, the term STAT has an accepted meaning that transcends the Joint Commission. The derivation of the word is from the Latin "statim," which means "immediately." Anyone who has watched medical shows on television has probably heard the word used in conjunction with a medical emergency, usually spoken urgently in an anxious, demanding tone. Regardless of what the Joint Commission requires, a radiology department that does not adhere to some form of "immediate" exposes itself to medicolegal risk if a delay results in harm to a patient.

This raises a number of challenges. First, doing something "immediately" is utterly disruptive. All other activities are displaced. Scheduled patients are delayed. Equipment is held open, awaiting the arrival of the "STAT" patient. The radiologist must abandon what he or she is doing and quickly switch to another activity, one with different preconditions and questions. In short, provision of this service degrades the efficiency of the department.

There is another problem. Designating an examination as "STAT" is done at the discretion of clinicians who may or may not be aware of (or care about) the impact on radiology department operations or on other patients. We have seen many examples of what we consider to be inappropriate "STAT" examinations. Among the most bizarre were orders for examinations such as "STAT, tomorrow, at 8 AM." The prescience required to predict that a medical emergency will occur tomorrow, at 8 AM, is awe-inspiring! The motivations behind such inappropriate requests may be selfish ones, such as clinician convenience, but often they seem to represent a sincere effort to expedite the patient's care.

The problem with this sort of "priority inflation" is that it can quickly become unmanageable, potentially delaying the care of a patient with a truly life-threatening emergency. A few years ago, we were faced with a "STAT crisis": STAT requests for certain types of imaging (CT) exceeded 50% of the total number of all CT requests! The number was so large it was literally impossible to prioritize the day's work, and the technical staff simply gave up. STAT examinations were treated in exactly the same way as routine requests. Something had to be done.

We decided to adopt a somewhat drastic approach. We defined a STAT examination as an examination that could not wait for hospital transport (Fig. 9.7). Therefore, if a medical team thought STAT imaging was necessary, they would have to transport the patient themselves, immediately. Our thinking was that, since providing a "STAT" service came with certain costs for the radiology department (and other patients), those ordering the examination would have to share in the cost by committing themselves to transport the patient. In exchange, the radiology department agreed that it would immediately accept all such STATs and would not make the patient (or the transporting team of nurses and physicians) wait.

Because of the dire situation leading to our suggesting this initiative, the hospital administration agreed to support it. Accordingly, after a series of meetings was held to explain it to physicians, nurses, and house officers, the new policy was implemented [7].

Starting November 9th 2010
STAT means NOW !

EMERGENCY USE ONLY
MISUSE OR ABUSE OF THIS
EQUIPMENT WILL RESULT
IN DISCIPLINARY ACTION
LIVES MAY DEPEND ON IT
BEING READY FOR USE IN
AN EMERGENCY

- If it can wait an hour, it is not STAT.
  - Examples
    - Sudden patient deterioration
    - In midst of procedure that requires imaging to complete
- STAT examinations deserve STAT reports
- Medical staff **must**
  - Call Radiology
  - Explain themselves
  - Be prepared to transport the patient immediately
  - If it can wait for patient transport, it is not STAT.

Fig. 9.7 Our attempt to manage the STAT crisis. This informational graphic emphasizes that the radiology department will not recognize an examination as STAT unless the clinical team is prepared to transport the patients themselves, without waiting for hospital transport

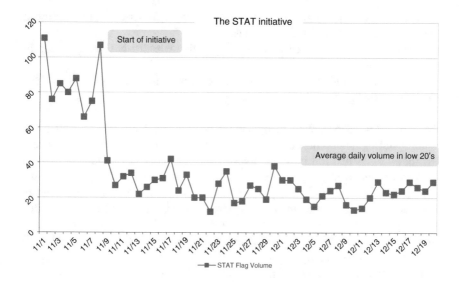

Fig. 9.8 We observed an immediate and striking decline in the daily number of STAT requests after implementing the new policy. The improved numbers have been sustained over the long term

The effect was both dramatic and gratifying!

Figure 9.8 shows a precipitous decline in the number of daily STAT requests, to a very manageable level of approximately 20 per day (including portable chest X-rays). This benefit was sustained for years, with no further education or scolding of clinicians needed. The key to the success of the initiative was the check it placed on clinicians' being able to order a STAT examination by a simple mouse-click, and the requirement that the clinicians transport the patient. Although it undoubtedly put a burden on the clinicians, the new "price" of ordering a STAT exam seemed to eliminate frivolous or self-serving requests. In our opinion, the effort was well worth it to protect the integrity of the STAT examination. Recently, institutional installation of a new EHR bypassed the direct personal contact required to order a STAT service, and again made it possible to select a STAT priority by a simple click of a mouse. Predictably, and depressingly, our numbers have now returned to their previous levels.

9.5 Priority and Radiologist Work Habits

If we view the question of priorities from the perspective of how they are implemented, we see three basic modes for organizing a day's work:

1. *Interruptive*: The radiologist stops what he or she is doing to address a specific case. We might see this happen if a clinician walks into a reading room and asks a radiologist to review a case. This is also the mode of operation of the STAT

case, in which a radiologist must step away from his or her current workflow to call up a recently completed urgent case.

2. *Prioritized*: A case is added to a currently active worklist but placed ahead of other cases on the list.

3. *Routine*: A case is added to a currently active worklist in the order it was received (a default "first in, first out" priority).

Most radiology departments recognize the need to provide continuous coverage (including during lunchtime, conferences, evenings, and probably nights and weekends) for all cases that fall into the "interruptive" category. If the number of such cases can be managed to the extent that there is adequate staffing to meet the demand, rapid turnaround is likely assured. However, it is important to recognize that, by its very nature, the "interruptive" workflow carries an efficiency penalty. Psychologists have known this for decades. The time lost in switching from one task to another appears to stem from having to reset one's mental controls (for the radiologist, this means switching the mental settings from "what was I looking for?" to "what am I looking for now" [8]). The difficulty in doing so increases with the complexity of the task involved. For this reason, practices should make every attempt to minimize the number of interruptions.

In contrast, rapid turnaround is not assured with the prioritized worklist. Even if continuous coverage is possible, the turnaround will depend on the number cases of similar or higher priority ahead of the case in question.

Radiologists exhibit the same human activity pattern we first encountered in Chap. 3. Figure 9.9 shows workstation usage (as measured by "dictation events" per every 6 min) among a group of chest radiologists. Notice the familiar "Asian camel" form with peaks at 10 AM and 2 PM. This pattern of activity will affect the timeliness of reporting for both routine and prioritized cases. In our institution, interruptive cases (such as STAT) are handled by a separate workflow with continuous coverage, which results in much more even performance over the course of the day.

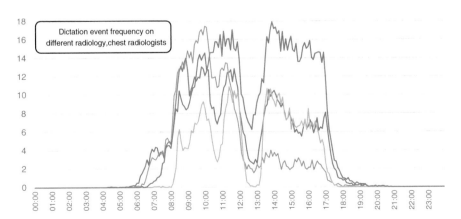

Fig. 9.9 Number of dictation events as a function of time of day among a group of chest radiologists. Each line represents the activity at a single workstation. Note the typical dual peaks with a break for lunch. Because the chart represents dictation events, it gives equal weight to plain films and CT scans, the major components of the radiologists' workload

A similar pattern is observed for neuroradiologists, who primarily interpret MRI (Fig. 9.10).

The addition of a second shift can produce a third hump on the camel, as demonstrated by our abdominal division (Fig. 9.11).

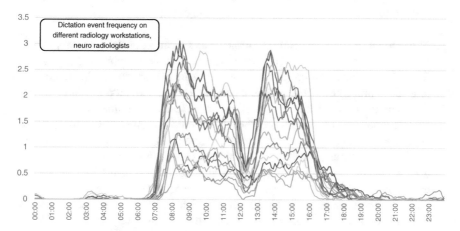

Fig. 9.10 Number of dictation events for a neuroradiology practice that mostly interprets MRI scans. Note that the pattern is the same as for the chest radiologists but the absolute number of dictation events is much smaller, reflecting the fact that the neuroradiologists interpret MRI and CT and do not need to manage a high volume of plain radiographs

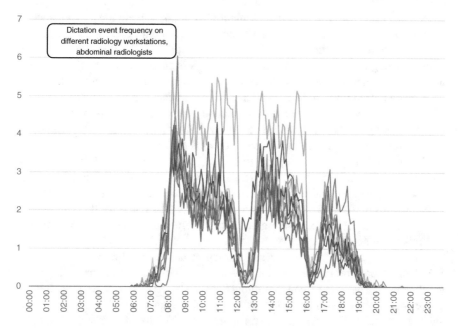

Fig. 9.11 Dictation events when a second shift is added. Note that there is a dip around the dinner hour (approximately 18:00), and that the overall productivity for the third shift is lower than during the daytime hours

9.5.1 Timeliness

Having established the priorities, the next step is to develop realistic and sustainable performance expectations.

Radiology departments' timeliness is commonly judged on the following parameters (therefore, they should judge themselves on the same):

1. The amount of time between performance and creation of a preliminary report: *complete-to-preliminary* (CtoP) time. The preliminary report might take the form of a trainee dictation (in academic departments) or it might be in the form of a "brief procedure" note or verbal communication about a procedure.
2. The amount of time between preliminary (if any) and final signed report: *preliminary-to-final* (PtoF) time. The latter should be completed as soon as possible as clinicians are generally uncomfortable taking action based on preliminary reports, knowing that they are subject to change. Further, if they do change, a long lag time can present significant communication difficulties as well as embarrassment and even negative health consequences. Oftentimes, we also compute *complete-to-final* (CtoF) time, which reflects the entire "radiology interpretation" interval (and can be translated into PtoF after subtracting CtoP).

Careful examination of these "simple" metrics can reveal hidden (and useful!) information.

For instance, let us examine the complete-to-preliminary (CtoP) interval in our hospital. Figure 9.12 illustrates mean times from completion to preliminary interpretation. This is the kind of data that might be used to evaluate the performance of individual or groups of radiologists. The figure demonstrates that the great majority of examinations are interpreted within 1 h of completion. Whether this is a good thing is a judgment we will leave to others. (This is an amoral book, after all!) We include it here not because of what it shows but because of what it conceals.

A much more informative presentation of similar data can be found in Fig. 9.13, which shows how the *complete-to-final* interval varies over a 24-h period as a function of the time the examination was completed. As in Fig. 9.12, the different color lines represent different clinical divisions or work groups.

To understand what the graph is telling us, begin on the very left (midnight). Note that, from midnight until approximately 8 AM, for most divisions, the time between performance and interpretation decreases in a more or less linear fashion. Examinations performed in each passing hour will wait 1 h less for their interpretation to be finalized. In fact, looking at the right-hand side of the chart, one can see that this trend actually begins in the afternoon, at approximately 18:00 h (6 PM). This hourly decline is due to the fact that cases are not read between 6 PM and 8 AM and, therefore, the earlier that they are done within that time period, the longer they wait. The linear trend is nothing but the unread exams "aging" with time. There is only one exception: Note that, for one of the divisions (ER), the time interval is the same at all times of the day, running generally between 1 and 2 h. This is because the emergency division is staffed more or less 24 h a day.

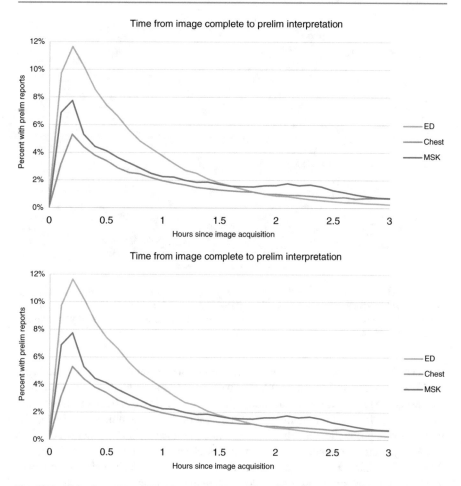

Fig. 9.12 Time from completing the examination to the first preliminary report, in hours. Note that, for the three divisions considered (ED, MSK, chest), the peak reporting time is the same, approximately 0.2–0.3 h. However, the highest ED curve *means that more cases will be read during this time overall, and fewer will be left for later hours*

The fact that the time interval falls by 1 h for each hour that passes suggests that overnight cases are finalized very quickly the following morning. This can probably be ascribed to the rapid review and approval of previously dictated reports (done by trainees, as in our institution, or by teleradiology services in others).

Note also that, for the thoracic and musculoskeletal divisions, another rapid decline occurs between 2 PM (14:00) and 5 PM (17:00). This reflects an effort to complete the day's work so the radiologist can go home. To this end, the end-of-the-day push likely excludes trainees from the workflow while minimizing discussion and consultation.

Though the rate at which imaging studies are produced generally increases during the day, all of the curves are relatively flat for a period during the first part of the day,

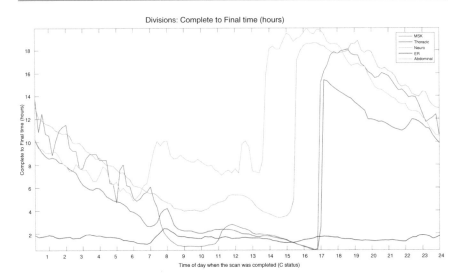

Fig. 9.13 The time it takes to produce the final report for studies completed at different hours of the day. The horizontal axis represents a 24-h period, from midnight to midnight. The vertical axis shows CtoF in hours. Studies interpreted by five different divisions are represented by the five differently colored lines

suggesting that the rate of interpretation is equal to the rate of performance. This could, we suppose, indicate miraculously balanced staffing in all divisions. However, we suspect the real reason is that radiologists adjust their work habits to maintain a steady state. Note that the relatively flat segment of the curve indicates *only* that the rate of image production equals the rate of interpretation. If this segment is close to "0," interpretation is consistently rapid; if it is elevated, the reports are consistently delayed. The horizontal part of the curve thus represents each division's comfort level with the backlog of cases to be done. Note that the emergency (purple), musculoskeletal (blue), and thoracic (orange) divisions achieve a relatively short interval (2 h or less), whereas the abdominal and neuroradiology groups tolerate longer times.

Why don't the curves ever reach "0"? In the steady state (that is, when number of cases done is equal to the number of cases interpreted), the height of the horizontal segment indicates the average amount of time it takes the radiologists to "deal with" a case. This is certainly not the same as the time spent actually reviewing the case and dictating a report. Rather, it must represent a combination of those activities and time lost in hand-to-hand transfers (as in the case of trainee dictation) and how large a backlog the radiologists are comfortable with seeing.

One more feature of importance can be gleaned from this chart. At various points in the afternoon, each of the curves has a vertical segment. This tells us that cases completed during these times are being left for the next day. Note the variability. The red and blue curves become vertical at 17:00 h (5 PM). The green curve (abdominal) becomes vertical at 3 PM while the yellow curve shows that, for this division, the last case of the day is finalized sometime between 1 and 2 PM. In this group of radiologists, the "quitting times" are related to how large a backlog the radiologists are willing to accept. Those groups that take longer to handle each case are also likely to stop accepting new cases earlier. For thoracic and MSK, the amount of time needed to handle a typical case is generally less than 2 h, trending even lower near the end of the afternoon and dropping to almost 0 as the quitting time of 5 PM approaches. Thus, it is possible for these groups to accept new cases almost up to the end of the workday. However, for neuroradiology, the typical processing time is so slow—8 h—that the radiologists have to stop accepting new cases by 1 PM in order to finish at a reasonable hour.

This is a perfect example of how divisional and personal culture can really eat departmental strategy for breakfast. In fact, it also eats it for lunch, and especially for dinner. This is also a good illustration of how pattern analysis can be much more instructive than averages. The patterns in Fig. 9.13 tell us which group does the job and for how long. They do *not* tell us about average or individual productivity, a subject we will consider shortly.

Radiologists reading these words may let out an inward or even audible groan. Aren't accuracy, diagnostic acumen, and clinical insight what it is all about? Aren't those the things on which radiologists pride themselves the most?

Perhaps. Unfortunately, accuracy is even more difficult to measure, and it could take days, months, or even years to properly do so. Turnaround time, in contrast, is seductively simple and immediate. It is likely that many management efforts focus on speed rather than on accuracy because speed is so much easier to measure.[1]

Finally, it is important to understand that CtoF—a major performance metric for radiologists—can be impacted by the lack of uniformity in the pace of image acquisition and the variations in delivery time discussed in previous chapters. Consider, at least, the following:

1. Surges in image acquisition volume, driven by everything from patient arrival patterns to technologists' meal breaks and work habits, can extend CtoF. Consider Fig. 9.14, showing MRI scanner utilization in two different radiology depart-

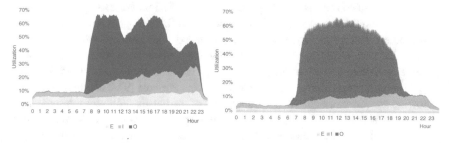

Fig. 9.14 MRI utilization at two large radiology departments. Three categories of patients are shown for each department: "E" (emergency), "I" (inpatients), and "O" (outpatients). Note the very substantial differences in utilization as a function of time of day. In department #1, shown on the left in blue, emergency patients (lightest shade) are relatively uniformly distributed throughout the day. Inpatients (intermediate color) are slightly less uniform, tending to increase over the course of the day. Outpatients, on the other hand, are very irregularly distributed, with several surges of activity throughout the day and lulls that appear to correspond to the lunch and dinner hours. In department #2 (green), scan productivity is much more uniform throughout the day

---

[1] We told you this was an amoral book!

ments. The MRI utilization on the left is not uniform, resulting in surges of new studies after periods of relative inactivity; the utilization on the right is load balancing, thus providing radiologists with a more steady stream of tasks. Maintaining consistent CtoF intervals is extremely difficult when there are surges in activity. As discussed earlier in the context of equipment use in the emergency department, there must be considerable reserve capacity to accommodate surges in demand if you want to keep wait times within certain limits.

2. Delays in image delivery: To be fair to the radiologist, one should probably start counting from the time the images become available for interpretation in PACS. CtoF includes the time to PACS (TTP), which makes it more a mixture of transmission and interpretation times.

In our institution, the time it takes for an imaging study to arrive at the PACS (TTP) is generally consistent, though not negligible, especially if we are trying to adhere to a standard of performance with a very quick turnaround time. As outlined in the previous chapter, we measure TTP as the interval of time between completion of the examination and when the full study is available for interpretation on the workstation. In our system TTP is consistently less than 40 min. Outliers mostly represent errors on the part of the technologist. As illustrated by the completion to reporting times in Fig. 9.12, a 40-min transmission time can represent either a significant or a negligible fraction of the total time, depending on the environment. In some cases, such as teleradiology, where image delivery can be slow, and where a premium is often placed on interpretation speed, the TTP can be critically important.

9.5.2   How Can Timeliness Be Improved?

There are two approaches to this problem, each of which merits consideration: workflow design and individual productivity.

There is little consensus about optimal workflow design. For example, how many radiologists should be co-located? In years gone by, all radiologists worked in a single central interpretation facility, sometimes endearingly described as "the pit." It now appears that such an arrangement impairs efficiency. Some have gone to the opposite extreme, believing that each radiologist should work alone, isolated in an office or cubicle somewhere. Others feel that small clusters are best [9]. This then raises the following question: Should all of the members of the cluster represent the same sub-specialty or should they be organized into multispecialty teams? To the best of our knowledge, none of these questions has been sufficiently addressed in the literature.

Another interesting approach to workflow redesign involves separating "image-interpretative" work from "non-image-interpretive" work. The authors of a 2017 study describing this approach did not specify exactly how they did this. However, based on surveys of radiologists before and after the "intervention," they claim that the interpretive work was improved by removal of the non-interpretive work. Perceptions of the effort required, stress, quality, training, and all other activities that were previously interrupted by non-interpretive activities had improved [10].

Yet another approach stems from the observation that individuals interpret different types of studies at different rates. Accordingly, worklists can be designed to assign studies to the radiologists who interpret that type of study most quickly [11]. Though one can achieve significant time savings with this approach, in our minds it raises concerns about job satisfaction, training needs, and sustained accuracy.

As was the case for the technologist work, for each case there is both pre-interpretation work (information gathering about the case) and post-interpretation work (report creation, editing, and communication). Unfortunately, because the same individual must learn the clinical context, interpret the images, and create the report, there is little opportunity for steps to be taken in parallel. At one time, report creation was completed with the aid of a transcriptionist while the radiologist moved on to the next case. This did permit some of the work to proceed in parallel. However, progress in speech recognition technology has drastically reduced the amount of time needed to create a report and most departments have found that the process of handing the report off to a transcriptionist and getting it back for editing and signature actually increases the time to finalization.

The electronic health record has resulted in increased access to clinical information. Though this increased access undoubtedly can improve the relevance and accuracy of reports, it also implies an obligation to review a potentially considerable amount of information. Thus, paradoxically, the availability of the records probably slows the work process by increasing the amount of time spent on pre-interpretation work.

Radiologists have become increasingly subspecialized. What a single physician used to do 100 years ago is now divided among an increasing number of specialized individuals. This can result in the individuals bringing greater expertise to bear on the interpretation but, just as in other parts of the workflow, separating a series of task into multiple queues degrades efficiency. The potential need for multiple radiologists also leads to a problem in synchronizing all the moving parts. Mismatches between staffing and demand are almost inevitable.

Keep It Real!

Though a mostly outdated practice, producing a report with the aid of a transcriptionist is a good illustration of how involving multiple individuals can add a synchronization "overhead." In one common scenario, the radiologist would record a dictation, the transcriptionist would type the report while playing back the recording, and the radiologist would review the typed report and sign off on it. Since the transcription was done off-line, several hours could easily pass between the original recording of the report and the radiologist review and signature. As a result, the radiologist's primary concern was not so much with transcription errors as with remembering what this case was about to begin with (sometimes it was even necessary to reopen it to refresh one's memory). Even when that was not required, it was necessary to synchronize the radiologist's availability (for both interpretation and signature) with the transcriptionist's availability. It is easy to see how nights, weekends, and vacations could become problematic!

Advanced image reconstructions, image post-processing of any nature, teleradiology, and even AI (when it takes too long) can introduce the same type of synchronization problems.

Creation of a diagnostic report is the least automated step in the radiology work-flow—at least for now. Here, the impact of machine learning has yet to be felt in any significant way, and reports depend completely on human interaction with the images. The alacrity and accuracy of this step depend on the radiologist's availability, expertise, and, in some cases, will to get the job done.

The timeliness of reporting is a function of three factors:

– The number of radiologists available
– The rate at which the radiologists interpret the studies (varying from radiologist to radiologist as well as from study to study)
– Radiologists' work habits

If the available radiologists interpret studies more slowly than the technologists produce them, a backlog will appear and continue to grow. If they interpret faster than the technologists, they often end up working intermittently, allowing cases to accumulate between interpretation sessions. Radiologists are accustomed to arriving at their workstation to find a list of examinations waiting to be interpreted. This is so commonplace that most may not perceive it as a bottleneck, but it is. The accumulating cases represent a pinch point. In a perfectly matched workflow, the interpretation would follow seamlessly upon completion of the images (Fig. 9.15).

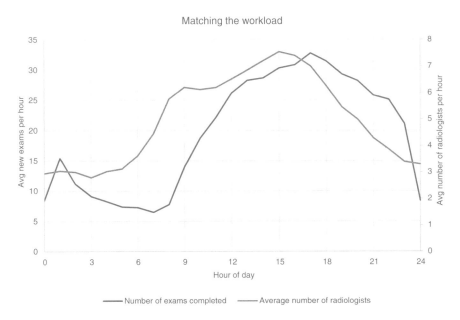

Fig. 9.15 Matching the workload in ED. To maintain a constant reading speed, the number of radiologists reading ED cases must increase proportionally with the number of cases to be read. Note also that the increase in radiologist count precedes the increase in the exam count, thus preventing backlogs

However, because we do not live in a perfect world, it is almost inevitable that either cases will wait for the radiologist or the radiologist will wait for cases.

Whether or not it is necessary to match interpretative capacity to image production at all times very much depends on value judgements about the need for timeliness. In many departments, these value judgements are not made explicitly. Even if they were, they might not have the full support of the radiologists. To a major extent, they are driven by the expectations of other clinicians, administrators, and patients, and these expectations are themselves a moving target. As all of healthcare has been subject to growing cost-consciousness, expectations for timeliness have gotten shorter and shorter.

Keep It Real!
Different radiologists can exhibit completely different work patterns. For example, all radiologists recognize that there are "slow readers" and "fast readers," and a significant part of the radiologist shift scheduling exercise goes into providing a good mix of both to keep things on time. How many times have you tried to push someone work faster and their only reply was, "I cannot sacrifice quality for speed"? In short, "service priority" does not meld easily with human nature.

9.5.3 Radiologist Mindfulness

Just as with the technologists, it can be helpful to keep radiologists informed about their "on-time" status. While they can derive this information from a review of the worklist(s), doing so requires that the radiologist actually be logged on to a workstation. The situation is further complicated by the fact that work is often divided into more than one worklist, making it difficult to obtain a global picture of the pending work. We have found it helpful to create a number of monitors that show the cases currently awaiting interpretation (Fig. 9.16). These large-format screens are placed in the reading areas and display examinations awaiting review by type.

Radiologists frequently refer to these displays during the course of their workday. Awareness of the pending work clearly alters practice patterns.

9.6 Radiologist Productivity

In the United States, all physician productivity (including for radiologists) is measured using relative value units (RVUs). Other countries have their own versions of this type of measure, or have developed different scoring systems [12, 13].

The American RVU for clinicians was created as the result of a large study authorized by Congress in 1989 and conducted jointly by researchers at Harvard

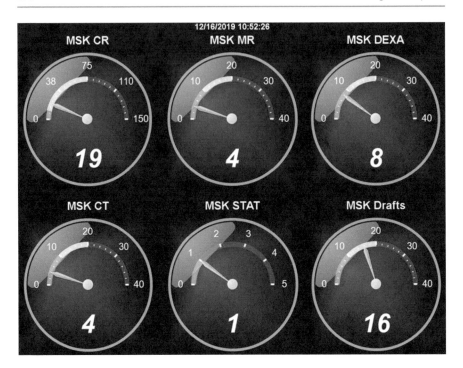

Fig. 9.16 A typical monitor showing the number of cases awaiting a radiologist's attention in our musculoskeletal division. The cases are organized by modality (CR, MR, DEXA, CT), except for "STAT" examinations, which are specifically called out, and "drafts," reports created by trainees but not yet reviewed by attending physicians

and by the AMA. In 1992, Medicare adopted the results of the study as a payment mechanism, which has been updated annually since then. Three components are included:

– Physician work (51%)
– Practice expense (45%)
– Professional liability (4%)

Note that the RVU value includes factors in addition to physician time. The RVU system was extended to radiology based on the results of a survey conducted by the American College of Radiology and the Health Care Financing Administration of the United States Government [14]. No effort was made to determine the actual value of a service—only its value relative to a plain-film (X-ray) examination of the chest. The RVU scale does not capture all of the activities that make up radiologists' contribution to healthcare, attending clinical conferences, teaching, and research. It does not even determine actual income, since the relative value unit must be converted to a payment through the application of a conversion factor that accounts for geographic variation. This is done by the government on a regional basis, and by insurance companies by contract.

Both academic [15] and community radiologists [16] have published benchmarks for the number of RVUs. These benchmarks have obvious shortcomings. In addition to the incomplete representation of the radiologist's role, some imaging studies are overvalued and others undervalued. For example, in proportion to the actual time spent, CT and MRI receive substantially more RVU "credit" than X-ray examinations. An MRI of the knee receives 1.35 RVUs without contrast or 2.15 with contrast. To obtain an equal amount of reimbursement a radiologist would have to interpret between 7 and 12 three-view plain-film examinations of the knee (0.18 RVUs each).

An interesting paper from Brazil reported the creation of an RVU system for CT interpretation. Here, the data was derived from actual time measurements, not from survey data. The authors defined "reporting time" as the difference between when the radiologist first accessed the imaging study and when the final report was signed, excluding cases in which the radiologist needed to do post-processing. The paper showed that interpretation times for CT scans ranged from 5.6 min (sinus examination) to 23.4 min (upper abdominal examination). When the authors compared their local RVU system to the US system, they found *no correlation*. They concluded that the US system significantly underestimated the time required for many exams [17].

Other alternative scoring systems have been designed to credit radiologists for the time they spend on nonclinical work, including teaching. These efforts appear to have grown out of radiologists' frustration that they are being "judged" only by their RVU output. Perhaps it is not surprising that these alternative measures tend to come from departments in which reimbursement is not based on RVUs (departments in Canada, for example) [18].

For the typical radiology department with no alternative sources of income, physician income derives from patient, insurance, and/or government payments, which in the United States are based on RVU productivity. The connection may be direct— i.e., a percentage of what the physician bills (sometimes crudely described as "eat what you kill"). Alternatively, patient revenues (still derived from RVU productivity) may be pooled and distributed among radiologists according to various formulas.

When radiologists do not see a direct relationship between their productivity and their income, questions of who should do what and when can become highly problematic. Internal policies, personal egos, confusing scheduling with ill-defined responsibilities, concepts of work-equity (sometimes ill informed), and financial incentives all conspire to make this a fraught issue. For example, an important source of conflict is the inherent tension between timeliness and accuracy. Because the risk for error can increase when less time is allowed for report creation, there may be a threshold for volume of work above which accuracy declines. This issue is complicated, though, by the fact that some radiologists routinely work faster than others, producing more reports with equivalent or even higher accuracy. We will discuss this issue in greater detail below.

Too rapid reporting may be problematic not only because work done in haste is error-prone, but also because additional information becomes available as time passes. This might include findings on other imaging studies, consultations with other radiologists and clinicians, more sophisticated clinical notes, and results of other types of testing. Is it better to create a rapid initial impression of the imaging or to accumulate all of the relevant data so you can compose a complete, comprehensive report? Some years ago, an extremely senior radiologist of our acquaintance represented an extreme outlier on the side of the complete and comprehensive report. In his practice, all reports remained preliminary until an autopsy had been performed! Obviously, it would not be possible to operate an entire radiology department like this.

Consider another slightly less extreme approach to the trade-off between timeliness and accuracy. If one interpretation is good, are two interpretations better? Detection of subtle findings can be highly subjective. The probability that they will be noticed depends upon the prior probability of disease (and thus radiologist expectations), observer experience, state of mind, and fatigue. As one expert put it, "All observers, no matter how skilled, periodically miss significant findings. It appears that this is an immutable phenomenon that ensures that every radiologist, even the most expert in the field, occasionally fails to see an abnormality that, in retrospect, is evident on an image" [19]. A second image review can improve lesion detection (sensitivity) in screening mammograms [20]. There is little doubt that similar conclusions would be reached for all imaging modalities; this has been one of the major motivations for introducing "complementary" AI image interpretation. Though large-scale clinical implementations of AI have yet to be created, when they are, they will surely improve accuracy, albeit at the cost of increased time.

The pressure not to miss anything is compounded by the medicolegal system, which does not recognize the concept of permissible error. If an abnormality "in retrospect is evident on an image," an expert witness can usually be found to testify that he or she would not have missed the finding. Consequently, a lawyer can argue that the error falls below the standard of care. This type of punitive approach encourages radiologists to take as long as necessary and seek as much assistance as possible to produce reports as close to perfect as they can (similar to our senior colleague who waited for autopsy).

On the other hand, powerful forces drive radiologists in the opposite direction. There has been a rapid expansion in recent years in the number of CT and MRI studies performed, as well as an increase in the number of images in each study (1300% for CT and 540% for MRI over a 12-year period). Radiologists have seen a sustained increase in the amount of work they are required to do [21]. In one study, the average radiologist would have to interpret one image every 3–4 s in an 8-h workday to meet workload demands [22].

The impact of this trend varies greatly with location. In the United States, radiologists in a 75th-percentile practice performed at least 65% more procedures annually than radiologists in a 25th-percentile practice [21]. The difference can be even more striking abroad. Japan, for example, has the highest number of CT and MRI scanners per capita in the world, and the second largest number of scans per patient (after the United States), but has a relatively small number of radiologists. Consequently, Japanese radiologists' workload is excessive by international standards (Fig. 9.17) and can vary by a factor of four from one region of Japan to another. Because there are simply not enough radiologists to do the work, more than

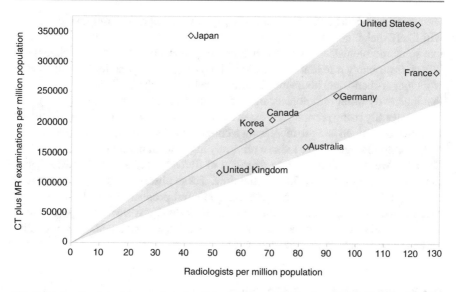

Fig. 9.17 Scatterplot of the number of radiologists versus the number of CT/MRI examinations performed in each country. The line represents a linear regression with zero intercept and the shaded area indicates 95% confidence intervals [23]

half of the scans done in that country are not seen by radiologists at all! This is not good for utilization management. If a patient visits a clinic with a scanner but no radiologist, the patient is more likely to undergo a scan and the scan is less likely to be appropriate. Australia is an outlier in the other direction, with far less work per radiologist [23].

Concurrent with the growing workload over the past 25 years, we have seen a sustained effort by payers to control expenditures by decreasing reimbursements for imaging [24]. Most likely, the increasing RVU productivity per radiologist in more recent years represents, at least in part, an attempt to preserve income in the face of falling reimbursements. Other factors, most notably improved technology, may also play a role.

9.6.1   How Much Is Too Much?

Studies have shown that radiologists who work long days and who see too many cases over the course of a day have a greater chance of making errors, and the potential for error increases later in the shift [25]. Working long days or nights can result in decreased visual accommodation and increased eyestrain. This is especially true for older radiologists but applies across all age groups. Physical fatigue also gets progressively worse over the course of a day. "Decision fatigue" is another form of fatigue often seen in radiology, especially in radiologists working longer shifts and who have inconsistent hours [26]. Malpractice attorneys have been all-too-successful in wielding the "too-many-cases" argument [27].

It also appears to be the case that radiologists who feel rushed or pressed for time will likely make more errors than they would otherwise [28]. That said, it is clear that some radiologists work faster than others ("thoroughbreds" vs. "workhorses") [29]. It is probably true that radiologists who try to push beyond their usual pace or work longer-than-usual hours may be prone to error, but there is little or no evidence that inherently faster radiologists are less accurate than slower ones [29].

The steadily rising productivity expectations combined with an increased demand for rapid turnaround and the increasing technology-driven physical isolation of contemporary radiologists have led to a relatively high rate of burnout in radiology [30]. Recently, we determined that an overload of unread cases affects our emergency radiologists approximately 50% of the time. These observations serve as a sort of red flag, telling us that the pressures for increased productivity and shorter turnaround times may have already gone too far! Unfortunately, we are not yet aware of any completely satisfactory benchmarks to determine when demands for productivity and timeliness have become excessive.

9.6.2   Measuring the Right Thing

We are great believers in the power of data and measurement. However, it can be extremely difficult to measure what is truly important. For example, consultants will often refer to national benchmarks for "average" turnaround times for reports.

An interesting and humane formulation of this issue was reported by Thompson [31], who noted that the time elapsed between detection of an abnormality on mammography and the results of biopsy led to a number of sleepless nights for the patient. Accordingly, his institution (Kaiser Permanente, Colorado) reports a "sleepless nights" metric that spans several medical "silos" (primary care, radiology, surgery). This metric is probably of no financial value but it reflects the value system of the institution in which it originated. Ultimately, the article cautions against a simplistic approach to performance metrics: "National approaches to assessing performance are doomed, at least in the current state, to fail … There are shifts and tasks that must be commoditized, but over-reliance on productivity as a measure is a big mistake and has significant unintended consequences" [31].

9.7   A Final Word: What Is a Radiology Report?

A great deal has been written about what a radiology report should contain and how it should be structured. Most of this concerns the practice of medicine and is therefore beyond the scope of this book. However, it is our belief that the recent and rather rapid transition to electronic health records has made much of it obsolete. For 100 years, more or less, a radiology report was a piece of paper. The American College of Radiology developed standards for the information that should be included in the report based on the expectation that it would be in this form.

Reports are still occasionally printed on paper, but clinicians increasingly view the reports from within an electronic medical record. Here, the "report" is in fact an extract of the electronic health record containing contributions from various sources, only one of which is the narrative produced by the radiologist. Contributing sources may include the name of the individual ordering the examination, the indications provided with the order, the name of the examination being reported, and various pieces of billing information including CPT codes. The report might exist in various forms depending on whether it is viewed from within the electronic record or externally.

When created in such a manner, the content and form of the report are malleable, which naturally raises questions. Should the impression section be first or last? Should the name of the requesting physician be included? Should recommendations be listed separately? Where does the order information belong?

Relatively little research has been done to determine the optimal content and structure from the reader's point of view. This is not a simple matter, as not all readers will agree on what is optimal. However, a relatively large survey of 3610 practitioners revealed that approximately half of report recipients read only the impression section, and nothing else [32]. Most studies show strong clinician preferences for structured reports, and especially for structured reports with images. Readers also prefer clarity about the radiologists' level of confidence.

We are living in a time of rapid progress in machine learning (also known as artificial intelligence). It is clear that this field will have a significant impact on the creation of radiology reports. In fact, and at least for now, medical imaging is the most actively studied subject in the field of deep learning in healthcare.

This has led to intense paranoia among some radiologists, especially those just beginning their careers. Articles with titles such as "The End of Radiology" [33], asserting that interpreting a CT scan is much less complicated than, say, driving a car, have conjured a nightmare vision (at least for radiologists) of obsolescence and unemployment.

In fact, machine learning is already being used for a number of different applications related to image interpretation. Machines are already doing a reasonable job of image segmentation, which is helpful to radiologists in labeling, lesion detection, and measurement. Data mining and classification of findings in radiology reports have been available for years. Business intelligence solutions based on machine learning, such as those described in Chap. 6, are already on the market. We expect that semantic error detection in radiology reports will be commercially available from the speech recognition companies very soon. Note that radiologists would likely view each of the above as a positive step forward.

Machines (or, to be precise, image processing algorithms) are already being trained to identify specific types of imaging pathologies (such as lung nodules or tuberculosis), and can produce automated reports with corresponding key images, measurements, and annotations. Automated processing can outperform humans because of its resilient, mechanical ability to carry out repetitive tasks such as lung nodule detection. Moreover, with sufficient computational optimization, it can almost certainly complete such tasks in much less time than a human radiologist could.

Does this mean that the end of the human radiologist is in sight? We do not believe so. The fact that an algorithm can detect lung nodules does not mean that it can detect pneumothorax, or cardiac disease, or rib fracture. For each finding, the machine requires specific training. Furthermore, accuracy rates derived from training at one site will likely be different at another, or sensitive to changes in hardware and examination parameters [34].

There is a profound danger that machine-generated diagnoses will contradict human reports, especially if they are made subsequent to the reports. During the current "awkward" stage of AI development, methods must be found to reconcile information from machine learning with reports created by radiologists, preferably before the reports are finalized.

Once this has been accomplished, we believe that machine learning will greatly enhance the value of imaging, and the importance of those radiologists who know how to make use of it.

References

1. Glasser O. W. C. Roentgen and the discovery of the Roentgen rays. Am J Roentgenol Radium Ther. 1995;165:437–50.
2. Czuczman G, Pomerantz S, Alkasab T, Huang A. Using a web-based image quality assurance reporting system to improve image quality. Am J Roentgenol. 2013;201(2):361–8.
3. ASRS. Immunity policies. [Online]. https://asrs.arc.nasa.gov/overview/immunity.html.
4. Gaskin CM, Patrie JT, Hanshew MD, Boatman DM, McWey RP. Impact of a reading priority scoring system on the prioritization of examination interpretations. Am J Roentgenol. 2016;206(5):1031–9.
5. Halford GS, Baker R, McCredden JE, Bain JD. How many variables can humans process? Psychol Sci. 2005;16(1):70–6.
6. Iyengar SS, Lepper MR. When choice is demotivating: can one desire too much of a good thing? J Pers Soc Psychol. 2000;79(6):995–1006.
7. Harvey H, Alkasab T, Stingley P, Shore M, Abedi-Tari F, Abujudeh H, Meyersohn M, Zhao J, Pandharipande P, Rosenthal D. Curbing inappropriate usage of STAT imaging at a large academic medical center. J Patient Saf. 2019;15(1):24–9.
8. Rubenstein J, Meyer D, Evans J. Executive control of cognitive processes in task switching. J Exp Psychol. 2001;27(4):763–97.
9. Benitez BFF, Cardoso R, Torres F, Faccin C, Dora J. Systematic layout planning of a radiology reporting area to optimize radiologists' performance. J Digit Imaging. 2018;31:193–200.
10. Lee MH, Schemmel AJ, Pooler BD, Hanley T, Kennedy T, Field A, Wiegmann D, Yu J. Radiology workflow dynamics: how workflow patterns impact radiologist perceptions of workplace satisfaction. Acad Radiol. 2017;24(4):483–7.
11. Wong T, Kaza J, Rasiej M. Effect of analytics-driven worklists on musculoskeletal MRI interpretation times in an academic setting. AJR Am J Roentgenol. 2019;212(5):1091–5.
12. Khan SH, Hedges WP. What is the relation between number of sessions worked and productivity of radiologists—a pilot study? J Digit Imaging. 2016;29:165–74.
13. Brady AP. Measuring Consultant Radiologist workload: method and results from a national survey. Insights Imaging. 2011;2(3):247–60.
14. National Archives and Records Administration. Medicare programs: fee schedules for radiologists' services. Fed Regist. 1989;54:8994–9023.

15. Lu Y, Zhao S, Chu PW, Arenson RL. An update survey of academic radiologists' clinical productivity. J Am Coll Radiol. 2008;5(7):817–26.
16. Monaghan DA, Kassak KM, Ghomrawi HM. Determinants of radiologists' productivity in private group practices in California. J Am Coll Radiol. 2006;3(2):108–14.
17. Dora JTF, Gerchman M, Fogliatto F. Development of a local relative value unit to measure radiologists' computed tomography reporting workload. J Med Imaging Radiat Oncol. 2016;60:714–9.
18. Walsh C, Aquino J, Seely J, Kielar A, Rakhra K, Dennie C, et al. The Ottawa Hospital RADiologist Activity Reporting (RADAR) productivity metric: effects on radiologist productivity. Can Assoc Radiol J. 2018;69(1):71–7.
19. Kopans DB. Double reading. Radiol Clin. 2000;38(4):719–24.
20. Anderson E, Muir B, Walsh JS, Kirkpatirick A. The efficacy of double reading mammograms in breast screening. Clin Radiol. 1994;49(4):248–51.
21. Bhargavan M, Kaye A, Forman H, Sunshine J. Workload of Radiologists in United States in 2006-2007 and trends since 1991-1992. Radiology. 2009;252(2):458–67.
22. McDonald RJ, Schwartz KM, Eckel LJ, Diehn FE, Hunt CH, Bartholmai BJ, Erickson BJ, Kallmes DF. The effects of changes in utilization and technological advancements of cross-sectional imaging on radiologist workload. Acad Radiol. 2015;22(9):1191–8.
23. Kumamaru KK, Machitori A, Koba R, Ijichi S, Nakajima Y, Aoki S. Global and Japanese regional variations in radiologist potential workload for computed tomography and magnetic resonance imaging examinations. Jpn J Radiol. 2018;36(4):273–81.
24. Levin D, Rao VM, Parker L, Frangos A. The sharp reductions in Medicare payments for non-invasive diagnostic imaging in recent years: will they satisfy the federal policymakers? J Am Coll Radiol. 2012;9(9):643–7.
25. Hanna T, Lamoureux C, Krupinski EA, Weber S, Johnson J. Effect of shift, schedule, and volume on interpretive accuracy: a retrospective analysis of 2.9 million radiologic examinations. Radiology. 2018;287(1):205–12.
26. Stec N, Arje A, Moody A, Krupanski E, Tyrrell P. A systematic review of fatigue in radiology: is it a problem? AJR Am J Roentgenol. 2018;210(4):799–806.
27. Berlin L. Liability of interpreting too many radiographs. Am J Roentgenol. 2000;175:17–22.
28. Sokolovskaya E, Shinde T, Ruchman R, Kwak A, Lu S, Shariff Y, Wiggins E, Talangbayan L. The effect of faster reporting speed for imaging studies on the number of misses and interpretation errors: a pilot study. J Am Coll Radiol. 2015;12:683–6.
29. Muroff LR, Berlin L. Speed versus interpretation accuracy: current thoughts and literature review. AJR. 2019;213(3):490–2.
30. Chew F, Mulcahy M, Porrino J, Mulcahy H, Relyea-Chew A. Prevalence of burnout among musculoskeletal radiologists. Skelet Radiol. 2017;46(4):497–506.
31. Thompson G. Measuring performance in radiology. Radiol Bus. 2011. https://www.radiology-business.com/topics/business-intelligence/measuring-performance-radiology
32. Heye T, Gysin V, Boll D, Merkle E. Structured reporting: the voice of the customer in an ongoing debate about the future of radiology reporting. AJR Am J Roentgenol. 2018;211(5):9640970.
33. Chockley K, Emanuel E. The end of radiology? Three threats to the future practice of radiology. J Am Coll Radiol. 2016;13:1415–20.
34. Tang A, Tam R, Cadrin-Chenevert A, Guest W, Chong J, Barfett J, Chepelev L, Cairns R, Mitchell JR, Cicero MD, Poudrette MGJJL, Reinhold C, Gallix B, Gray B, Geis R, Canadian Association of Radiologists Artificial Intelligence Working Group. Canadian Association of Radiologists White Paper on artificial intelligence in radiology. Can Assoc Radiol J. 2018;69(2):120–35.

Part III

Some Final Thoughts

Ars Longa, Vita Brevis

10

Contents

10.1   Tricks of the Trade

As we have said many times throughout this book, healthcare data requires serious, in-depth analysis. Fortunately, data scientists have developed a variety of tools that can help us. A few approaches and concepts deserve a brief mention here.

10.1.1 Queueing Theory

Queueing theory is an important tool for anyone doing operations analysis. We have referenced ideas derived from it quite a few times in this book.

Queueing theory was introduced in about 1910, when the Danish statistician Agner Erlang (known for the "Erlang distribution") was tasked with analyzing bottlenecks in the booming technology industry of that time: telephone communications. As a true applied scientist, Erlang started with a real problem and developed a solid and highly useful theory that grew well beyond the problem it was originally created to solve. Queueing theory deals with queues in a generalized, abstract way: A queue can be any list of tasks (or customers) to be processed by a "server" (defined here as a person, a device, or a workflow; not to be confused with a computer server). Phone calls waiting to be answered, patients waiting for a CT scanner, coffee shop customers lined up for a barista, completed radiology examinations piling up to be read by a radiologist—all of these workflows fit nicely into the same

© Springer Nature Switzerland AG 2021   219
D. Rosenthal, O. Pianykh, *Efficient Radiology*,
https://doi.org/10.1007/978-3-030-53610-7_10

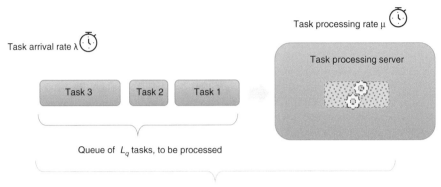

Fig. 10.1 Queueing theory view of real-life processes. Line size L_q corresponds to the number of tasks waiting to be processed, and L, to the total number of tasks in the system. (Note that the server can be either busy or idle)

task-server paradigm, which makes queueing theory applicable to a wide range of processes (Fig. 10.1).

What are some of the most interesting inferences we can draw from queuing theory?

The two principal takeaways involve Little's law [1] and the Pollaczek–Khinchine formula [2] (already mentioned in this book).

To understand these ideas better, let us define some key terms (a good occasion for using fancy Greek letters). First, let λ be the average arrival rate of tasks (such as the number of patients arriving to your imaging facility per hour).

Know Your Tools

It makes sense to assume that each patient arrives independently of others. Queueing theory models this by assuming random Poisson distribution. This also means that λ becomes the mean of the distribution and corresponds to its deviation.

Little's law defines a simple relationship between the number of tasks waiting to be processed (L_q, Fig. 10.1) and the average time W spent in the queue:

$$W = \lambda L_q$$

In essence, the formula states that the tasks/customers will be waiting for a period of time that is proportional to the waiting line size, and the rate of their arrival. This is not completely intuitive. What makes the law remarkable is that it holds true regardless of how the customers are arriving, and of how they are being served. Note that this is independent of the rate of processing! Several years ago, when we decided to predict patient wait times by analyzing a multitude of operational parameters, one model identified line sizes as the most important predictor [3]. Thus, we literally rediscovered Little's formula empirically.

The Pollaczek–Khinchine formula refines this result further, estimating average line size and wait times based on service rate, utilization, and variability.

For example, let μ be the service rate (the number of tasks that can be processed per hour). Then, given λ and μ, one can express the server utilization u as

$$u = \lambda\big/\mu$$

Indeed, this makes perfect sense: If your facility can process $\mu = 5$ patients per hour but only $\lambda = 3$ of them arrive, the facility runs at $u = 3/5 = 0.6 = 60\%$ utilization. This is an averaged estimate, and, as we have seen many times throughout this book, the variability of both arrivals and processing time will affect the waiting line as well. Since the variability in arrival times is already incorporated into the Poisson distribution assumed in Pollaczek–Khinchine, we need to include the variability of the service time, denoted as V. Then the Pollaczek–Khinchine formula states that, given all of the above, the mean size of the waiting line L_q (number of arrived tasks waiting to be served) will be

$$L_q = \frac{u^2 + \lambda^2 V}{2(1-u)}$$

And the total number of tasks in the system will be

$$L = u + \frac{u^2 + \lambda^2 V}{2(1-u)}$$

All of this may look like a fruitless theoretical exercise but examining the Pollaczek–Khinchine formula closer brings us to few very practical observations.

First, pushing utilization u close to 1.0 (or 100%) has bad operational consequences. As the formulas show, as u approaches 1.0, the denominator $1 - u$ becomes very small and the values of L_q and L become extremely large (Fig. 10.2).

Know Your Tools

The steep growth of the curves that describe pending tasks and waiting time is often called "exponential," but in fact it is not. This is a hyperbolic curve and, unlike the exponent, it reaches infinity at the finite value of $u = 1$.

We illustrated the practical consequence of this in our chapter on image acquisition, in which we discussed the waiting time in a walk-in facility as a function of utilization. Idle time is necessary to absorb and buffer unanticipated events. Therefore, having some amount of idle time is important for the stability of the system. This raises the question, "how much idle time is desirable," a proverbial can of worms that no theory can fully address. Each practice must evaluate the trade-offs based on their business model and the cost of their server time (such as a scanner or a physician).

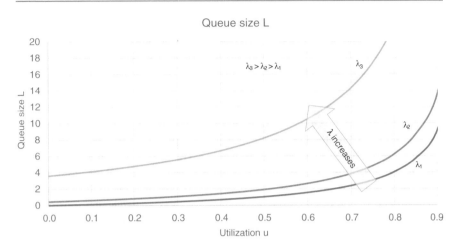

Fig. 10.2 Queueing theory "in system" line size L as a function of the utilization u, for different choices of the task arrival rate λ. As expected, increases in λ (such as more frequent arrivals of walk-in patients) result in longer line sizes. When utilization u approached 1.0 (100%), all three curves will grow to infinity

> **Keep It Real!**
> The horrifying events of the recent coronavirus pandemic illustrate some of the issues that arise when facilities already close to capacity (testing facilities, ventilator supplies, ICU beds) experience a sudden surge in demand. The system is unable to absorb the increase, and delays grow to unacceptable lengths of time!

Second, a high degree of service time variability is bad. We have played this tune many times throughout this book. It may by now sound like a broken record, but it just feels better to be backed up by a solid theory. As the Pollaczek–Khinchine formula plots in Fig. 10.3 demonstrate, an increase in V leads to more tasks waiting to be processed—like walk-in patients crowded into the waiting room.

Note that waiting lines can happen even for processes that seem to have considerable excess capacity (serving patients much faster than they arrive)—as Fig. 10.3 suggests for u close to 0. Indeed, for the small values of u, both L and L_q line sizes grow proportionally to $\lambda^2 V$. Cutting your service variability V is essential for keeping your waiting rooms empty!

Third, as Little's formula suggests, service wait time $W = \lambda L$ will be proportional to the task arrival rate λ. Keep this in mind if you want to increase your patient flow or the number of studies that are read. In these cases, unless more server capacity (rooms, equipment, radiologists, etc.) is provided, the wait and turnaround times will increase proportionately.

You might ask: If theoretical queueing theory is so good, why have we spent so much time looking into the details of specific operations? The answer is, you pay a

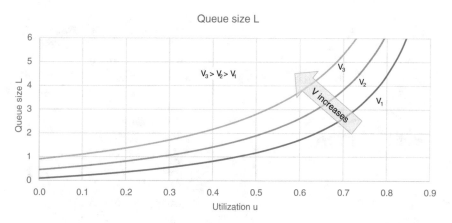

Fig. 10.3 Queueing theory "in system" line size L as a function of the utilization u, for different choices of the service variability V. An increase in V results in longer lines (and proportionally longer wait times, according to Little's law)

price for any theoretical abstraction: As the abstraction becomes more general, it also departs further from any specific instance. The queueing theory equations are remarkably true *overall*—just like the averages we discussed in the beginning of this book are—and they provide a number of useful insights. Yet, using them becomes less practical when applying them to real numbers: Their derivations were based on assumptions and simplifications, which may not hold all the time, and definitely will not hold in all cases. They also fail to account for some other important parameters—such as temporal fluctuations in λ and μ—that we have addressed many times in this book. Queueing theory can help as a general guide, but we must always look deeper into specific processes to understand their individual traits.

10.1.2 Process Mining

Process mining is not a theory but rather an interesting set of tools. As its name suggests, it was designed to extract the actual process flow from the real data a process has generated. Process mining, and the information it yields, should appeal to any manager. Yet, strangely, it is often overlooked in the course of analyzing a process or workflow. Why? Perhaps because managers believe that they already know all of the processing steps. However, the myriad variations and deviations from standard operating procedures that occur in real life can easily go unrecognized.

Figure 10.4 illustrates the power of process mining through a comparison of two diagrams of emergency department (ED) process.

The simple "textbook" chart on the left, which might be used by management, corresponds to an idealized understanding of how the ED works. The messy chart on the right was produced by a process mining algorithm based on a full year of ED data. The algorithm looked at the ED data as an event log—taking timestamps and locations of different steps patients went through. This enabled the algorithm to

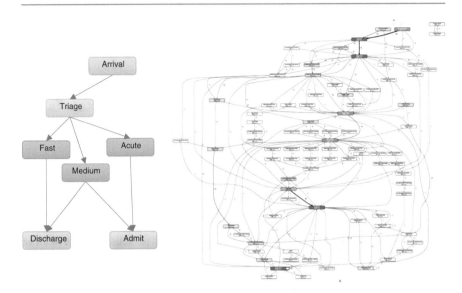

Fig. 10.4 Left: A highly abstracted conceptual view of how an emergency room might work. Such a diagram is more likely to represent an ideal than it is a reality. Right: Diagram of an actual process-mined flowchart for an ED department. Each box corresponds to a specific step in ED patient processing (triage, waiting room, different care areas, imaging examinations, and more) and each connection shows how the patients travel between different states

extract ("mine") the flowchart of the actual process. A great deal of math was applied to remove noise and the least important branches, resulting in a much simpler representation of reality (yes, the chart on the right is a *simplified* version of the fully mined process). When we presented the process-mined chart to our ED management, it took all of us several weeks to figure out what it was showing us.

Still, it was worth it. The gap between reality and a simplified, idealized representation can be colossal. For example, with one of the most common approaches for ED workflow analysis, known as discrete event simulation (DES), the simple chart on the left is "populated" with patients, propagating through the various steps or stages under a set of equally simple rules. While DES can be used to create nice videos of simulated workflow, it misses the main point: the messy, interconnected, probabilistic spaghetti-ness of the real process.

For this reason, you should never analyze a process based on an idealized image—you need to face the reality and make sense of it. Process mining is a good way to do so. Commercially available software packages (Disco [4] for sufficiently basic, and ProM [5] for those who like challenges) can help you get started.

10.1.3 Artificial Intelligence and Machine Learning

Artificial intelligence (AI) and machine learning (ML) have caused a great deal of handwringing in radiology in recent years, with more certainly to come. Therefore, it is essential to understand these tools correctly, and use them when (and only when) they offer the most efficient solutions.

The general idea of AI is that machines can perform actions in what appear to be a "smart" way. This "intelligence" can be achieved using highly sophisticated rules programmed into the machines. Machine learning (ML) provides these rule-inferring mechanisms, by representing ("modeling") real data with complex mathematical functions, "learning" their shapes from real data patterns.

Know Your Tools

By definition, learning is only possible using historical data. So, if your ML model predicts a huge surge in exam volume for next Thursday, there should be something in all of the previous Thursdays (and other related features) that suggests this trend. When we used to explain this to managers, the reaction was often: "Oh, so these models predict only from the history?"

What else would you expect?

"It's difficult to make predictions, especially about the future," a Danish proverb suggests. The power of ML can do a lot to improve upon human guesswork. But do not expect it to do the impossible. And remember, many future problems are rooted in the past.

Though the concepts behind AI and ML are not particularly new, recent advances in computing have provided sufficient computing power to make practical application possible. Thus, they are well suited for solving many operational problems.

As an example, consider the terrible process mining chart from the previous section. Clearly, with so many features coming into play, the chart is virtually incomprehensible. In fact, many contemporary processes exist that are well beyond our ability to comprehend. This is not to belittle the human brain. We are far better than computers in many ways. As it happens, though, processing complex data with large numbers of variables is not one of them. We desperately need an efficient analytical tool to sift through these complexities and arrive at the most important and meaningful features. Such a tool would help us come up with the best decisions and smartest possible strategies.

Machine learning is the perfect instrument for doing this work. In radiology operations, it can be particularly useful for identifying the most important variables that affect outcomes. ML exhaustively searches through all of the features and feature combinations in the data, seeking to determine which of these contributes most to the final result with no preconceptions or biases.

Consider again the linear regression in our chapter on scheduling (as shown in Fig. 10.5). In this case, we started with a hypothesis that duration might influence variability and the mathematical technique of linear regression was used to show that this relationship was significant.

However, suppose we had no idea duration could influence variability but had a large number of possible variables that might be important (technologist, technologist age, time of day, day of week, weather, examination volume, etc., etc.). If presented with enough such data, as well as the outcome "variability," ML algorithms could look for all possible patterns and associations without cutting corners due to

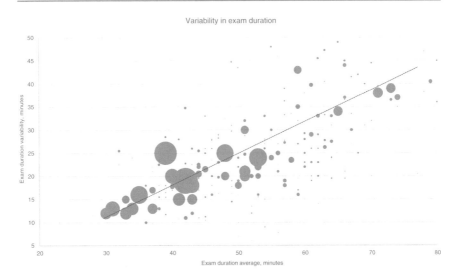

Fig. 10.5 MRI exam duration variability as a function of the average exam duration. The data was taken from 372 different types of MRI examinations; the size of each blob is proportional to the examination frequency. Variability was computed as the difference between the 75th and 25th percentiles of exam duration. There is a visible linear trend, confirmed by the statistically significant linear regression

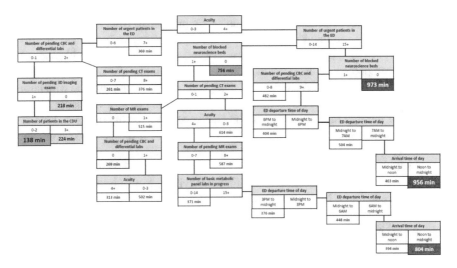

Fig. 10.6 Decision tree model of ED processing. Compared to the more complex process-mined chart above, a decision tree extracts the principal and humanly interpretable branching logic of ED workflow. Courtesy of Steven Guitron, MGH Medical Analytics Group

preconceptions. Moreover, ML can consider all of the factors at once, taking into account all of their interactions, while we humans can look only at two-dimensional charts. And though a straight line represents the simplest fit, other, more complicated relationships (curved lines, multidimensional clusters, decision trees, etc.) can also be extracted, possibly providing an even better fit. Figure 10.6 shows a decision tree model (one of the most popular ML model types) that was fitted into the ED workflow data. Compared to the complex process-mined Fig. 10.4, this decision tree extracts only the most important features, making it much more comprehensible. It would be simply impossible to build the same tree manually.

As we increase model complexity, ML models tend to become more accurate but harder to interpret. For example, we could have fitted our ED data with a more complex model (such as an *ensemble* of many trees, known in ML lingo as a *forest*). This likely would have provided an even better approximation to reality, though it would have done so at the cost of comprehensibility.

Uninterpretable models do not play well with healthcare projects: Understanding how the process works is essential for any operational work. Therefore, additional work has to be done to make model results more comprehensible. ML offers the tools to be able to do so. This brings us to the same mantra we have repeated so many times in his book: *Understanding* is the key. ML models, just like the data behind them, need to be examined and understood to bring them back into the "human" domain, and to make them actionable. They also have to be implemented in ways that are transparent, where their quality and results can be seen (and thus controlled) by any number of interested parties. Finally, they have to be retrained on a regular basis to stay in touch with their ever-changing environments. ML can be a very efficient tool when it is used wisely.

What happens when ML fails to achieve good model quality? Certainly, the initial blame falls on the model—it may be ill chosen, poorly trained, or based on an insufficient feature set. But when incorporating all possible knowledge about your process still results in a poorly predictive ML, stop blaming the model and look at the process itself. ML works under the assumption of deterministic, rational outcome. When operational decisions are highly subjective, when random variabilities prevail, and when judgements are done with a coin flip, even the most sophisticated modeling will be pointless. Make sure that the process logic makes rational sense.

10.1.4 The Optimal Trap

In many ways, this book is about optimization—making things better in the most rational, mathematically correct way. We like to rely on data and numbers to lead us toward the most logical improvement. But can we go too far?

Here is a brief experiment: Imagine we ask you to place a ball at the highest point of the "mountain," as shown in Fig. 10.7. Theoretically, you should put it at A, aiming for the "optimal" solution. However, a slight breeze would make the ball drop, possibly all the way to the bottom.

Point C, while lower than its prominent neighbors A and B, is protected from small disruptions. Though it is lower ("worse"), in a practical sense it is better. We sacrificed the optimal placement to gain stability. "Perfect is the enemy of good" (Voltaire, Dictionnaire philosophique, 1764).

Over-optimized solutions are fragile. Just as you should allow for some idle time to make a schedule more robust, it will often make sense to accept slightly

Fig. 10.7 Optimization choices. If your goal is to place the ball at the highest point of the mountain, then clearly point A is the best. However, if your goal is to keep it there, then point C is a better choice

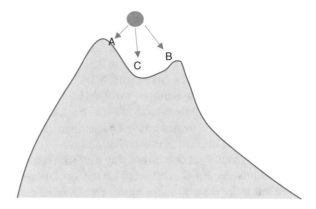

suboptimal solutions if they help absorb random shocks. Therefore, an optimal solution should be tested not only for its highest possible gain, but also for its sustainability.

Know Your Tools

One of the best ways to test process models for stability is to add random noise to their parameters to see if they remain close to optimal.

Another approach can be borrowed from machine learning, where the initial data is broken into two sets, one to train and the other to test (typically with a 70/30% randomized split). The model is trained on the training data but its quality is evaluated on the test data over several train/test splits. If the model is stable, it should not depend on the train/test split and thus should demonstrate consistent quality with the test data.

10.1.5 Efficiency vs. Quality

One final but important question: Does efficiency compromise quality?

"We are slow because we are careful …" When business intelligence and concepts of efficiency drive the delivery of healthcare, questions are inevitably raised as to whether quality is being compromised. There are certainly instances where this could be true. For example, attempting to shorten the acquisition time of a CT scan by using thicker slices, or shortening MRI acquisitions by fewer NEX (number of excitations), will result in lower quality imaging. However, other methods for shortening the acquisition times may not result in perceptibly worse images. Shorter pulse sequences decrease the risk of movement during the acquisition while increasing the likelihood that the patient will be able to tolerate the examination. In this case, a more efficient examination might even be a better one.

A very interesting and highly technical paper in the field of economics explored the question of whether the efficiency of hospitals or individual departments within hospitals is achieved at a cost in quality [6]. In its analysis, the paper used the economic theory of "principal agent relationships": relationships in which an individual cedes control to an agent who has substantially more information (such as a doctor, a hospital, or an attorney) and trusts the agent to make decisions on his or her behalf. However, because the agent's and the individual's respective interests may differ, one of the parties could benefit at the expense of the other. The study looked at the hospital itself, as well as individual departments, as potential principal agents to see if optimizing the agents' costs took precedence over the quality of care, as measured by an ongoing national survey (Dutch). As of the time of writing (2010), and in the location evaluated (The Netherlands), the analysis found that improving the efficiency of a hospital did not result in a lack of quality. In fact, efficiency and quality went together.

Still, while these findings are encouraging, one can imagine that, under certain circumstances, the push for efficiency can be taken too far.

We are not sure if he was trying to be funny but one author offered a nightmarish example of exactly this. In a 2011 paper [7], he noted that distance runners use "rabbits" to pace themselves during training. Cyclists do the same, and competitive swimmers might employ "pacing goggles."

The author suggested creating a pacing system for radiologists that would take into account case complexity and individual past performance. Here, at the beginning of each case, the radiologist is presented with an estimate of how long it should take to evaluate and report the case and then receives alerts at the halfway mark and the expected finish time. This is supposed to provide motivation to perform at top speed. If he or she begins to lag, another alert will announce that it is time to take a (short) break because fatigue is setting in! [7]

Yikes! We have no intention of going there!

10.2 Credo

Throughout this book, we have emphasized that the electronic systems used in radiology are a vast treasure trove of data that can be used to guide management and operations. It has been our unhappy experience that healthcare managers often do not make good use of this data. Business leaders seem to be both more aware of and better able to use data sources in their operations. Almost everywhere you look in the business literature, you can find articles with titles like "How data drives change …" "Data-driven management", and so on.

Please note, though, that the terminology used in such articles can be misleading: *Data does not drive change. People drive change.*

Who solves problems in your institution? Who even recognizes when problems exist?

Some years ago, a particularly ineffectual vice president of our organization frequently complained he could not possibly provide leadership because no one ever told him anything. He never realized how ridiculous this sounded! If a manager really needs information (or data) to work, he or she will insist upon having it. However, as you can see from the many examples we have offered, understanding data and applying it to the particular problem at hand can be hard work. If a manager does not actually require data, it will not be used. Providing it in any form—charts, reports, dashboards, etc.—no matter how accessible or visually beautiful, is like casting pearls before swine.

How can we create a culture in which managers need data to do their jobs? The expectation that decisions will be based on real data must permeate the entire organization, since individuals at every level of management are influenced by their peers and by those in the levels above them. Guesses, estimates, and seat-of-the-pants approximations may be an acceptable starting point, but they should always be superseded by information derived from data as soon as is feasible.

Let us face facts, though:

"Ars longa, vita brevis"
("The art (of medicine) is long, life is short."—Hippocrates)

Running a radiology department is difficult. Analytics cannot be divorced from operations, and one cannot simply purchase an operations analysis as though it were a new car. Managers need to have a basic understanding of what data is available, how to collect and process it in a meaningful way, and how to recognize results that are wildly implausible.

It would be unreasonable to expect all managers to have a deep knowledge of neural networks and Markov chains. Still, basic statistics is a must. You may find that you have to educate both yourself and your staff. Embarking on an analysis without knowing the difference between an average and a median is very much like sailing without a compass or a map: You might discover America but believe you are in India!

The basic background needed to understand an analysis can be difficult to acquire, especially for adult learners who have any number of other demands on their time—but it is worth it! Even if you do not intend to do your own analysis, a pragmatic understanding of the issues and methods involved will help you evaluate the advice you receive. Ultimately, your own—or your team's—skillset cannot be limited to science, medicine, or engineering only.

Fundamentally, there are three different types of data projects:

(a) One-time purpose-driven collection and analysis: This type of project might serve to answer a question such as "Do we have sufficient demand to justify purchase of a new MRI?"
(b) Periodic reporting for data patterns and trends: for example, tracking availability of appointments, or turnaround time for reports.
(c) Real-time data that might prompt an immediate intervention.

The first type is probably the most common, and the most popular, because the results are usually of more or less immediate interest, and because it does not require sustained attention.

In contrast, the second and third types are the "problem children" of management, requiring the drudgery of regular surveillance. A former chairman liked to refer to managing these issues as "mowing the grass" because no sooner have you cut the grass than it begins to grow back. It never ends. We should try to make good, data-driven management easier by taking steps to lessen some of the drudgery!

Take the initiative.

Operational metrics that require regular surveillance should be reported automatically. Do not depend on someone to request a report.

Do not be distracted.

More data is not necessarily better than less. It is said that fish swim in schools because it helps to confuse predators. Similarly, excessive or overly frequent data can be a distraction for managers. Do not create or perpetuate reports that are not being used. Generate useful reports at time intervals that are appropriate to the metric. For example, if you are only going to act on a trend that develops over a month, do not report the data more frequently than once a month.

Understand action thresholds.

A surveillance metric can be regarded as being "in control" when its variations fall within an accepted range. When it falls outside this range, the deviation should be promptly brought to managers' attention. In our department, we have made extensive use of automated pages to alert managers when metrics fall outside an accepted range and when immediate attention is required (just one example: delayed examination completion). For less time-sensitive issues, we build dashboards that only display actionable items (reports that are overdue, for instance).

Expect action when an action threshold is reached.

This is a key aspect of building a culture in which managers use data to do their jobs. Each manager should be responsible for one or more surveillance metrics and for taking action if the metric falls out of bounds.

Rely less on outside consultants and build strong ties between managers and data scientists.

A corollary of this is that dashboards and surveillance metrics are not likely to be effective when they are imposed from the outside. Managers need to take full ownership of the metrics that describe the operations for which they are responsible.

There are countless potential uses for data science. Publish a paper? Write a grant? Convince senior management you are doing a wonderful job? Persuade your chief financial officer that you need more equipment or manpower? Decorate your office wall with some deep learning regalia? Make something work, like really work? In these and innumerable other cases, data science can work for you.

However, no data science group, be it internal or external, will be able to satisfy all demands. Therefore, we have adopted a set of criteria for ourselves and refer to it before undertaking any project.

The criteria are summarized in Fig. 10.8.

We began by saying that this was going to be an amoral book. But now we realize we have undercut our initial premise.

Our book is not amoral at all. We feel a moral obligation to improve our healthcare system. We abhor waste and inefficiency. We denounce cost without benefit.

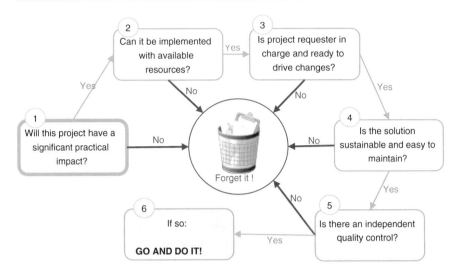

Fig. 10.8 Planning for a data-driven project. If the answer to any of the questions is "yes," proceed along the green arrow. If it is "no," the project goes in the trash

We value results. We want our efforts to benefit patients, as well as the healthcare system as a whole.

Above all, we hope that the fruits of our efforts will be useful to you, and that you will take the work we have done and find ways to improve upon it.

Acknowledgements This book would not have come about without the support and interest of many of our colleagues. It would be impossible to name them all here. But we would like to thank the Radiology Department of Massachusetts General Hospital and its Medical Analytics Group for providing us with opportunities to investigate, solve, and implement. We would also like to thank the many leaders and managers of our department for their willingness to try new ways of doing things. We would also like to thank our current and past chairmen, Dr. James A. Brink and Dr. James H. Thrall for their support, insights, and encouragement.

References

1. Wikipedia. Little's Law. [Online]. https://en.wikipedia.org/wiki/Little%27s_law.
2. Wikipedia. Pollaczek–Khinchine formula. [Online]. https://en.wikipedia.org/wiki/Pollaczek-Khinchine_formula.
3. Pianykh OS, Rosenthal DI. Can we predict patient wait time? J Am Coll Radiol. 2015;12(10):1058–66.
4. Flexicon. Disco. [Online]. https://fluxicon.com/disco/.
5. ProM. ProM. [Online]. http://www.promtools.org/doku.php.
6. Ludwig M, Van Merode F, Groot W. Principal agent relationships and the efficiency of hospitals. Eur J Health Econ. 2010;11(3):291–304.
7. Reiner B. New strategies for medical data mining, part 2: the customizable productivity pacer. J Am Coll Radiol. 2011;8(1):33–8.

Correction to: From Images to Reports

Correction to: Chapter 9 in: D. Rosenthal, O. Pianykh, Efficient Radiology, https://doi.org/10.1007/978-3-030-53610-7_9

The original version of Chapter 9 was inadvertently published with an incorrect year in the first line of Section 9.1. It is corrected as "1895".

The updated online version of the chapter can be found at
https://doi.org/10.1007/978-3-030-53610-7_9

Printed in the United States
by Baker & Taylor Publisher Services